What If Freud Was Wrong to Push Jesus Christ Out of the Counseling Arena?
David Cliff
Spring, 2014
Uncovering Long-Discarded Counseling Truths

ISBN 978-0-9812183-5-9

Proverbs 1:5, 7—*A wise man will hear and increase learning, and a man of understanding will attain wise counsel. The fear of the LORD is the beginning of knowledge, but fools despise wisdom and instruction.*

Solution-Based Ministries: Healing the heart by building up the soul

Unless otherwise specified, all Scriptures are taken from The New King James Version® (Copyright © 1982 by Thomas Nelson, Inc. Used by permission. All rights reserved.)

Scripture quotations marked KJV are taken from the King James Version of the Bible.

Scripture quotations marked (NIV) are taken from the Holy Bible, New International Version®, NIV®. Copyright © 1973, 1978, 1984, 2011 by Biblica, Inc.™ Used by permission of Zondervan. All rights reserved worldwide. www.zondervan.com The "NIV" and "New International Version" are trademarks registered in the United States Patent and Trademark Office by Biblica, Inc.™

Introduction

In his first book, *Changing the Way We Feel Inside*, Dave Cliff told of his struggles with depression and explained how, despite years of medications and the best efforts of mental health professionals, he was nowhere nearer a solution. Then, after a series of foundational revelations, he carefully rebuilt his mental health using sound scriptural principles. In this second book, What If Freud was Wrong?, David reveals that the teachings of Freud and his followers are faulty because they are attempting to use natural reasoning to solve spiritual problems. It just doesn't work!

Instead, he shows that spiritual solutions from the Word of God provide clear answers for mental health problems. David gives further insights—such as the seven pillars and the seven rooms of our soul—into why mental health problems arise, how to counter them, and how to enjoy lasting results. This book offers no instant cure. Rather, it is a call to a renewed lifestyle, one of closer relationship with the Lord and of a greater devotion to His Word. Only then do things begin to change!

What a Peculiar Title: "What If Freud Was Wrong?"

This book title was crafted to grab your attention, because for far too long we've allowed unbelieving professionals and a modern-day counseling system to set the bar, and totally dictate the content of mental health instruction. But as the mounting casualties appear before us, and others remain in distress despite endless counseling and heavy medications, we must finally ask the question, "What if Freud was wrong to push Jesus Christ out of the counseling arena?" Every time I hear that one in six of the North American public is clinically depressed, or I hear of the alarming side-effects of depression medications, I plead with the Lord that He would open doors for me to teach His wonderful counseling truths.

I'm qualified to answer this "what if" question because I lived for many years under a heavy blanket of fear, anxiety, and depression, always hoping that one day I would fully recover using this world's methods. But that was not to be. So I finally abandoned my own attempts to regain my inner health and threw myself at the Lord's feet. With hot tears, I desperately sought His counsel. I had tried everything, first as a non-Christian, and then as a Christian. But all to no avail. My inner problems remained, and I was becoming ever darker within.

As I waited before Him, I asked a number of *what if* questions. To my amazement, He opened up the Heavens over my altar, and began speaking in a clear manner. He told me that He was going to answer all of my questions, and fully heal me;

but He also warned that my healing would not be according to this world's methods. So, in Chapter 1, I would like to share some of the "what if" questions He posed, and reveal His way of counseling. I knew that He hated any method of counseling that excluded Him, and I became excited as He opened up Psalm 1:2. It states, "But his delight is in the law of the LORD, and in His law he meditates day and night." Here we see the Lord's challenge to our generation. Modern-day wise men made a very foolish mistake by shoving Jesus Christ out of counseling; and in this verse, the Father is telling us to bring back our King, and return Him to His rightful place in Christian counseling.

Later, I will discuss how the fathers of modern counseling struggled just to maintain their own mental and emotional health. Yet in spite of their personal mental health struggles and opposition to Jesus Christ, their teachings serve as part of the foundation of modern-day counseling. As we see the casualties increasing around us, it's time to loudly proclaim that Freud and his associates were definitely wrong in removing Jesus Christ from the mental health counseling arena.

A Tragic Accident

The scene was set. The audio/video expert had been hired to film an exciting free-fall event that included many well-known participants. He was to be on the outskirts of the fall, and record all of the breath-taking action. His fee was enormous. In fact, it was large enough to start him on a whole new career in the film-making industry. But there was zero room for error. His equipment had been repeatedly tested until it was flawless, and there was no danger of a foul-up. The free-fall proceeded perfectly until the set signal was given for all of the participants to open their parachutes.

He grasped for his own parachute cord, but he couldn't find it. He frantically searched over his equipment for the rip cord, but something was terribly wrong. To his horror, he realized in the urgent preparation to make certain all of his gear was operating perfectly, he had neglected that which was vitally important—his own parachute. He maintained his composure, and he has now gained some fame by calmly recording his own death fall. Yet there is a lesson to be learned from his tragic oversight. Many suffering from mental health afflictions will desperately canvass everyone they know to find relief from their suffering, but in the midst of their urgent search, they forget to put on what is vitally important—the Lord Jesus Christ.

In my own life, I saw that Freud was very wrong in removing Jesus Christ from counseling. After all, it makes clear sense that the One who created the human spirit and soul is the One to whom we must turn for answers and ongoing advice. As we spend time in His Word, we will find hidden there a wealth of neglected counseling nuggets. It is time that we opened those pages and made them known to a dying world. Many people have wrongly concluded that there is no permanent answer for the mental health woes of mankind. If we follow the problem-chasing methods of this world, that may be true; but if we're willing to work with the Lord, and allow Him to build His solid and secure house within us, then we'll discover that we're growing ever stronger within our soul. In time, our "insoluble" inner problems will begin to fade away. The end result is that there will be no tragic accidents. We will make it safely to Earth, and will find true life once again.

Dedication & Acknowledgements

I would like to dedicate this book to the many desperate people who don't yet know that they can be fully healed inside. The Holy Spirit is hovering over them yearning to increase their inner strength so that they can be successful in building up their soul.

I would like to acknowledge the help of Ed Strauss, Brian Rodda, and Justin Manzey who all assisted me to get this material into a form where it could be printed and distributed.

The words "man" and "mankind," where used, refer to women and children as well. When I speak of the soul, I am often (but not always) referring to the spirit/soul combination. Our inner man is tightly joined and intertwined and cannot be separated by human means.

Another book by David Cliff:
Changing The Way We Feel, Solution Based Ministries, 2013

For Further Information
email: daviddcliff@gmail.com
Website address: www.daviddcliff.com
Ministry Covering: City Life Church, Chilliwack, B.C.

Table of Contents

Section 1 Two Distinct Types of Counseling
Chapter 1 Some Serious "What If" Questions 7
Chapter 2 Establishing a Clear Counseling Sequence 13

Section II The Hidden Architecture of the Soul
Chapter 3 Soul Support: Its Seven Pillars 32
Chapter 4 Soul Rooms: Their Seven Names 56
Chapter 5 A Fighting Soul: Its Seven Parts 71
Chapter 6 A Growing Soul: Its Seven Additions 87
Chapter 7 An Overcoming Soul: Its Seven Challenges 102

Section III Foundations and Substances of the Soul
Chapter 8 Building a Basic Soul: and the Wise Builder Parable 120
Chapter 9 The Soul's Foundation and Pathway 130
Chapter 10 Filling the Soul: A Top 10 Shopping List 149

Section IV A Very Fruitful Soul
Chapter 11 Coffee-Cup Counseling: Sharing Your Freedom 171
Chapter 12 Maintaining Our Freedom Forever 184
Chapter 13 Conclusion: The "What If" Questions Answered 192
Chapter 14 Wrapping It All Up 197

Section I
Two Distinct Types of Counseling

Psalm 1:1-2—Blessed is the man who walks not in the counsel of the ungodly, nor stands in the path of sinners, nor sits in the seat of the scornful; but his delight is in the Law of the LORD, and in His law he meditates day and night.

The Lord of Heaven draws His line in the sand concerning all types of counseling. We clearly see from these two short verses that God wants nothing to do with any type of counsel that excludes the Lord Jesus Christ, and He clearly tells us exactly what will happen to such negligent people in the remainder of this Psalm. He warns that the counseling that pleases Him must be based on the tried and true principles found in the Word of God.

CHAPTER 1
Some Serious "What If" Questions

As we search the pages of Scripture, we find a hair-raising story in the Old Testament that causes many people to shout out, "That's not fair!" In 1 Kings 13, a prophet of Judah is commanded by the Lord to travel to Bethel and pronounce judgment against a pagan altar that had been built by King Jeroboam. As the king rises up in fury against the prophet's words, seeking to arrest him, an incredible miracle takes place. The king's hand withers in front of many frightened onlookers, and the altar is split apart with all of its ashes spilling out onto the ground. In mercy, the prophet entreats God to restore the king's hand. In response, the king requests that this prophet dine with him. The man of God refuses, declaring that he has been forbidden by the Lord to even touch food in that place. To emphasize his urgency, he immediately heads home in a different direction.

Along the way, he is deceived by an elderly man claiming to also be a prophet of God. In complete confusion, the young prophet disobeys his previous instructions from the Lord. The sudden result of his disobedience is that he is killed by a lion who then refuses to eat him. In fact, the lion stands side by side with his donkey gazing on the prophet's corpse. Eventually, the prophet is hauled away by the old man and buried. As I try to get my head around this story, my immediate response is to ask, "What would the outcome have been if the prophet hadn't allowed himself to be deceived, but had carefully listened to and obeyed the Lord's instructions?"

Let's not stop here, because every story in the Word of God is given to us for our benefit and our learning—we just need to scratch past the surface to apply it to real life. If we don't do some digging, we'll merely see the Bible as a bunch of interesting stories, and move forward in life unchanged like many people around us. But if ask the Holy Spirit to show us how to apply these stories to life, we'll find that they have great value. In this story, the man needed to understand the seriousness of the warning given to him, and to know the consequences of disobeying the Lord's command. It doesn't matter if someone seems to have a better idea; we're responsible to hear the Word of the Lord for ourselves. Let's bear this story in mind, but change the scenery. This allows us to return to the thought-provoking question, "What if Freud was wrong?"

Centuries ago, Jesus Christ gave His Church a clear mandate to evangelize the world by declaring the love of God, and making clear the seriousness of His instructions to all who would listen. For a time, great miracles flowed from the hands of those who loved Jesus Christ. But eventually, the voice of deception became much louder to the point where the Church became like this prophet who abandoned his original instructions and lost his way. To fill the void, a different altar was built by men like Darwin, Freud, Jung, and Nietzsche who proclaimed to the whole world that God was either dead or irrelevant in modern day society. They soon pushed Jesus Christ out of the picture, and blazed a whole new counseling trail: so much so that the lion now stands over the dead bodies of those who forgot that God's Word is still true.

To their shame, many in the Church world also allowed themselves to be deceived, and began to walk along the same pathway. The result is clearly seen all around us today where more than one in six of the North American public is clinically depressed. To remedy this crisis, we see endless counseling as the norm supported by all manner of soul-numbing medications. In city after city, counseling offices can no longer handle the caseloads as the problem-chasing method of counseling stretches on endlessly; and in the medical laboratories, many new varieties of depression medications are still being developed. We still see both the lion (the devourer) and the donkey (the Church) gazing on the carcasses of those who have died; and all around them men are running to and fro without any answers—so much so that most have given up hope, and there seems to be little chance that these barely-living casualties will ever be brought back to life.

Thankfully, there is good news! Some Christians are rising up and asking, "What if Freud and company made a serious mistake when they pushed the Lord out of the counseling arena?" and "What if the Church made a serious mistake in sitting down with the world to discuss ways to counsel?" "What if we had insisted that the Author of the spirit and soul was alive and well, and that He knew more than they did?" As we ask these questions, we see clear answers that have been placed in the

Word of God for our learning. There we are taught that mankind was fashioned in the image of God, and that every person has a repairable soul and a rechargeable spirit. This is significant because we can see that the long-despised Book of Genesis gives a reference point for accurate counseling back to mankind. And it also gives us much-needed answers to impossible questions. It places the tools in our hands that we need to live our lives.

This question, "What if Freud was wrong?" is also extremely important in the subject of human mental health. If Freud was wrong, it would most certainly explain the huge frustration that we see in the current mental health practices… people searching endlessly for solutions to bring relief for their inner pain. If Freud was right, we should be seeing some really good success from his practices, and from his multitude of ideas. Needless to say, from the confusion that is happening all around us, we can see that Freud made a serious error in judgment by removing the Lord and His words from the counseling equation. Tragically, many in the Church have also followed Freud, and ignored the counsel written in Psalm 1 where we're warned that those who seek ungodly counsel will end up in great confusion.

When we repent, and begin to walk in "the counsel of the godly," we soon see that we no longer have to chase down problems. We can now have at our fingertips a reference manual that will enable us to build up that soul, and repair the parts that have been damaged by life's storms. I found in my own life that as I worked with the Lord in this way, I began to grow ever stronger within my spirit and soul, and in time, the whole landscape changed before my eyes, and I gained a new view about life.

One of the most unusual passages in Scripture takes a video clip out of the life of a prophet named Jonah. He is painted as somewhat of a rebel who liked things to go his way, and didn't like it when God kept turning his world upside down. Now, God told Jonah to go and warn the Ninevites about His impending judgment of them and their city. But Jonah and the rest of the Israelites despised the Ninevites and their cruel, warlike ways, and would have liked nothing better than to see them wiped out. When they did repent, and God decided to spare the city, Jonah became upset, and told God so. How dare He spare the whole city of these cruel Ninevites! But it was through this merciful act of kindness that the Lord decided to reveal to oncoming generations a little bit more about His own amazing character. The story also reveals to us that God was gracious with Jonah, and tried to reveal to Jonah's heart what He was doing. But Jonah wasn't willing to listen.

He was very angry with the Lord and refused to change his thinking. That was a big mistake because we see that Jonah disappears completely from the Lord's register of heroes in Hebrews 11. And so it is with anyone who contends with the Lord, and refuses to get on board with His plans and purposes for mankind. They may make a big splash for awhile, and everyone seems to notice them, but in time, they're only remembered for their notoriety.

But this principle isn't just confined to the pages of Scripture. I find it really startling what happened to those who worked so hard to remove the name of the Lord Jesus Christ from being honored amongst men. I am horrified as I see how Friedrich Nietzsche ended his days on this Earth. He was a German philosopher who loudly proclaimed to the world that God was dead, and that man could do anything through the power of his own will. Yet this advice was obviously false because in 1889, he was declared hopelessly insane, and ended the last 11 years of his life either in an institution, or under the care of others. He was unable to continue to write or proclaim his ideas.

Life didn't go much better for Sigmund Freud who was terrified that he was going to die at the age of 62. He did live past that date, but the pressures of life became too great, and as the years progressed, he became a raging cocaine addict, and actually prescribed this drug to others. Strangely, in spite of his fears and addictions, the teachings of this man have been raised up by our society to oppose the Word of God.

But he didn't stand alone. On his heels came another supporter, Carl Jung. He also contended with the Lord concerning man's inner health. His philosophies have continued to receive some strong attention, but we see that in time his dance with the enemy also caused him to end up in serious mental/emotional difficulties. The literature widely reports that he had a serious nervous breakdown in his latter years, and was known to frequently consult with the occult realm. Yet he is highly regarded—even in some Churches—as one of the fathers of the modern day counseling technique.

Another man who changed the face of counseling was Charles Darwin. In his famous book, On the Origin of Species, he argued that there was clear evidence that evolution was occurring. But what if he had examined the evidence a little more carefully? He would have discovered that there was indeed variation within "kinds" of organisms (such as the variety that we can observe between a Chihuahua and a St. Bernard), but there is certainly not the evidence in the fossil records to support the claim that species barriers had been crossed.

However, many people concluded that there was no need for God because one kind of organism could actually become another kind given enough time. It wasn't long before many were also claiming that there was no God...everything we see around us had come about by time, chance, and natural selection. This fuelled a worldwide uprising against the Scriptures, and many began to see them as irrelevant to modern day life, and further accelerated the push to get any reference to the Scriptures out of our schools and universities.

Even though this decision was made to dishonor the Lord, the fact remains that if you're going on any kind of journey, you need a reference point to start your trip, a compass to find your directions, and a clear road map to follow. Yet modern day counseling doesn't have any of these. It appears that every man is instructing others according to his own ideas. But what if mankind humbled itself and gave honor once again to the Scriptures? Would we see less mental health problems? In God's Word we would find a whole different approach to counseling, and these would give us the principles that we would need to begin a very different type of counseling journey. As we leaf through the pages of Scripture, we see the heart of God clearly revealed, and His strong invitation to become ever more like Him.

So let's step back, and look at counseling through a different set of glasses. Let's now consider the full question, "What if Freud was wrong to push Jesus Christ out of counseling?" This opens a whole treasure chest of new counseling information. We see written all throughout the Scriptures amazing and very effective counseling truths. And contained within these truths is the power to change and revive a man's soul, and cause it to function correctly once again. In this book, I have taken hold of a few of these long-hidden counseling truths, and enlarged upon them.

Some believe that Freud and his associates were right in rejecting biblical counseling truths. But as Christians, let's assume that these men were wrong, and let's set forth a different set of questions. For example:

a) What if Jesus Christ was right when He inspired David to pen these words in Psalm 1:1?—"Blessed is the man who walks not in the counsel of the ungodly…" If we look around us, we'll see that the ungodly aren't providing a whole lot of people with solid answers for their inner problems.

b) What if Psalm 1:2 is a better counseling choice? It instructs us, "But His delight is in the Law of the LORD, and in His Law he meditates day and night." If we can accept this Scripture, we have now inserted an easy-to-follow road map into the counseling equation.

c) What if mankind is indeed made in the image of God, and does contain a soul/spirit combination? If we can accept this biblical statement, we also have a clear reference point to begin our counseling.

d) What if this spirit/soul combination is the seat of our mental and emotional health? Not only do we now have a reference point and a road map, but by factoring in the Holy Spirit, we have in our hand an accurate compass that always points toward Jesus Christ.

When speaking, I sometimes like to use various skits. One of my favorite is about a beautiful sunrise. After gazing intently into the darkness for a long time, I finally look over my shoulder to see where the strange light is coming from. To my amazement, I behold the sun coming up in all of its splendor. I am so excited that

I run up to the next fellow who is also peering into the darkness. He argues vehemently with me, stating that I am some kind of nut, and that he is perfectly content to continue staring into the darkness. Finally, he takes a peek over his shoulder and is absolutely astounded. He looks at the sunrise for a brief moment, and then quickly runs to another fellow to try to get him to look over his shoulder. The same argument ensues all over again. The point of the skit is that we can get so fixated on the darkness that we don't realize that God has something beautiful for each one of us. If we will respond to His counsel, we'll eventually find the answers that we're looking for. This skit is so clearly summarized in Proverbs 4:18-19, which states, "But the path of the just is like the shining sun that shines ever brighter unto the perfect day. The way of the wicked is darkness; they do not know what makes them stumble."

As I close this section, let's return to the Okanogan Valley for a moment and revisit the truth that you can't distinguish one type of apple tree from another until you've seen its fruit. This also applies to mental health. As I look back now, I still feel great respect toward the many counselors who spoke to me, some even prescribing medications, and others offered a battery of medical tests trying to help me. Yet the fruit of their efforts was not there. I spent many years of my life trying to come free using their methods, but had little success. At a later date, when I began to use the biblical principles that the Lord was revealing, I began to grow rapidly internally, and I could observe a lifetime of blackness slipping away. So let's proceed into the next chapter with a clear understanding that the Lord has a far better method of healing our inner man.

Chapter 2
Establishing a Clear Counseling Sequence: The Need for Landmarks in Counseling

In the past, when we were planning a Scouting hike, we'd map out our route and give someone in authority a starting and ending point so that if we did get lost, searchers would know where to look. In mental health counseling, it must be the same—we must have a clear starting point if we want to have success. Even though the need for a reference point, road map, and a counseling sequence is obvious, yet it's sadly lacking from modern counseling. When the image of God, the Word of God, and the soul/spirit combination were rejected, men were left to find their own way through life. Today, there are many replacement techniques such as psychotherapy, anger therapy, scream therapy, etc. When they're combined with medications, some may help for a time, but it's only the Holy Spirit and the Word of God that have the substances necessary to bring healing to a broken and damaged soul. So, if we desire to have success, we must have an action plan that draws its precepts from the Word of God. This chapter gives some of those insights, and provides an accurate road map.

The Sincerity of Doctors and Nurses

When I first went to my family physician in North Vancouver with my depression problems, I was amazed by his interest and his sincerity. I didn't know Christ at that time, and neither did he. But he did all that was humanly possible to help me using his medical perspective. He spoke with me at length even though other patients were waiting, and he set up some possible recovery strategies for me. First, he arranged for a psychiatric specialist to see me, plugged me into some group counseling, set up glucose tolerance testing at the local hospital, and offered the most current medications. In his sincerity, he was following along all of the well-marked worldly trails that he knew. Even though he did all that he could, however, at the end of all of his efforts, I was still depressed. In looking back, we can have the best advice and medications, yet still be on the wrong trail. That's why I grabbed onto Isaiah 42:16 as one of my life-rings many years after I came to know the Master. It clearly promises, "I will bring the blind by a way they did not know; I will lead them in paths they have not known. I will make darkness light before them, and crooked places straight." This verse described my story so accurately. The Lord took everything that I thought I knew about depression, and pushed it out of the way. Then He opened up a new pathway. So let's take what we now know, and bring it together into a clear counseling trail.

Defining the Counseling Pathway

There are so many different reasons why a person could feel oppressed in spirit, and there are many different types of inner afflictions. In fact, there are so many that it'd be impossible to describe them and their proposed solutions in a thousand volumes. The reason is that the counseling systems first defined by Freud and Jung made a serious error. They tried to chase down the countless problems of mankind and provide some kind of answer for each one of them. In their blind zeal, they pushed Jesus Christ out of the way saying that they wanted nothing to do with His simplistic answers. The key mistake is that most of these counseling systems have an evolutionary base, so start off on the wrong trail. The result is generations of hurting people, lost in their afflictions, not knowing what route to follow, and finally going to the grave with many of their afflictions still unresolved. Yet the Lord Jesus Christ continues to stand beside them with His arms outstretched, waiting for them to open their hearts to His wise counsel. We must tell them that it's still possible to place Christ back into the center of their counseling. If they're willing, they'll then find the answers that they so desperately need. When we humble ourselves and admit that we've made a serious error, we will see that the Lord offers a much different counseling approach. He's very sympathetic toward our inner afflictions and the horrible feelings that may currently be inside of us, but He may refuse to listen to our outpourings of blackness. If we'll adopt Him as our counselor, He will take all of our problems and put them into the disposal bin. Then He will command us to close our mouths for the time being, and to follow Him. This is where I loudly objected, but thankfully His voice prevailed.

Defining Mental Health & Grasping His Definitions

God speaks about mental health often in Scripture. Many of us are familiar with the term "peace" but that's not the one that the Lord most often uses. As I have studied the subject, I finally saw that God uses the comprehensive term "life" to describe our inner health; and He makes it clear that it's His will for us to have it. I love Jesus' statement in John 10:10: "I have come that may have life, and that they may have it more abundantly." I needed to have sharp definitions like that because I was in the crucible alone with God. In fact, I was feeling so terrible inside that I knew if it wasn't 100% His will to heal me then I was a dead man. So I went after Him aggressively with faith in my heart, and He gave me everything that I asked Him for, and so much more. In 3 John 1:2 we're told, "Beloved, I pray that you may prosper in all things and be in health, just as your soul prospers." So, not only does God want us to prosper in all things, but He expects our soul to have a full dose of His vibrant mental health.

Where to Begin

Let's start at Genesis 1:1, the Scripture that the worldly wise love to hate. There we're told that God is responsible for this world and everything in it. The Lord has no intention of introducing opposing philosophies in order to disprove them. But for our benefit, He does make His point very clear later in Romans 1:22-23. In this passage, He puts the so-called wise men in their place by declaring, "Professing to be wise, they became fools, and changed the glory of the incorruptible God into an image made like to corruptible man—and birds, and four-footed animals and creeping things." This bold statement sounds like God is speaking directly to the evolutionists. If God is truly all that He claims to be, then we need to be careful what we learn from worldly sources.

The world may have their thousands of volumes about mental health that confuse even the most qualified experts, but the Lord answers them in 2 Corinthians 11:3 by declaring, "But I fear, lest somehow, as the serpent deceived Eve by his craftiness, so your minds may be corrupted from the simplicity that is in Christ." The Lord wants us to know that He has set before us a clear counseling pathway, and that it's very simple. So let's accept that God made each one for a definite purpose, and loves every human being passionately. Whether we respond to His love is entirely our decision, and will have eternal consequences.

The 50/50 Split

Love is always a two-way street; and even though God adores us, we must respond to His love and do our part. Our link with Him is a 50/50 contract, the terms of which have been clearly set forth in the Word of God. Even now, multitudes are sitting by the side of the highway puzzled by their afflictions, and wondering why life is passing them by. Without knowing it, they are fulfilling the famous song penned by Otis Redding many years ago where he described how the tide would endlessly advance and retreat. He felt that nothing could ever break this cycle; in the same way, those blanketed with mental health afflictions would feel the same sense of hopelessness. Yet, in the midst of this despair, God stands in front of us with His arms outstretched, waiting for us to respond to His offer of love. Tragically, many refuse His voice.

If you enjoy the outdoors, particularly gardening, then you realize that you have some serious work to do before your dream of a lush, backyard garden comes into reality. Firstly, the garden beds must be turned over, weeded, fertilized, and watered. Secondly, the plants and seeds must be carefully selected to bring forth your desired result. When all is prepared, the seeds, plants, and shrubs are placed into the ground. You have basic maintenance from now on, but your 50% is mostly done, and now God takes over. He brings forth the wonderful miracle of growth and fruitfulness.

It's exactly the same as we discuss our recovery from serious inner afflictions. We must be integrally involved in the recovery process. If we're willing to roll up our sleeves and do our 50%, then God will do His part. The tragedy with inner afflictions is that they tend to be very paralyzing, and it takes real determination to rise up and fight.

The Feelings Fight

Now comes "the feelings fight." As we move forward in our counsel, we soon realize the spirit and soul are the seat of our feelings as well as our mental health. And the condition they're in often determines the way we think, and the way that we feel inside. If these parts are strong and healthy, we'll have a sense of inner well-being; if they're not, our feelings will be all over the chart. If we want to change our feelings, we have to do something about the condition of our inner man. Hence, this manuscript is all about "finding life" as we change unpleasant and unstable feelings. But the great challenge in this mental health battle is overcoming the feelings that tell us to give up and die. For me, it was a bit more dramatic. I knew that if I didn't do something, I'd probably be shut away in a mental institution for the rest of my life, or I'd eventually end my own life. So in spite of these strong negative feelings, I was determined to learn what God had to say about the matter. It wasn't easy at first because I didn't feel like fighting, and I always wanted to describe to God how I felt inside—whereas He wanted me to rise up in faith, not to verbally reinforce my black feelings. So He'd respond that I was to lay aside my unstable feelings, and follow His instructions by faith. I purposed to obey Him, and as I did, the end results were glorious.

Our Salvation Contract Is the Starting Point

Many reading this book will already be Christians, and can immediately move on to the next point…but it's good to remind ourselves of the wonderful story of His precious salvation. For those who have never been introduced to Jesus Christ, it's vital to stop and carefully consider John 3:16. It states, "For God so loved the world that He gave His only begotten Son, that whoever believes in Him should not perish but have everlasting life." We must clearly understand that God has sent His Son into this world to serve as His model for mankind, demonstrating His pure and righteous life to those who are wise enough to be instructed. At this point, we need to stop and repent for going our own way, and ask for His forgiveness. We need to humbly admit that His way is correct, ask Him to save us, and purpose to follow Him for the rest of our lives.

The Psalm 1 Counseling Pathway

I knew the Word of God would be important in my recovery so I began to spend more time reading it. As my search proceeded, I wasn't disappointed. I could see clearly from Psalm 1:1 that God wasn't impressed with ungodly counseling methods that excluded Him. It states, "Blessed is the man who walks not in the counsel of the ungodly, nor stands in the path of sinners, nor sits in the seat of the scornful." I knew that if God was dismissing one system, then He must have a much better system in mind to replace it.

In Psalm 1:2, He identifies His method. He tells us, "But his delight is in the law of the LORD, and in His law he meditates day and night." The answers that we need about life are to be found in the counsel provided in His Book. If we'll accept His ways, then we're given the results that we need in Psalm 1:3. It states, "He shall be like a tree planted by the rivers of water, that brings forth its fruit in its season…and whatever he does shall prosper." This is the fullness that God has planned for every life. He desires that we should be very fruitful, as well as being mentally and physically healthy.

Our Spirit and Soul

As we walk along this new counseling pathway, we leave the teachings of Freud and Jung far behind. They talk about consciousness, the Ego, and the Id, but the Bible wastes no time in redefining our inner makeup. The Lord instructs us early in Genesis that He has made everything for His pleasure, including mankind. He tells us in the first chapter that we are made in the image of God, and in the second chapter that we all possess a spirit and soul. As I continued to press God for more information, I understood that my soul was the house that God desired to build up in me, and that it was His breath that infuses the life component into each one of us. I also saw that this perfect inner architecture had no initial flaws. It was not until mankind chose to go his own way that sin entered the picture, and our inner design was wrecked. Along with this initial damage came a whole host of inner problems. Thankfully the story didn't end there, or there would be no hope to ever recover from our inner afflictions.

Personal Responsibility

In Genesis 2:15, we're told, "Then the LORD God took the man and put him into the garden of Eden to tend and keep it." So, from the very beginning of Creation, we see that mankind was given a twofold responsibility. First, he was given directions to make the world surrounding him even more beautiful, and second, he was expected to carefully maintain what he had already been given. This certainly goes against the sense of entitlement so common in our present-day society. Many think that God owes everything to them. They don't understand that it's their responsibility to care for and to keep that which they've been given. If we don't break out of this wrong attitude, then our inner health isn't going to be very good.

An Enemy? Spiritual Pressures? What Are You Talking About?

If we're going to believe the Lord this far, we might as well go all the way. In Genesis 3, the Lord introduces us to His archenemy, Satan. Many laugh at such a concept, but when we examine the terrible suffering and darkness that he has inflicted upon the whole human race, it might be time to allow the Lord to open our spiritual understanding so we don't get swallowed up by his deceptive lies (2 Corinthians 2:11). The critical thing we must know is that he can't exceed the authority structure and the boundaries that the Lord has placed around him (Job 1:9-12; 2:4-7). Even though we've been given authority by God over the devil (Luke 10:17-19), Satan takes advantage of our ignorance, and is able to set up his strong spiritual pressures against all mankind.

These spiritual pressures are very real. Not only did they wreck man's perfect inner architecture at the beginning of time, but they're also responsible for the powerful mental, emotional, and physical afflictions that currently trouble the human race. As we continue in Genesis, we see that anger, depression, disobedience, deception, and fear soon became commonplace, and continue even to the present day. The great tragedy is that many counselors have gone into serious error because they have spurned the Lord's Word, and have set their sights on counteracting these surface symptoms.

Obedience—The Core of God's Soul Rebuilding Program

If disobedience to God's command was the destroyer of the human soul, then it makes perfect sense that obedience to God's commands should be the restorer. This is exactly what we find in Matthew 7:24-25. There Jesus says, "Therefore, whoever hears these sayings of Mine, and does them, I will liken him to a wise man who built his house on the rock: and the rain descended, the floods came, and the winds blew and beat on that house; and it did not fall for it was founded on the rock." Our soul is the house mentioned in this verse. When our soul is rebuilt correctly, paying close attention to Scripture, mental and emotional strength are part of the package. But we're warned in the next few verses that those who ignore His words are inviting serious inner problems.

The Proverbs 9:1 Seven Pillars Challenge

I knew that Proverbs 9:1 had a very significant part in God's mental health solution, but I didn't yet know what it was. It tells us, "Wisdom has built her house, she has hewn out her seven pillars." Several years later, the Lord revealed that the seven pillars that strengthen the human soul, and the seven pillars that support His mighty universe, are one and the same. He didn't throw away His blueprints. I'll discuss this topic in a later chapter, so I won't enlarge on it here.

But the key point is that we must put real effort into gathering wisdom. This enables the Lord to do His mighty soul-strengthening work. The results of that work will determine whether our inner support pillars are strong and well-formed, or whether they're the size of mere toothpicks. If they become strong, our inner health is going to be on the mend, but if they're weak, we'll remain in our affliction. We see that the five foolish virgins made very poor life choices, and wasted away their days of opportunity on this Earth. For us, there can be a different conclusion if we make a different decision.

The Proverbs 24:3-4 Mental Health Directive

God knew before time began that foolish men would reject Him, and that their emotions would go into chaos, so it should not surprise us that the Lord addresses the issue of counseling directly. In Proverbs 24:3-4, He gives us the exact information that we need in two small verses. There He declares, "Through wisdom a house is built, and by understanding it is established; by knowledge the rooms are filled with all precious and pleasant riches." The directions are different from anything that this world can offer because we see nothing here about man's problems, or our need to chase down human problems. Instead, the Lord takes our human house (soul) in His hands, and restructures it. We've already learned that we must be involved in the process, but we see that He's directing the whole reconstruction operation.

In these verses, we're told once again that our soul is constructed and strengthened on the inside by a spiritual substance known as wisdom (described in Chapter 10). But He also exhorts that we need a healthy dose of understanding so that we know how the spiritual world surrounding us is designed to work. This gives us a firm foundation on which to build our soul. In addition, I discovered that one of the greatest side-benefits of understanding is that it removes all fear. Lastly, we are shown that the knowledge of God is the vital spiritual substance that is designed to fill us in such a manner that it squeezes out all of our negative garbage, and keeps it from ever returning. What amazes me is that this world's libraries are filled with thousands of volumes of mental health literature, yet God tells us in this short statement how to be successful in this area.

Spiritual Strength

After a lifetime of problem-chasing, it was a shock to see that the Lord doesn't focus on our human problems—instead He focuses on building up our inner strength, and filling our souls with His spiritual supplies. This is stated so clearly in Proverbs 24:5-6. There we are told, "A wise man is strong, yes, a man of knowledge increases strength; for by wise counsel you will wage your own war, and in a multitude of counselors there is safety." The obtaining of wisdom is the tool that builds up our strength, and the pursuit of knowledge causes our strength to continually increase.

God warned in Psalm 84:5-7 that there would be times of tears in every life, but if we hold onto Him, we'll grow from strength to strength. Another powerful statement about the necessity for soul strength is given in Isaiah 40:29-31. God encourages us that "He gives power to the weak, and to those who have no might He increases strength. Even the youths shall faint and be weary, and the young men shall utterly fall. But those who wait on the LORD shall renew their strength; they shall mount up with wings like eagles, they shall run and not be weary, they shall walk and not faint." What an incredible promise!

Here we see that inner fainting is not just happening in our lives, it is common in all men (1 Corinthians 10:13). The remedy is to grow strong internally so that we might overcome this enemy of our souls. The key point is that all of us must wait upon the Lord if we want to build up inner strength, but many fail because we're not told how long we'll have to wait.

Consistency of Devotions

When I am counseling, I often begin by asking about a person's devotional life. Sometimes people will look at me with the most puzzled expression, and ask what that has to do with their depression. But as we are now beginning to look at counseling from the Lord's perspective, the answer should be obvious. If we're going to help build the house that the Lord desires, then the first step is to obtain the necessary construction materials; and the quantity and quality of our daily devotions has a large part in this. As we're diligent to obtain proper spiritual nutrition we're handing to the Lord the materials He needs to do His reconstruction in us. We must not lightly pass over Matthew 4:4 that warns, "Man shall not live by bread alone, but by every word that proceeds from the mouth of God." Every word of God is significant in the building up of our souls. The need for consistency in our daily devotions is further highlighted by this next verse. Proverbs 8:34-35 encourages us, "Blessed is the man who listens to Me, watching daily at My gates, waiting at the posts of My doors. For whoever finds Me finds life, and obtains favor from the LORD." I see this theme of consistency and diligence woven all through the Scriptures. I remember one time when I was absolutely desperate for an answer concerning an impending threat against me. As I was agonizing before the Lord during my devotional time, I clearly heard God speak to my spirit man. He spoke to my heart, "Be at rest. I've already defeated the problem." I believed what He said, and to my amazement, as the days passed the impending crisis never came about, and the vicious threats seemed to melt away as if there had been no emergency at all.

Hearing the Lord

In the previous example, I clearly heard the Lord and it brought rest into my soul. In Proverbs 8:34 we see yet another spiritual secret. As we maintain consistency in our daily devotions, God wants us to listen for His directions. As our spiritual senses are sharpened to hear Him, He will reveal to us what the problem is, and will give us the instructions we need so that we'll know what to do about it. Yet the world's counseling system has no such luxury because they pushed the Holy Spirit away from them, and are forced to spend endless days looking through medical journals hoping to find an answer for each individual affliction. We are also told in the Scriptures, "Hear, and your soul shall live" (Isaiah 55:3). The Lord is pleased when we ask for His guidance and counsel, and it is His delight to give it to those who diligently seek it.

Spiritual Intimacy

In Psalm 2:12, we are given an unusual command. We are told, "Kiss the Son, lest He be angry, and you perish in the way, when His wrath is kindled but a little." There is an expectation from the Father that the immensity of our pardon, and the magnitude of His offer of eternal life, will cause us to respond to Him in great love. The Father won't give the Son a weak and listless bride as His reward. So we must become intimate with the Son of God, and as His love fills us, the knowledge of God will push things out of us that have been hurting us inside. The next exciting step is that as these things are pushed out, this ever-increasing knowledge of God now keeps them out. In my life, it was my determination to become intimate with the Holy One that brought the greatest changes in my mental health. As I drew close to Him in the secret place, I heard His voice, and the directions that I received helped me to break the shackles, and opened the way for me to write this mental health material.

The Holy Spirit

The great tragedy in worldly counseling circles is the absence of the Holy Spirit. Freud and a host of others felt that He was unnecessary, so they eliminated both Him and His advice. This was a very sad day for mankind because it makes perfect sense that the One who created the human spirit and soul is the only One who knows how they are designed to operate. His presence is vital for counseling success. When He's present in the counseling equation, He brings hidden problems to light, and provides us with solutions for problems that are too complex for the human mind. Acts 1:8 says it so well: "But you shall receive power when the Holy Spirit has come upon you…" He gives us the power to know what the problem is, and how to solve it.

Another truth that infuriates the enemy is found in Jude 1:20. There we're encouraged, "But you, beloved, building yourselves up on your most holy faith, praying in the Holy Spirit…" The enemy resists the idea of praying in a heavenly language. The reason is that communicating with God this way is like attaching a trickle charger to our soul. Ever so slowly, our spiritual man is built up. I refuse to get into the argument with others about praying in a heavenly language, but I know from much firsthand experience that when I prayed this way, I would feel relief from the heaviness of the depression.

The Absolute Necessity of Prayer

We must communicate in a deep and sincere manner with the Lord. As we search the Scriptures, we see that prayer is the vehicle that enables us to do that. Prayer is our vital communication link, so much so that James encourages us all that "The prayer of a righteous person is powerful and effective" (James 5:16 NIV). I love the insights provided by Billheimer in his book, Destined for the Throne. He restates the belief of so many others before him that God does nothing except in answer to our prayers. He insists that we are in on-the-job training to rule and reign with Christ, and prayer is the vehicle of communication that He has chosen. If God moved in spite of our prayers, then He would be frustrating His own purpose of teaching us how to take up the reins of rulership while we are here on this Earth.

Prayer is not a light thing to me. It was huge in my own mental health recovery, and has continued to play a large part in the freedom that I still enjoy today. Although God stopped me from continually pouring out my black thoughts and feelings to Him, He allowed me to speak forth by faith those things that I needed from His Throne. The results are now obvious…a life free of black, choking depression. If I ever feel a return of these pressures, I immediately increase my prayer time, and it is soon gone again.

The Tree of Life

We need to realize that the Genesis "test of two trees" is still not over yet. Many Christians think that the Tree of Life was done away with in the Garden of Eden, but that's not so. After the fall of man, the Lord rearranged things in Heaven and on Earth. He took away the physical form of this tree, changed it into the Word of God, and commanded us to eat of its fruit. He knows that whenever we ingest the Scriptures, and take time to assimilate their contents, we are actually building Jesus Christ into our soul. Even in our present day, people must still choose what spiritual substances they will allow to fill up their innermost being. It's not wrong to enjoy the fruit from the neutral trees all around us but they do nothing to build up our inner strength.

Proverbs 4:20-22 emphasizes this same thought in a different way. It declares, "My son, give attention to My words; incline your ear to My sayings. Do not let them depart from your eyes; keep them in the midst of your heart; for they are life to those who find them, and health to all their flesh." When we let these words sink in, we see that the fruit from the Tree of Life is designed to repair both soul and body. Volumes of helpful information could be written about the power of the Word of God to repair damage in the human soul that the Tree of the Knowledge of Good and Evil has done; yet we still see many struggling to find life and sustenance under its branches. Many in our day spurn the Tree of Life, and choose to eat exclusively from the Tree of the Knowledge of Good and Evil. As a consequence, their souls are starving within them, and their mental and emotional health suffers greatly. How I remember the long and lonely days in university where I would have given my eye-teeth to understand some of the truths that I now know. I remember one time when I was so low in spirit that the staff psychiatrist made a special trip to see me even though he was very ill because he thought that I might not make it. I was thankful for his care, and he did counsel me to the best of his ability. He simply didn't have the right fruit to bring life into my weak and troubled soul.

Mockery of God's Word has become so prevalent in our hallowed halls of learning, that schoolteachers and professors are hardly able to mention the Tree of Life for fear of reprisal. No wonder we have a generation of young people desperately searching for a reason for their existence. Their mental health is in tatters as their precious souls are starving within them. If we're going to be effective in our counseling, we must first get some spiritual nutrition into them. Rick Warren noted in *The Purpose Driven Life* that in response to his survey question concerning the meaning of life, one prominent university professor responded that he didn't know the answer, but if Rick ever found a reasonable solution, then he should let him know immediately.

Natural and Spiritual Substances

When I was in my early 20s, a restaurant chain opened in Vancouver called the Keg & Cleaver. They offered a piece of delicious steak and a small lobster tail for $5.99. Now these were two substances that I really wanted in my belly. Unfortunately, everyone else did as well, and the supper lineups would be halfway down the block. After a delicious supper there, I felt warm and fuzzy inside, and looked forward to my next meal in that place.

From another perspective, I'm repeatedly using my computer printer to get a paper copy of my book manuscripts. This requires that I continually restock the printer with paper and ink. In the same way, we must frequently restock our souls if we want them to work properly. The supplies that God gives are also consumable, and must be topped up frequently. In the natural world, lobster tails and printer paper have a definite use; in the spiritual world, wisdom and understanding also play a critical part in the proper functioning of our souls.

As we examine this subject, we need to know that the spiritual substances that are resident in us when we first get saved won't be the same substances that are going to be in us when we're ready for Heaven. God wants to sweep away that which is not pleasing in us, and replace it with something that delights His heart. As we read His Word, and seek Him, He fills us with an abundance of wisdom, knowledge, and understanding. That's why we're so clearly warned in Romans 12:2, "And do not be conformed to this world, but be transformed by the renewing of your mind, that you may prove what is that good and acceptable and perfect will of God." The five wise virgins provide an excellent example. They were filled with God's holy oil and were eternally rewarded for their efforts and their diligence (Matthew 25:1-10). We must do the same.

Getting Wisdom

Solomon's hard-working ants knew that they needed to collect the right materials for the winter if they were to survive through difficult times (Proverbs 6:6-8). So while the summer was at full strength and times were good, they were very busy enlarging the anthill, and gathering an abundance of materials. They all worked feverishly together to make a well-supplied and well-prepared home. If we jump over to Aesop's Fables, we see that the friendly, musical grasshopper did no such thing. He arrived at the ants' door in late autumn looking to find shelter in one of their underground caverns, and hungering to be fed from their winter's supply of food. The ants weren't being cruel in telling him to go away. They knew that the life of their colony was at risk, and they dare not feed him if their colony was to survive. Hence, the underlying principle is that we must be diligent to prepare ourselves if we want to survive both naturally and spiritually.

I've always felt that Jesus Christ Himself is the purest form of wisdom that could ever be found (1 Corinthians 1:24, 30). And if we truly want to find Him, then we must immerse ourselves in the Scriptures (John 5:39). If we are to recover from our inner afflictions it's vital that we hear Him speaking to our troubled heart. Proverbs 6:21-23 states, "Bind them [His words] continually upon your heart; tie them around your neck. When you roam, they will lead you; when you sleep, they will keep you; and when you awake, they will speak with you. For the commandment is a lamp, and the law is a light; reproofs of instruction are the way of life." We can tune in to His voice by becoming a lover of His Word; then as we learn to hear Him in this manner, He will speak to our problems, and give us personalized solutions. Some say they can't hear the Lord speak, but from personal experience, I'm convinced that the more we get His words in us, the stronger His voice becomes.

But what is an everyday working definition of wisdom, and how can it become a spiritual filling substance for our souls? I tried to ask those around me for a clear definition but everyone had a different answer. Yet I knew that wisdom must occupy a significant space in my soul if I was to be healed, and to grow spiritually. Thankfully, the Holy Spirit delights to make things clear, and in this case, He used a natural thing to give spiritual understanding. When people turn on their *bump app* and join two cell phones together, there is a transfer of selected information between the phones. In the spiritual world, it is almost exactly the same. When we take the Word of God and bump it against our hearts, the essence of the Word of God flows into us, and in time, it transforms us inside (see Luke 8:43-47).

This somewhat mysterious Christ-like substance that flows into us as we bump up against the Word of God is the best definition of wisdom that I know. As the essence of His words soothes and builds up our troubled soul, it progressively transforms us into the image of Jesus Christ. The Lord is thrilled to see this change taking place in us, and as a side benefit, we're granted inner wholeness, prosperity, and long life.

Gaining Understanding

As we "get wisdom" in the manner that Proverbs instructs us, we must now apply this wisdom to the circumstances of everyday life. As we do, we will grasp how God's spiritual systems are designed to work. We are now beginning to "get understanding." It all sounds so easy, but we can't gain true spiritual understanding until we make the Word of God our primary passion. Godly understanding is something that the Lord yearns to see in every Christian, and He wants it to grow in us year by year. If you doubt this, just read through Proverbs 1. It's quite an eye-opener to see what God thinks of those who ignore His words and the counsel of the Holy Spirit. As I worked to gain greater understanding in my life, it changed my outlook on things, and gave me strong hope for the future.

One of the pieces of godly understanding that has impacted my thinking is this: my bouts of depression were not some unexplainable malady or mere chemical imbalance as I had previously been led to believe; they occurred because my soul was both weak and damaged. As the Lord repaired the damage, and used the substance of wisdom to strengthen my inner pillars, the spiritual pressures of depression, anxiety, and fear no longer had the same effect on my soul. This has enabled me to walk in glorious freedom for the past ten-plus years. As an added bonus, I no longer fear the return of these terrible things because I'm now strong enough internally to fully resist these soul pressures.

Storing Away Knowledge

Hoarding has become a real problem in our day. My mother went through the terrible Depression of the 1930s and had become a mild hoarder. We would get so frustrated with her because she believed in saving absolutely everything, thinking that it might come in handy some day. The point is that our soul is filled with rooms, and it is God's design that they should be filled with the spiritual materials of His choosing—not the hoarded rubbish of this world. Proverbs 2:5 and 24:4 tell us that God's chosen substance is called "the knowledge of God" (Proverbs 2:5).

The missing piece of information in gaining this knowledge is that it doesn't build in us by natural means. God must reveal it to us, and He does that as a reward for our diligence in seeking Him. As it fills room after room of our soul, we discover that it's an amazing spiritual substance indeed. Its presence squeezes out the many negative things that previously gripped us. Not only that, but it also stops the enemy from ever reoccupying the soul areas that he was previously forced to leave. In Matthew 12:43-45, Jesus describes a man who had been delivered from demonic oppression. Not long after he had come free, however, he allowed himself to be reinvaded because he didn't know that the knowledge of God was consumable, and he needed to seek after it and replenish it. The message in the Parable of the Wise and Foolish Virgins (Matthew 25:1-13) is designed to teach us that we must constantly refill ourselves with the knowledge of God. If we ignore all of Christ's warnings, the consequences can be serious indeed.

The Filling Power of Love

Love is not just some gushy feeling like you see portrayed in Hollywood movies. Love is a definite heartfelt commitment to those things which are real and important. In fact, we are told in 1 John 4:8 that "God is love." In other words, God is love itself, and it is His intention to fill our hearts to overflowing with this love. God also binds Christians together in unity with this same substance of love so that we become a living, functioning body. Many years ago, when I was under attack from a spirit of fear, a revelation of God's love flooded my being, and it completely set me free. It is this same love that continues to fill me, and keeps the fear of the past from ever returning.

I shudder when I reflect on the Parable of the Sheep and the Goats in Matthew 25:31-46. We see that those who shared their love with the unlovely were held in high regard by the Master; those who despised and bullied others were sent to the place of punishment designed for the devil and his angels. From this we see that love isn't an option; it will be the trademark of everyone in Heaven. We won't find people there with the attitude of selfishness; so we must deal with those things now. In John 3:16 we are told that "God so loved, that He gave..." Also, we're plainly told, "And this is His commandment: that we should believe on the name of His Son Jesus Christ and love one another" (1 John 3:23). If we can catch this vision from the heart of the Father, it will add a great sense of purpose to our lives, and in so doing, it will help to put mental health problems to flight. When I felt that I was being consumed by problems, I forced myself to rise up in worship and praise. This literally pushed the blackness out of me.

Spiritual Violence / Resistance

It's difficult for depressed people to understand that we must fight against how we feel inside. During difficult times, it seems like feelings spiral downward to the lowest point; so much so that God had to warn Cain that he would rise up and do the correct things, he would be able to overcome how he was feeling. A powerful mental health principle is that it is critical to force ourselves to be positive despite how we feel. As we do, we are building up inner muscles.

Whenever we pace ourselves through an exercise circuit, we must expend much effort. It's the same in the spiritual world. If we desire to overcome the things that come against us, we must put out effort to defeat them. The natural world also teaches that as we exercise vigorously, our muscles will increase in mass, and it's no different in the spiritual world. As we aggressively resist how we feel inside by forcing ourselves to worship and rejoice, spiritual muscles will begin to bulk up. From much experience, I know that as I made myself praise despite how I felt inside, I grew ever stronger. I didn't like the effort involved, but it worked. I now know that the more I violently exercised spiritually, the stronger my soul grew.

Rejoicing, Singing, Worship, and Praise

I often quote to myself, "This is the day the LORD has made; we will rejoice and be glad in it" (Psalm 118:24). The Lord isn't asking about our feelings here. He's telling us to make a willing choice to rejoice. In other words, we must all start our day by actively rejoicing in faith—whether we feel it's a great day or not. When we do, we're using our faith to fight against our feelings, and this is a vital part of the soul-building exercises that the Lord requires of every person. God also tells us to "rejoice in the Lord always" (Philippians 4:4). He wants us to remain strong.

When we determine to rejoice and to worship often, we're keeping our soul filled with the right things, and demonstrating our thankfulness to the Master. God has designed us to be like the Sea of Galilee where He pours His living Spirit into us, and expects us to pour out to others in thankfulness and joy. As we continue to rejoice and sing, the Spirit of God flows out of us and blesses others. And as we share God's Spirit, He continually refills us. It's almost as if we were breathing out, and when we reach the end of our breath, God breathes back into us once again. In this way, we keep ourselves full, and we give the enemy no place to flood us with his cruel negativity. What a difference this can make in our mental health!

The Place of Demons

I know that demons and the spiritual pressures that they can apply do affect human mental health, but the danger is that people focus on them and their acts rather than on building intimacy with Jesus Christ. When we hear about the Lord's work in the New Testament, we know that He didn't hang out His shingle and open up a mental health clinic in the Lower Galilee region. He dealt with demons face to face, and told the person to go and sin no more (John 5:14; 8:11). In other words, the anointing He carried freed the person from their inner afflictions, but then He wanted them to fill themselves up with God. He was warning that it was possible to break the demonic strangleholds from our soul, but if we did not put God and His Word in its place, then we would experience the same problem again. Some, however, get so wrapped up in exploring the demonic realm that they become totally blinded to the reality of Christ's power. I remember one confused individual commanding the demons to tell who they were, and why they thought they had a right to stay in an individual. He got some very interesting answers back. I think his funniest question was asking the demon whether he was lying or not. I really cared for those people, but I certainly didn't like their strong focus on demons. Demons have the power to afflict mankind, but they seem to only be able to move in and do damage if they can find a spiritual opening. If we are intimate with Jesus Christ, getting rid of demons and keeping them out is just a normal part of the healing process.

Faith and Overcoming

We're being groomed to rule and reign with Jesus Christ. So our battle in life is to overcome every one of our afflictions by faith so that we might receive a glorious entrance into Christ's Kingdom. When we examine the life of Abraham and other saints in Hebrews 11, we know that their faith allowed them to overcome all trials because they could see in the spirit a city whose builder and maker was God (Hebrews 11:9-10). What they focused on gave them a great deal of inner strength.

If you're currently facing mental and emotional afflictions, I encourage you to eat from the Tree of Life by faith. As you build up your soul in this manner, you will realize that you now have the power to drive afflictions out of you. From much personal experience, I can assure you that if you remain intimate with Jesus Christ, your faith will not lead you into confusing pathways. You will see your answers, and understand what you must do to overcome.

In Closing

Recently, a young man about 50 years old was exercising near my home when he suddenly dropped dead from a surprise heart attack. He had some of the natural principles right for living a long, healthy life, but he was missing that which was critical. Proverbs 4:22 tells us that the secret of vibrant mental health and long life will be granted to us as we hunger for wisdom. In the same way, I have given clear pointers in regaining our inner health, but this is by no means a comprehensive list. You will have to do some of your own searching. This book gives some of the highlights of my writings, and it lays a strong foundation for becoming free internally. If you continue to struggle and feel that you're not making headway, there are those in the Church who have been given a specific ministry of deliverance. They can help you start the process of coming free in your soul. They may have to first break the logjam over your life so that you can grasp these truths more clearly.

In closing this chapter, I must stress that it's possible that mental health problems will return. But you now have some knowledge, and some definite spiritual substances in you. This will allow you to face these problems from a new position of understanding. This gives you great inner strength. As you continue to grow in knowledge and faith, you'll be able to knock away any returning pressures, and you'll discover that these spiritual pressures will once again fade away. As you continue to maintain your spiritual strength, your freedom will become permanent.

Section II
The Hidden Architecture of the Soul
Psalm 23:3 (KJV)—"He restoreth my soul..."

What a powerful statement of encouragement! If our soul was whole, then there would be no mental health problems, and it wouldn't need to be restored. Yet, I see that in our day, mental and physical problems have become so rampant that thousands are dying many years before their time. I myself was in that targeted group, and faced serious depression issues for a long season. I wasn't able to overcome this nightmare until God restructured my troubled soul using the biblical wisdom that I was now storing up in my heart in my daily devotional times.

From this very difficult experience, it has become my opinion that restructuring the human soul is connected to God's command to gain wisdom, knowledge and understanding. If we ignore His directions, we leave our souls improperly structured and unable to resist the many strong spiritual pressures targeted against them. But if we will be diligent to "get wisdom," it enables God to build our house (soul), and allows Him to build His seven mighty pillars in us. As we set ourselves to "get understanding," He re-sets the foundations of our lives, and makes our pathway plain. I'm also acutely aware what happened to the five foolish virgins (careless Christians) because they lacked the knowledge of God...and I'm determined not to fall into the same trap.

Because I see this restructuring and restoring of the human soul as vitally important, I have used the next section of this book to describe the many strategies that God used to strengthen me. As He did, my depression slowly ebbed away, and my anxiety levels began to diminish. Then, as I worked with God to continue this process, a lifetime of mental health problems left completely, and the cure became permanent. It has now become my life's passion to continue to grow in wisdom, knowledge, and understanding because I firmly believe that they're the key players in our mental and emotional health. As we continue to build these into ourselves, we'll see that He is truly restoring our souls.

Chapter 3
Soul Support: Its Seven Pillars

In Philistine architecture, the bearing pillars of the house were very important indeed. They were what held up the whole superstructure. When Samson asked to rest between the two central support pillars of the temple, he knew exactly what he was doing. As he pushed sharply on them, they collapsed, and the whole structure came crashing down. So it is with our soul. God has given us seven critical bearing pillars, and He asks us to "get wisdom" so that He might make them strong in us. In the Parable of the Wise and Foolish Builders (Matthew 7:24-27), we're taught that the man who paid no attention to the foundations and bearing structure of his house suffered great loss as the house constructed by God to contain his mental health came crashing down. We must respond to these examples given to us by God, and not repeat this man's folly.

The trouble in the human race all started when Adam and Eve sinned. Their inner pillars and architecture were completely wrecked, and mental health problems flooded into the human race. But God didn't desire to leave mankind in that sorry condition. It was in His heart to offer up His only Son so that this terrible inner damage might be repaired in us. This mighty salvation was designed to be His first step in the reconstruction of our inner pillars, and the repairing of the human soul. Once we take this salvation step, we give God permission to work within us. He also expects us to be closely involved in His soul rebuilding process. To do this, we must become passionate lovers of wisdom so that He might change our inner architecture. His first major task is to begin forming His seven pillars of strength that support our souls. When in place, they keep us from the terrible mental health afflictions that are so prevalent in our day.

> *Wisdom has built her house, she has hewn out her seven pillars...*
> *Proverbs 9:1*

As I was struggling through one of my black periods of depression many years ago, I received an unexpected surprise from the Lord. He suddenly revealed that Proverbs 9:1 was one of His mental health powerhouses, and He wanted to teach me what it meant. I stopped in my tracks to listen. He then revealed that this verse contains three vital soul construction secrets. First, Wisdom, Jesus Christ Himself, is the Master Builder of our human soul (house). Second, wisdom is the material that He uses to construct every healthy soul; and third, He looks for sufficient wisdom in each one of us so that He might begin forming these soul-strengthening pillars. I was warned that I must make the gaining of wisdom my primary passion so that He would have ample material to begin this very important construction project in me. If I failed to do my part in gathering the necessary wisdom, then I was giving Him no materials to build with. Even though I had submitted myself to the Lord and was heavily involved in Church, I still hadn't understood that wisdom was to be found in the Word of God alone. If we get our wisdom from everywhere, we end up with a confusing mixture. Let me use a natural example to clarify this point. Several years ago, an agricultural group bought a farmer's field that had been previously infested with horsetails. They had plowed and cleansed the field, and then planted vast rows of strawberries. Within a few months, the horsetails were back in full force, once again smothering the field and choking out the new strawberry plants. For the past several years it has been an expensive uphill battle for these farmers just to keep the horsetails contained so that they can harvest their annual crop. It's the same with the gaining of wisdom. If we neglect the Scriptures, and comb the world for ungodly advice, we'll not end up with the material necessary to heal our ongoing inner afflictions, and the problems will keep returning.

As I considered this example, I began to parallel it with modern counseling. Desperate counselees often spend vast amounts of time and money talking to the counselor about an endless stream of frustrating problems. No sooner is one problem solved than another one pops up. Even with the best efforts on both sides, there may be progress for a time, but all too soon the problems begin to choke the counselee once again. I went through this same endless process for many years, but I never received healing in my troubled soul. When the Lord finally spoke to my situation, He told me that He was not going to fight my weed infestation—instead, He was going to completely root up my field and restructure it. As He did, He rebuilt my soul so that the problems of the past no longer had any place in me. He had truly set me free.

His Ways Are Not Our Ways

I soon discovered that my situation was not unique. God doesn't waste too much time trying to deal with the details of a person's problems. Instead, He lifts their sights onto Christ as their solution, and begins His incredible soul re-structuring process. He had promised me in Jeremiah 33:3 that if I would call unto Him, He would show me things that I didn't even know about. So call I did. When it came to mental health, I desperately reminded the Lord that wasn't just me that was having trouble... no one I had ever talked to seemed to really know how their mental and emotional health worked. They frequently referred to ideas from countless volumes on counseling, but I was certain that the answers I needed were not to be found in them.

As God began to speak personally to my situation, He bypassed the world's literature and took me right into the Book of Proverbs. In its pages, He began to reveal to me some of His construction secrets about the human soul. Included in this was His amazing "seven pillar" strategy. Even though I had read these verses many times over, they had made no sense until the Lord opened them up. When I first thought about pillars in houses, the only thing that came to my mind was the previously-mentioned example of Samson between two pillars, standing blind before the taunting mobs of Philistines. I always joked that they must have liked his act because it wasn't long before he brought the house down.

Samson's Tragedy

The story of Samson's life is a sorry tale indeed. Even though he carried an incredible Holy Spirit anointing, and had a clear call of God, he answered to no one, and wasted his days in pursuit of wine, women, and song. As his life was drawing to its tragic conclusion, God directed him to push down the pillars of the Philistine temple. In this last great act, he did more to destroy the enemy than he had done in his whole life. Samson knew how Philistine buildings were constructed, and understood that the two central pillars supported the entire structure of this huge temple. He also knew that if he collapsed them, he would be crushed and die along with everyone else. But he saw that this last act of collapsing these pillars would finally bring some sense to his life that had gone so wrong. But these massive supporting pillars weren't something that the Philistines had invented. This architecture had been around for some time, and God uses the ideas of pillars and foundations to better describe His universe, as well as the construction of the human soul. In Proverbs, He tells us much about human architecture, and often describes how we're built internally.

As I look back now, I see that Freud and his followers did a terrible thing to lead suffering men away from the truths of the Scriptures. These incredible writings by our God should be the leading document in all of this world's mental health studies. In them are found a treasure house of vital information about our internal construction, and we're given many details how our soul operates. To me, it makes perfect sense that if you want accurate information about any product, it's a good idea to consult the original manufacturer of that product. Why have we taken so long to come back to Christ for our mental health information?

An Unusual Scripture

In God's Word, we discover amazing information about the human soul. In it, He not only tells us about our human character, but He also unveils secrets about the spiritual substances that make up the core of every person. Although these secrets about the soul's complex architecture are also scattered throughout the length and breadth of Scripture, a very significant treasure is opened to us in Proverbs 9:1. It states, "Wisdom has built her house; she has hewn out her seven pillars."

On the surface, this verse merely seems to contain a few poetic words about architecture, but hidden within these words are powerful secrets about our inner construction. As previously mentioned, when I first stumbled across it, I was going through another one of my deep bouts of life-threatening depression. At first, I thought it might have some significance concerning my own mental health, but it took a direct word from God several years later before it really made sense. As I first meditated on it, I grasped that Christ was Wisdom in the flesh, and I realized that the house that Wisdom was building was my own soul. I soon suspected that my house had some very serious flaws in its construction because of my terrible inner blackness. I also didn't have a clue what these seven pillars might be; but I knew that my own soul pillars seemed very shaky.

A Construction Secret

Before examining these seven pillars more closely, let's pause to look at the natural world. If I tell you that I live in a white, two story, split-level house with a basement, and a back patio, I am informing you about some of the construction details concerning my home. When God tells us in Proverbs 9:1-6 that He has used Wisdom to build us a house supported by seven pillars, and has filled its rooms with furniture and delicious food, He is likewise giving us some important details about the construction of the human soul. Before we charge off on the millions of other rabbit trails concerning human mental health, we would be wise to pause and really hear what the Creator is trying to say to us. After all, He knows what He's talking about.

We know from the natural world that a house must be constructed from solid, tangible materials. It's no different in the spiritual. Our soul is built from the difficult-to-define but very real material that God calls wisdom. As we search the Scriptures and put the effort into building up a block of wisdom in our soul, God responds to us by forming His seven internal support pillars. It would appear that each pillar is responsible to strengthen a different room of the soul. But again, even though the Lord forms His pillars in us, He never works alone. He requires that we work side by side with Him to determine the strength of these pillars that He gives us. From much experience I have learned that the intimacy of our personal devotions will have a huge bearing on the strength of these pillars. If we respond correctly to Him, they can be magnificent columns indeed; but if we have hit-and-miss devotions, then they can be the size of mere toothpicks. It all depends on our efforts.

The "Seven Pillars" Revelation

The amazing revelation about these seven pillars came in a most unusual way. A fellow teacher was frustrated because in a recent survey, she was finding that less than one third of her high school students were attending church most Sundays. I responded that my Grade 5 students always attended church regularly. She laughed and challenged me to find out. So the next Monday, I did a little survey, and asked the kids what they had learned in church on the previous Sunday. To my utter dismay, she was correct. Less than one-third of my kids were attending church regularly even though they went to a Christian school. After several children in a row gave very weak excuses why they were not in Church, I exclaimed to all of them, "How dare your parents steal the second pillar of discipline from your life!"

As soon as these words were out of my mouth, I stopped in my tracks, and asked myself, "What did I just say?" That was the exact moment the Lord chose to give me one of the greatest revelations of my life. He said, "I want to answer your question about the seven pillars." I was shocked at the timing. Here I was sitting in front of my class leading them in their daily devotions, and the Lord was speaking almost audibly to me. In spite of the circumstances, I was all ears. I had heard His personal voice several times before, and I didn't want to miss it.

He continued, "You have been wondering how to define the seven pillars, so I am going to give you a key. The seven pillars of your soul and the seven pillars that I used to construct My universe are one and the same. When I finished building My universe, I didn't throw away the blueprint. I used it again in the construction of man's soul. I want you to set yourself to study the early chapters of Genesis, and I will make this revelation clear to you."

I was both thankful and in awe of what the Lord had said just said to me, but I also found it very amusing. He was pointing me back to the incredible depth of wisdom contained in Genesis 1. Here I had spent seven long years in university, and no one in the "higher halls of learning" ever took Genesis 1 seriously. We thought that people who did must belong to the Flat Earth Society, and the joke in my college days was that man's troubles didn't start with an apple in a tree, they started with a pair on the ground.

In this passage from early Genesis, God began to open up His incredible pillar-building strategy. First, He required that I read the chapter over and over again to set it in my heart. Then, when I was getting frustrated because I wasn't really seeing anything, the Holy Spirit began to speak to my heart—and that's when this Seven Pillars revelation finally began to make some sense.

Pillar I—Spiritual Photosynthesis

> *Then God said, "Let there be light";*
> *and there was light."*
> *Genesis 1:3*

I saw that on the first Creation day, God commanded, "Let there be light." But I couldn't see how it related to my mental health until the Lord asked me why light was so important in the plant world. It was exactly the right question, and it kick-started my thinking process. I have a Master's Degree in Botany, and the old material now began to come alive. I remembered that in the presence of strong light, plants combine carbon dioxide and water in their leaves to make all of the basic sugars, storage oils, and oxygen that they need to live. In the spiritual, it's exactly the same. During our intimate devotional times, the Lord reveals Himself to us, and combines the Word and the Spirit in our souls to create life, strength, and wisdom. Those who obey Him will grow strong inwardly. It's the ongoing formation of these products that creates this first critical pillar of our soul.

I immediately saw that the life that I had been so desperately searching after wasn't to be found in earthly things at all; it was produced in us by the Lord as we spent intimate devotional time with Him. What a revelation indeed! In our day, people are searching the face of this Earth hoping to find life, yet the Lord hungers to create it deep within the human soul. Our task is really very simple: we must slow down and wait before Him. No wonder the Word says that "those who wait on the LORD shall renew their strength" (Isaiah 40:31). Yet this astounding pillar remains hidden to most of the secular and Christian worlds.

Some Natural Examples

Let me use another practical example: If you had a houseplant in trouble because it was set in a low light location, you could change its pot and soil, and give it an abundance of nutrients and water, but it would be all to no avail. In time, it would still wither and die unless you put it in a place where it could receive sufficient light. It's exactly the same with the human soul. We were designed to draw close to Christ so that we might receive an abundance of His spiritual light. This enables us to spiritually photosynthesize. If we ignore this very important soul need, then we should expect to see exactly the things that we are observing in society right now…overcrowded mental health institutions, psychiatrists' offices crammed with very desperate people, and countless people reaching for the medicine bottle for something to calm their inner storms.

We were doing some experiments with potato plants in my Grade 5/6 class one year. I noticed that one particular plant had grown really tall, and was leaning toward the window to catch the maximum amount of sunlight. I told the students to observe what happened when I turned the plant around so that it was now leaning away from the light. In a matter of just a few days, it had readjusted itself and was now bending toward the light once again. This response in plants is called phototropism. Doesn't it make sense that if the lowly plants know that they need to adjust themselves so they can get the maximum amount of light, then we as human beings should also be doing the same things, and hungering after the spiritual light that God so freely offers to us?

A Passion for the Light

To highlight this point even further: when a huge, over-mature tree finally topples over in the woods, a large green space opens up on the forest floor. Soon, there is an explosion of new growth in this well-lit area. It seems that colonizers of every kind fill this open space, and begin to actively send forth their branches. But over a period of time, an amazing thing happens. Certain species have more of a passion for the light than the rest, and their growth quickly outstrips the others. Soon they are stretching out their limbs and blocking the light from reaching the other plants growing on the forest floor. In time, it seems that only the plants with the greatest passion for the light survive, while the other plants slowly wither away. It's exactly the same in our churches and youth groups. Many people come to Christ, and there is an explosion of great joy in them for a time. But if they don't passionately pursue the light and ground themselves in the Word, eventually the previous problems return, and their zeal for Christ can ebb away.

If you have been facing mysterious inner problems for some time, this would be a good time to carefully examine the strength of this first pillar in your life. Are you getting sufficient light (revelation) from the Lord about your particular difficulties during your intimate daily devotions? Stop and ponder this question. He promises throughout His Word that He will speak to each one of us (Jeremiah 33:3), so it's important to take these promises very seriously. Remember, the priests who waited faithfully at the altar got the juicy cuts of meat, and hot, fresh bread (1 Corinthians 9:13). Building this first strong pillar of intimacy into our lives doesn't mean that we won't go through some difficult trials in life; it just means that we'll gain an amazing inner strength to face these trials and overcome them. As this first strong pillar develops within our souls, we've taken a huge step toward the development of vibrant mental and emotional health.

Between the Pillars—The Night Season

Once this first pillar begins to operate in us, a "night season" always follows. This dark time can be frightening for those who don't understand how spiritual things are designed to work, but it certainly doesn't have to destroy us. This is the time where we must actively use our newly-developing soul muscles to defend what we have just been given. Even though the darkness tries to overwhelm us again, as we work at it, we soon find that we can resist the previous pressures much more effectively. By staying close to the Lord in prayer during these times, and spending some time in Scriptural meditation, we'll continue to grow inwardly, and in short order, the dawn will break upon us once again.The construction of this pillar of light in us, and our understanding of the purpose of this dark period, is the first and most critical step in the regaining of human mental health. We're now set for the forming of His second soul pillar in our lives.

Pillar II—Inner Discipline

> Then God said, "Let there be a firmament in the midst of the waters, and let it divide the waters from the waters." Genesis 1:6

The light now revealed a universe in utter chaos, so God set about to change that. It's in the heart of God that when He sees disorder, whether it's in His Creation or in the soul of a person, He desires to set it right. And this is what the second pillar is all about—the restoration of order to His Creation. Once He had carefully done that, everything was designed to follow set systems of order, and God declared all things to be very good. And the careful maintenance of this God-given order is the second pillar of our human soul, and of His universe.

But tragically, Adam's sin changed all that, and mental health problems began.

Even though Satan had promised Adam and Eve some wonderful things, he was lying through his teeth. In an instant of time, mankind lost the peace and joy that had been their wonderful portion and their souls spiraled down into darkness. God's intricately-designed systems of order had now been thrown into utter chaos. This act of disobedience was also the point when fear penetrated the human race, and humanity lost its mental health. Thankfully, this is also the place in Scripture where God gives information on how it might be restored once again.

The Adamic Curse

Thankfully, God did not reject mankind at this time, but purposed to send His Son to bring the soul of man back into order once again. It was God's plan to use the sinless model of His Son as an example for all of mankind. Those who would respond to His call would receive all of the help that they would ever need to escape from this terrible pit of sin and disorder. The second pillar becomes the benchmark that allows us to attain to 1 John 3:3 which states that "everyone who has this hope in Him purifies himself, just as He is pure."

Whether we accept it or not, this world is reeling from the ongoing effects of the terrible Adamic curse, and the mental health problems in our society demonstrate utter soul chaos. The first pillar taught us that we need an abundance of spiritual light so that we might know how to turn our soul around. Immediately following, the dark period clearly revealed that our soul muscles must be strengthened and developed. Now, as we carefully study the second pillar, we recognize that we must discipline our lives if we're going to give God the opportunity to heal our inner damage. To their dismay, the people of the Old Testament discovered that self-cleansing didn't work. In fact, during some of the darkest times of the Earth's history, almost everyone who was born rejected the warning voice of the patriarchs, and went to a Christless eternity. Thankfully, we now have a model to fashion our lives after because God sent His own Son to die for our sins, and be our everlasting example.

The Need for Discipline

Some foolishly think that they'll just walk into Heaven one day without any effort on their part, but Solomon found out the hard way that careful discipline is needed in a man's life. He became careless concerning wine, women, and song, and eventually, his godless wives turned his heart away from the Lord. As we observe his life, and read more deeply into the Scriptures, we see that Heaven is a disciplined place, and we must submit to the Master's discipline.

In one passage, Christ spoke about a foolish man trying to enter Heaven without wearing wedding garments. To his dismay, he was discovered, rejected from the wedding feast, and sent into the outer darkness (Matthew 22:10-13). Only Jesus' blood cleanses us from our sins. We must wash our robes "in the blood of the Lamb" (Isaiah 61:10; Revelation 7:14).

There was a time in England when the systems of measurement were in chaos. Every time the king died, the "foot" changed. This was thankfully replaced by a carefully-designed metric system. This natural example points to the strict measuring standards that God has instituted in His universe. In fact, we see in the Scriptures that Satan tried to interfere with God's measuring standards by convincing many others that God's systems were unjust. He was so convincing that he trapped one third of the angels in his deception. They fell with him when God threw him out.

When I was a young lad, I went to a British private school. How well I remember the old headmaster standing over us as his cane descended onto our bottoms, loudly declaring, "Spare the rod, and spoil the child." The many stripes I received on my backside helped to bring my very undisciplined soul into order. In the same way, the sting of discipline in Joseph's life brought forth a man who was very thoughtful of others, and capable of ruling all of Egypt. The same was not to be said for Eli's two sons, Hophni and Phinehas. Their father didn't discipline their lives properly, and they were severely judged for their unrestrained conduct.

Is it possible that depression is also a beneficial ordering force that is only able to attack a soul in chaos? I believe that its black sting across our frail human soul was never meant to destroy us; but it can most certainly wake us up to the need for restructuring and discipline in our lives. "Blows that hurt cleanse away evil, as do stripes the inner depths of the heart" (Proverbs 2:30).

After high school graduation, many young people struggle in their walk with God. Up to this time, they have always had parents, pastors, and teachers as an outside source to help them fight the downward pull of sin. Now they're finally free, and they must discipline themselves. In some, it becomes a tough fight indeed. But they're not the only ones fighting this battle. We live in a society where divorce amongst adults is rampant. Yet God set these parents in place to be an example of godly discipline for their children. When the parents pull apart in divorce, this second restructuring pillar is badly damaged, and their children are no longer as fully protected from the terrible downward pull of the Adamic curse. Later in life, when these hurting children enter into a marriage of their own, their problems become further compounded.

The Power of Demons

In the New Testament, Jesus revealed that demons could cause some serious problems for mankind. Once the Lord cast out a demon, people needed to now discipline themselves in that particular area of their life so that the demon could not return (Matthew 12:43-45). We must realize that even though demons can apply spiritual pressure against our soul, it's our steady commitment to discipline that will keep us from doing evil. I've observed that they're able to exert their greatest power against those who are going through troubles in their lives. They seem to be like vultures that sweep in on the fallen, and cause suffering when and where they can. When Jesus warned individuals to discipline themselves, He was setting forth a new pattern whereby we could go to God with a problem, and it would be His delight to set us free (John 8:31-32). Then He expects us to fill up with Christ and exercise discipline so that the problem can't return.

If we'll permit God to form this second pillar of discipline in our souls, and allow Him to restructure us inwardly, it will have a huge bearing on our ongoing inner health. We all fight against pressuring spirits, so we must be strong in our resistance, and in our determination to place them under our feet (Luke 10:19). If we want to fully recover our mental and emotional health, and find the abundant life that the Bible so clearly promises, then we must all "press toward the mark for the prize of the high calling of God in Christ Jesus" (Philippians 3:14 KJV). As we push forward, we'll be able to overcome this demonic pull, and our inward health will gradually improve.

Discipline vs. Legalism

A person with a religious spirit is fairly easy to spot. In their opinion, nothing seems to be done correctly, and they're quick to judge others. This is legalism at its worst, and must not rule in our lives. Discipline under the Holy Spirit's guidance is very liberating (John 8:36). In the New Testament, God contrasts Jesus Christ with the Pharisees. It's amazing to watch how Christ's discipline brought men into freedom, whereas the discipline of the Pharisees brought men into bondage. We can hear the voice of legalism indignantly screaming out that the disciples aren't allowed to pluck heads of grain on the Sabbath; yet Christ assured His followers that they were permitted to eat if they were hungry. Legalism cried out that a lady who had suffered with a crippled spine for eighteen years must continue being Satan's prisoner because it was the Sabbath day. Thankfully, Christ ignored their raging, and stretched out His hand to set her free.

How well I remember my visit to Jerusalem many years ago. We were driving in the wrong section of town when the Sabbath descended upon us. In an absolute rage, one of the devout Jews attacked our car with his umbrella because we were "Sabbath-breakers." Later, I paid for the evening meal in the cold storage room at the back of the restaurant because we were forbidden to make any financial transactions on the Sabbath. No wonder people turn against organized religion! As we put this second pillar to work in our lives, we must always remember the importance of mercy. By keeping our eye on the One who forgave the woman caught in adultery (John 8:1-12), we're going to change for the better inside, and not be gripped by this same cruel hand of legalism.

Pillar III—Solid Ground and Faith's Formation

> *Then God said, "let the waters under the heavens be gathered together into one place, and let the dry land appear"; and it was so.*
> *Genesis 1:9*

What would a life without faith be like? God doesn't want us to experience that terror, so on the third Creation day, He added some solid substance to His world. First, He created the rocks, and then added an ongoing weathering process to sandpaper these rocks apart so that they become deep, rich soil. Then as these soil-formation processes began to operate, He filled the Earth with magnificent trees, flowering plants, and much fruitful vegetation.

God creates the third pillar of the human soul in a similar manner. First, He places the rock-like substance of faith within us to create an abundance of inner strength. Then, He uses life's many storms to weather our faith into a deep, rich soul soil. It's into this soil that we set down an abundance of spiritual roots, which causes an explosion of new life and fruitfulness in us. And it's this inner richness that gives such zest and excitement to life, and keeps the darkness from finding room in our souls.

This third day process plays a very important part in the development of vibrant mental health, and must not be taken lightly. In fact, it's the daily outworking of this pillar that grounds us in the faith. Whenever rock-like faith is placed in us, it causes us to recognize how wonderful the Christian life truly is. Yet it is through the tears and trials to come that we take hold of the promises and draw near to God. By doing this frequently, our newly-forming faith is weathered into soil that can bear much life.

If we fail to draw near to God at these times, it allows bitterness to creep in instead. This tragic scene was often played out by the Children of Israel after they left Egypt. God was working with their stubborn hearts, but instead of drawing close to Him in love with each testing, they pulled back in anger. Finally, He exclaimed, "Forty years long was I grieved with this generation, and said, It is a people that do err in their heart, and they have not known my ways" (Psalm 95:10 KJV). Thankfully the results were much different for Moses, Joshua, and Caleb. They responded correctly, and this third pillar became a strength in them, and yielded much fruit.

Roots and Soil

The Parable of the Sower (Mark 4:1-20) is a powerful warning that we must not allow ourselves to ever be distracted from fruit-bearing. As the story unfolds, we see that each person determines the type of soil that forms in them by the way that they yield their hearts to God. If we respond to Him correctly in love, the touches, revelations, experiences, and understandings about Christ form a deep and complex rooting system within our soul. And it's from these powerful new roots that we're able to draw up great strength into our innermost being. In time, we're able to bring forth much fruit.

But the contrary can also be true. If we have had a series of bad experiences in our lives (especially various types of abuse), or we respond bitterly to life's circumstances, then poisoned roots may have formed deep within us. These will draw up blackness into our minds, and frequently cause much dark thinking in our soul. If we don't stop this process, and we allow these wrong responses to continue, they'll eventually hinder our ability to bring forth fruit. In time, this can seriously affect our mental health. So we must learn early how to cauterize these poisoned roots in us. Because I had such an abundance of damaged roots remaining from my earlier life, the Holy Spirit taught me how to lay hands on my own head, and then pray over my own blackened roots. I asked that He would replace these old dying remnants with new vibrant roots that would draw from my soul properly. Over time, I had the privilege of seeing this happen deep within my own heart, and I now experience great joy.

The Reward of Faith

I always enjoy the story of the two frogs that fell into a farmer's cream jug. One was a frog with deep-rooted faith; the other was not. As they were desperately swimming around in the cream, one kept saying that it was no use…they'd never get out of the jug alive. The other told him to keep swimming, and to have more faith. This conversation proceeded for some time, but finally the negative frog said he knew that they'd never get rescued in time. The faithless frog gave up, sank to the bottom of the jug, and croaked. Meanwhile, the faith-filled frog kept affirming that he'd be rescued. As he continued to swim vigorously in the cream, his toes began hitting something solid. He swam even more fiercely now, and all of a sudden he was sitting atop a large island of butter. His faith had paid off, and he soon leaped to safety.

This is exactly what happens as we go through our trials: some cling to God and are eventually rescued, whereas others stop swimming, and sink deeper into their blackness. Thankfully, my daughter was one of those who listened to the Lord, and was helped by Him. She had graduated from high school, and then went through a year of struggles where we had to constantly hold her up before the Lord in prayer. She had been pulled away from her foundations by a group of older teenagers who weren't serving the Lord.

At the end of that year, while she was struggling to find her feet in Christ, she was invited to go to Tibet on a mission trip with a group of young adults from another church. Near the end of the trip as she was standing alone on the top of a mountain in Tibet looking down on the desperate plight of the poverty-stricken villagers, the Lord clearly spoke to her. He said, "Is this what you want for your own life?" "No, Lord," she replied. "Then go back to Chilliwack, and join the Master's Commission program, and I will speak to you again." She obeyed the Lord, and solidly reconnected with her roots. To our great delight, she has never looked back. The true meaning of roots and soil can often be lost in the extreme busyness of our everyday Christianity. But if we'll slow down long enough to allow the soil-forming process to work in us during times of trial, then our soul soil will deepen, and we'll become mighty in spirit. The answers that He gives because of our correct responses will become a strong, stable rooting system in our souls. This step-by-step development of God's third pillar eventually leads us into times of great fruitfulness as the dark thinking of the past is destroyed, and our mental health becomes ever stronger. We should now be able to offer some help to others because these newly-forming pillars can start bearing some weight.

The Soil-forming Process

When God wanted to form soil in the Children of Israel, it wasn't an easy or comfortable process. They had left Egypt in great victory, but now they were trapped against the Red Sea. A little later in the desert, they became thirsty, but the only water that they could find was bitter. At a later date, they were hungry, and urgently needed food. In each case, God was looking for a trusting response from them, but He didn't get it. Instead, He received much complaining, and even some insults. After ten major testings in the desert, He'd finally seen enough. With a sad heart, He had to cast aside that whole complaining generation, and He began with renewed zeal to build faith into their children (Numbers 14:22-31).

Thankfully, all was not lost. He was able to show great mercy to Moses, Joshua, and Caleb because they displayed a very different spirit. When this soil-forming process happened to them, they responded correctly by placing their faith in God, and their soft, pliable attitude soon brought forth incredible blessings from the Lord. Soil-like faith will always believe that God has our best interests at heart, and if we will allow this process to work in us, it will become the third strong pillar in our lives.

Pillar IV—Guidance Systems

> *Then God said, "Let there be lights in the firmament of the heavens to divide the day from the night; and let them be for signs and seasons, and for days and years..."*
> Genesis 1:14

One of the most horrible sensations I ever experienced during my dark periods of depression was the recurring feeling of being lost in life. I frequently felt that I was drifting endlessly through my days without any real purpose or direction. Thankfully, as the fourth soul pillar formed in me, it completely removed these feelings, and in its place gave me a strong, well-functioning GPS.

Many years ago when I was a boy, we went on a scouting expedition to fairly rugged place on Saturna Island, B.C. Being trusting boy scouts, we all thought that the other guy had the pocket knife and the compass. But when they were really needed, we realized that no one had remembered to bring them, so it wasn't too long before we were thoroughly lost. Even now, I can still remember those sharp feelings of panic at not knowing where we were. All twenty of us wandered around for awhile in the dense underbrush, but finally cooler heads prevailed, and we climbed to a much higher location on the island to get a clear bearing. As we gazed around, we received a real shock! We all thought we were on the right track, but it turned out that we had wandered about ten miles away from our base camp. From our high vantage point we immediately set a true course, and soon found our way home again.

At the time, the sense of being lost was somewhat frightening; but I still remember the feelings of great exhilaration when we finally got our bearings. If we apply this story to everyday life, we see that God makes our pathway somewhat narrow and complex. Why complex? Because He longs for us to learn to depend on His Word and on the voice of His Spirit to find our way home. It was never His desire that anyone should lose their way.

God has also placed within us a keen desire to know our future. Hence, we see material from psychics and astrology predictions posted everywhere. It has such a big following because many people are absolutely desperate to know something about the days that lay ahead of them. Every year when I go to a large agricultural fair in Vancouver, I pause beside the psychic booth just itching to go in and tell the fortune teller that she needs to get saved, so that she might be truly used by God. I haven't done that yet because I'm certain that I'd quickly get thrown out on my ear. I sadly watch people streaming into her booth with heavy wallets, and see them come out again with their billfolds much lighter thinking that they've received some valuable information. Their intense desire to know the future is valid, but they're going about it the wrong way.

This shows that the fourth soul pillar is active in them, but if they'll turn to the right source, they can legally satisfy this need. God has given us a hearing ear, His Holy Word, and a prophetic voice in His Church so that we might find the information that we need.

Hearing the Lord

A number of years ago, a Christian businessman was attending to his affairs in a South American bank. All of a sudden, he heard this clear voice whisper in his ear, "Pick up your papers and walk out of the bank." Being used to hearing the voice of the Lord, he obeyed without question. A few moments later, there was a large earthquake in that area, and all that remained of that bank was a huge pile of rubble. Hearing and obeying the voice of the Lord saved his life. In Northern Ireland in past years, there were so many car bombings that the Christians had become used to hearing the Lord whisper to them. He would often tell His people when to go out, and what streets to avoid in their morning shopping (Isaiah 30:21). God still speaks in this manner today, and it's an important part of our fourth soul pillar.

The strong push of evolution that we see in our present day really troubles me. Even though God speaks so clearly, and intelligent design is all around us, learned people still proclaim that there is no voice of God, and that there is no design in nature. They teach schoolchildren that everything happened by time, chance, and natural selection—causing many of these young people to feel lost in life because their sense of future destiny and daily purpose has been stolen away. No wonder God declares, "Professing to be wise, they became fools" (Romans 1:22). It's now well past time to stand up against this strong negative voice because it's nothing more than Satan's attempt to steal the fourth soul pillar out of our hearts and the hearts of the next generation.

Another wonderful feature of this fourth pillar is God's desire to give us variety in life. He does this by surrounding us with a profusion of different sights and sounds as well as changing the day length and the seasons. My favorite time of the year is when the days begin to lengthen in the spring: I'm a botanist at heart, and I love to see the explosion and the beauty of the new growth. This joy that we have from the changing seasons, and the incredible diversity of living things surrounding us in nature, are all part of this amazing fourth soul pillar. The full operation of this pillar can bring a genuine richness into our lives, and it's a very important part of our ongoing mental health.

Learning to Hear God for Yourself

Many Christians complain that they have difficulty hearing the voice of the Lord. But what they're really saying is that they're running too fast through life. If this is the case in your life, slow down a bit and take some time to meditate on passages of Scripture such as Psalm 91. Whenever we get the Word inside of us, it opens the way for the Holy Spirit to speak back to us in the middle of the night, or when we first wake up in the morning—or throughout the day.

When the persecutions were really bad in Russia, the pastors didn't announce the location of the next church meeting for fear of the secret police. The congregation members had to go to God, and find out from Him when and where it was to be held. Through such times of difficulty, these people learned to clearly hear the voice of the Lord for themselves. What a great way to mature quickly in the Christian faith. After my first great encounter with the voice of the Lord, it never occurred to me that others had trouble hearing Him. Since He had said, "Call to Me, and I will answer you" (Jeremiah 33:3), then that is what I fully expected. As I look back now, I see that much of my self-deliverance from depression came from His ongoing guidance, and a large part of the information given here is a result of hearing the voice of the Lord, and carefully obeying it.

Pillar V—Inner Resources

> *Then God said, "Let the waters abound with an abundance of living creatures, and let the birds fly above the earth across the face of the firmament of the heavens."*
> *Genesis 1:20*

I could hardly imagine walking though life with a constant feeling of emptiness inside. A few deep touches of this horrible empty sensation during my own long periods of depression were enough for me. Yet many in our society struggle with such emptiness constantly. These terrible, driving feelings will often force them across the face of this world in search of something to satisfy their souls. They've never learned that the life that is within them needs a source of fuel to continue. But thankfully, as God adds His fifth pillar to our soul, He greatly enhances the quantity and quality of our lives.

Sometimes, the people that we're so earnestly trying to help aren't in as bad a shape as we might first think…they have simply run out of "soul fuel." So our primary task is to teach them how to spend quality time with the Lord so that they can be fully refueled. Unless they learn to spend this time with the Master, they may never discover what soul fuel is. Every time I learned something new about the Lord in His Word, or by the voice of His Spirit, I would feel enriched inside, and would have a strong desire to share with others what the Lord had just shown to me. After a time, I began to realize that this soul fuel is "the knowledge of God" (Proverbs 2:5). Our human soul has been designed to run on this fuel and it always gives us exciting things to look forward to in Christ. That doesn't mean we can't enjoy the wonderful things around us; it just means that earthly things will never bring us the same kind of lasting satisfaction.By definition, the word "know" speaks of an intimate physical union between a man and a woman. In marriage, such times of union are important and enjoyable, and also critical to produce offspring. Just as a man can't wave to his wife from across the room and expect her to bear children, so it is spiritually. It is God's desire that we come to know Him intimately; and as we do, He plants His Word in us, and then brings these words to life. In time, this causes us to bear spiritual fruit. This continuous refilling gives us a driving passion to know Him even more, and as a result, we become even more fruitful. The end product of this intimate union is that we are topped-up with rich inner resources, and we feel a zest for life, and an incredible joy within.

Hitler and Napoleon

In past centuries, both Hitler and Napoleon had grandiose plans for world conquest and domination. These men desired to take over the lush green steppes of Russia. But both of their campaigns were very poorly planned. Each leader, in turn, sent their troops far out onto the steppes of Russia, but they made a very big mistake. They failed to build any kind of supply lines for their armies. They were certain that the soldiers could gather all of the food that they needed from the rich farming areas as they moved forward. This was not to be the case.

They never dreamed that the Russians would perform a "scorched earth" policy. During both invasions, as the Russian soldiers retreated ahead of the rapidly-advancing armies, they burned their own crops. In doing so, they destroyed every possible scrap of food. When the invading armies arrived in those areas, there was nothing for them to eat. Then as winter set in, the troops began to starve and freeze in the middle of a barren land. As the armies were perishing, or tried to retreat, angry villages picked off the stragglers.

This happens constantly with Christians. People start out well in their walk with Christ, and then settle into a busy church life. Out of ignorance, or laziness, they never learn to the importance of resupplying themselves spiritually. Then, as they run out of inner resources, they lose their first love, their church attendance lags, and they gradually fall away from Christ.

It's very important to know where these many resources are hidden that are so critical in the resupplying of the human soul. Earlier in my Christian walk, depression would drive me endlessly through my days, and I often felt very empty within. Through necessity, I've learned to resist the urge to run, and have trained myself to spend time in the Word of God. When I take the time to meditate, I find such rich food there. Then as I talk with the Lord, He reveals His words to me in so many unusual ways. This produces great excitement and the emptiness drains away. To my amazement, I seem to fill up with a fresh zeal to know even more about Him. This is what we should expect, because John 1:1-2, 14 tells us that Jesus Christ is actually the Word of God in the flesh. As we consume His words, we are spiritually ingesting the Lord Himself. No wonder the prophet Jeremiah so excitedly cried out, "Thy words were found, and I did eat them; and thy word was unto me the joy and rejoicing of mine heart" (Jeremiah 15:16 KJV).

I have taught in Christian schools for over thirty-five years now. I find it so refreshing each September to receive a fresh crop of students, eager to learn all that I can teach them. I know that it's important to capture the moment, because by late May, all they can think about is their upcoming summer holidays. As a teacher, it's my task to add to their store of knowledge so that they can easily move along to the next grade level. Some accept their tasks well, while others would rather play or talk. Nevertheless, as I build up the resources within them, I'm preparing them to accomplish more in their lives. This has such clear application in the spiritual world where we're expected to constantly build up our inner resources, and grow year by year. The fifth soul pillar also has a very great bearing on our extended mental health. Even though your gas tank may be full at this time, and your cupboards may be stocked with groceries, in time they'll empty, and you must go on another shopping expedition. This fifth pillar has been specifically designed by God to remove those feelings of emptiness from mankind, and restore our spiritual energy levels. I'm now certain that one of the key players in finally bringing my inner afflictions to a halt was learning to take the time to keep myself spiritually full.

Building Up Your Own Inner Resources

As I speak to Christians about depression, I'm shocked that many have never really had any close personal encounters with the Lord. Yet God is no respecter of persons, so what He will do for one person, He will also do for others. Because of the severity of my depression, I was desperate to have help from God, and I always took Him at His Word. If He said He'd do a certain thing, then I would hold onto Him tightly until I got an answer. This faith that He will always give me an answer has become a valuable resource in me.

Throughout the course of my Christian life, as God has revealed Himself to me personally by words, soul touches, and revelations, these have become like a rich fuel in my soul that makes me know that there's no limit to what God can do. Some may struggle with the idea of God touching our spirits with His Holy Spirit, but I have had many soul touches over the years that have repaired my damaged areas, and given me a new vision for living. At other times, He's given dramatic revelations that have answered my deepest questions. I know that He wants to give the inner resources, but we must demonstrate a hunger for them.

Pillar VI—Surrounding Environment

> *Then God said, "Let the earth bring forth the living creature according to its kind: cattle and creeping thing and beast of the earth, each according to its kind"; and it was so.*
> *Genesis 1:24*

Gang violence is a problem in the area where we live. Thankfully, the gang task force associated with the local police are making some headway, and now beginning to see a difference. But the root of the problem is not the gangs; it's the bleak environment that some parents provide for their children. When young people have no one to affirm them, they begin to look for places where they can be accepted. Tragically, some turn to gangs. It was never God's plan to leave the new Christian without support. That's why He designed the sixth soul pillar. He purposed that we should be surrounded by a strong supportive environment so that we might succeed in life.

I find it fascinating that when plants photosynthesize, they play a part in sweetening their own surrounding atmosphere. Not only do they make their own sugars, but they create the oxygen that is essential for other life to exist. God desires to see this sweetening process also operate in our lives. When the poet John Donne said, "No man is an island," he was very accurate indeed. All of us have an influence on those around us, and it's very important how we live. As Christians, we're designed to continually encourage one another to grow in relationship with the Master (Hebrews 10:25 NIV). A clear demonstration of this sixth pillar can be seen in marriage. If we'll work to continually love and encourage our marriage partners, we'll greatly sweeten the atmosphere for our children.

Seniors and Loneliness

We can see one of life's great tragedies played out in seniors' homes every day. God didn't plan for these aging parents to be locked away in lonely rest homes where they only occasionally see their children and grandchildren. As long as they're still able, He planned for these "hoary heads" to be an integral part of their families where they could teach the wisdom of the ages to their children and grandchildren (Leviticus 19:32 KJV). This is one of God's ways of passing spiritual truths on to the next generation. In this way, the "hoary head" can sweeten the atmosphere, and fully function in the environment that God has designed for them.

Neither was it God's intention that we should live out the words found in Otis Redding's famous song, "Sitting on the Dock of the Bay," penned so many years ago. There he portrays the desperate loneliness and lack of purpose of a man without destiny or any kind of lifelong vision. These words so clearly reveal the loneliness and lack of purpose faced by so many in this present generation. If only he could have known about this amazing sixth pillar of the human soul! When we make things better wherever we go, we truly start to live. If you're lonely and want to make some true friends, get involved in some church projects that count. At one time, I had a struggle making friends, but I connected with others on a wall-building project. As we worked and ate together on a number of Saturdays, we found we had something in common, and friendships just seemed to happen.

Job's Struggles

Many stand back in shock at the events that transpired in Job's life. But before we react that way, we need to carefully examine the words coming out of Job's own mouth, as well as his environment. His words in Job 3:25 are very significant: "For the thing I greatly feared has come upon me, and what I dreaded has happened to me." Even though Job was far above the others in righteousness, and was held in high regard by the Lord, he had a gaping hole in his hedge. He was filling his surrounding environment with thoughts of fear and dread. We need to learn well from this example, and always fill our environment with praise and faith-filled remarks. If Job couldn't get away with it, neither can we! When Job got his faith working properly, God was able to give him twice as much as he had before—and Satan wasn't able to steal from him again.

We live in a society that's really confused, so we need the institutions of the family and the Church like never before. As we each take our faith and our gifts into a Church environment, we create a spiritual womb where the young can be born. When they're brought forth into Christ, gentle pressure helps them to grow and conform to Scriptural principles. I well remember during my dark days of depression how important the Church and family were for my own support and encouragement. Their love and continual strengthening often helped me to carry on for another day.

Many years ago, an elder withdrew himself from the Church body, and opted to stay at home and watch sermons on TV. It was his decision that he didn't need the body of Christ. Since that time, he and his pastor had often met, but came to loggerheads over the subject of Church involvement. This evening was no different. Finally the pastor stopped contending with him, and the two were quietly watching the flames die away on a log that had fallen out of the fire. Finally, it even stopped glowing. Without speaking, the pastor took the large blackened piece and placed it back onto the fire. All of a sudden, it roared back to life once again. No more had to be said. The elder promised to be back in Church the next Sunday. He suddenly realized that the environment of the Church was the best thing for his spiritual life and growth.

Many years ago, when I was principal of a small Christian school, I had a lot of trouble with a hurting family. I tried to explain how they needed to support our discipline; otherwise the children would be severely damaged by life's storms. I got a verbal tongue-lashing, and they stormed out of the room. Life proceeded downhill from there for them. They family broke up, and years later, I heard that the children walked away from God as they became tangled in all of the frustration. If these people had responded to the discipline and love offered by a caring Christian environment, the outcome may have been quite different.

Pilate & His Troubles

A surrounding environment isn't always a positive thing. I'm still amazed whenever I hear the story of Pontius Pilate, and how he was pulled down by those who were supposed to be supporting him. He was a well-respected man in his day, and God found some good in him. Pilate knew that Christ was innocent, and did what he could to confirm that innocence. Even God tried to support Pilate by sending his wife to him with a dream confirming what he was already thinking. But the pressure of his surrounding negative environment was too great. After he had condemned Christ, he tried to wash away his feelings of guilt. But certain historians tell us that he walked into a river one day until the waters closed over his head. He was screaming that he couldn't get the blood off of his hands. He discovered the hard way that we mustn't yield to wrong surrounding pressures.

On the sixth day, we see that God had taken considerable time and effort to put things in place that were necessary for life to succeed. In the same way, He longs for each one of our lives to be a success. In order to do that, we need to recognize the value of the sixth pillar. When all six pillars are fully functional, we should be finding a new richness in life. This prepares us to discover the seventh great pillar of our soul…that of inner rest.

Pillar VII—Inner Rest

> *And on the seventh day, God ended
> His work which He had done, and
> He rested on the seventh day from
> all his work which He had done.*
> *Genesis 2:2*

To date, the greatest minds in the world have failed to solve the mental health problems that plague mankind. Yet God has provided the answer for this dilemma. It's His plan that seven great pillars should support our souls, and keep them solidly in place for both time and eternity. This last great pillar of inner rest functions best when all the other pillars are set properly in place. It really doesn't matter what you or I think about all of the different ways that society has proposed to improve our inner health. The Great Designer knows exactly how He has put us together, and it's very important to listen to what He has to say about our complex inner makeup. When it's Friday afternoon in my classroom, it's hard to get the children to focus on their studies. In fact, during the last study block on Friday afternoons, I don't fight against the children's excitement. I usually plan a Bible video or an art project. They all know that there's a time of play and rest just ahead, and they're really excited. I always find it humorous that they don't understand that the teachers look forward to these times of rest and recreation more than they do. These rest times are the seventh great pillar of the human soul, and we'll soon discover that rest is an eternal principle.

There are many in our society who think they have too much to do and that rest isn't important at all. But they're very wrong. If God makes rest one of the seven pillars of our human soul, then we can be certain that it's very important indeed. This can be better illustrated by the following story. Earlier last century, the Russian communists decided that people didn't need a day of rest. They demanded that food production continue full speed ahead for seven days per week. All seemed to go well for the first few weeks, but after about fifty days, people started breaking down both mentally and emotionally. Production dropped off so sharply that they decided that it would be good to have a day of rest once a week. God's way won out once again.

A Lesson From Nature

I'm always fascinated by the things that we can learn from nature. In daily life, the body is fresh and ready to go in the morning after a good night's sleep. During the day, as the muscles are used, lactic acid builds up in them little by little. By evening time, lactic acid levels are high enough to make us want to lie down and rest. During our sleep, the lactic acid is broken down, and the sense of fatigue leaves. If this didn't happen, eventually lactic acid levels would build up to such high levels that the organism would burn out or die. In overall life it's exactly the same. If we don't take adequate time for rest and recreation, we'll eventually suffer from mental and emotional burnout.

In this era of ever-expanding social media, there's a much greater chance of the seventh pillar being ignored. It's not uncommon for young people to stay up most of the night on the social media, and then be barely functional in school the next day. This lack of rest is further compounded if an emotional issue should arise in the middle of the night. A typical comment might be: "By the way, I saw Suzy with your boyfriend earlier last evening." Now Jane is up all night wondering if it's true, and what to do about it. Rest has long since departed from her.

I still remember the earlier days of my Christianity when we were all so super-spiritual. In our youthful zeal, we thought that rest was just for backsliders. If you weren't out doing something for Christ every night of the week then something was wrong with you. But then the practical aspects like laundry, shopping, and family commitments began to catch up with us, and we finally realized that there was another very real side to life…and in time, we all discovered a greater balance.

Through the operation of this pillar, we see that God also loves times of fellowship, rest, and recreation. So in His wisdom, He has created this seventh pillar, and declares that we all need it. Those who listen to Him find that their mental health will grow strong; those who ignore Him find themselves in great mental and emotional difficulty, and in danger of burn-out.

Seven Pillars—Conclusion

Even though much of the counseling world has tossed away God's wise advice about the construction of our inner man, the Lord doesn't wilt before their foolish accusations. He quietly tells those who will listen that He has placed seven support pillars within every human soul. Those who will turn to Him and strengthen these pillars will be blessed with vibrant inner health; whereas those who ignore this provision will eventually suffer from great weakness of soul.

In the natural world, we understand that a house built without bearing walls and pillars will collapse. So when the Lord tells us that He has used seven pillars in the construction of our soul, He wants us to learn more about our bearing walls and foundations. He doesn't delight to see anyone suffer mental collapse, and has made full provision at Calvary to prevent this. But if people live carelessly, and ignore His call to gain the vital substances designed to support life, then they can't blame God for their lack of internal strength. If we obey Him and live our lives carefully, we'll grow internally strong as He puts our seven pillars in place—and over a period of time, our life will flourish, and have significant impact for the Lord.

Chapter 4
Soul Rooms: Their Seven Names

By knowledge the rooms are filled with all precious and pleasant riches. Proverbs 24:4

When my wife and I purchased our first home in Sechelt, B.C., it was exciting indeed. Even though the place was a mess, and the animals of the previous owners had urinated everywhere, we looked forward to all of the additions and changes that we were about to make in our new castle. No sooner was the title deed signed than smelly carpets were flying out the windows, and the urine smell engrained in the old floor was being sealed in by a strong covering of oil-based paint. But most exciting for me was the additions I planned to make in the unfinished basement. It was our desire to take people into our home and help them to regain their feet, so I set about in earnest building partitions and creating extra rooms.

Purchasing my own home and then making additions provides a perfect opening for this chapter where I discuss the seven rooms that God desires to restructure within every hungry soul. As I was meditating on this concept of soul rooms and soul growth, a question began circulating in my mind: "Could these hidden soul rooms be the place where God desires to meet with mankind, and provide for our deepest needs—the mysterious 'secret place of the Most High'?"

Before I answer that question, let me say that years ago I thought I was all ready to go out and speak about vibrant mental health and this most unusual "seven pillars" revelation. But the Lord stopped me in my tracks, and spoke to my heart again. He said, "Son, I'm not finished yet. You asked me to give you a greater understanding about your soul. I've only just begun to reveal some of My construction secrets. There is so much more to know."

Then to my complete surprise a few mornings later at about 4:30 a.m., He began enlarging on this already exciting revelation. His gentle rebuke about my lack of information reminded me of the Bible story about Ahimaaz (2 Samuel 18:14-33). He was the courier, and became really embarrassed when he stood before King David because he could only give an incomplete report about the recent battle. Yet the second courier, who arrived shortly after, had taken the time to get the full story together with all of the proper details. My following story about man's inner construction would have also been incomplete if I had missed this important additional information.

Rooms In Our Soul

As the Lord began to speak, He reminded me about Proverbs 24:4, which states that "by knowledge, the rooms are filled with all precious and pleasant riches." God said, "Son, when a man opens His heart to Christ, it is Our desire to become intimate with him. To fulfill this need, We have prepared 'rooms' deep within the human soul where We can commune with that man on a regular basis. It is in these special meeting rooms where your mental health is forged, and your soul gains great confidence."

Then He gave me a tremendous revelation. He reminded me about the seven redemptive Names of God that I had once studied, and showed that each room of the human soul had a name according to one of our seven redemptive needs. I was struggling to grasp this truth when He added, "As we commune together in these rooms of your soul, and I meet your needs, a strong pillar of confidence is built into each one of your soul rooms." Now I was getting excited. As I began to ponder this in more depth, I could see that He was actually answering my long-standing question about the "secret place of the Most High" (Psalm 91:1). During my long years of depression, I had often inquired about this place thinking that if I could ever get there, my ongoing mental health troubles would be over. Well, I was perfectly correct! I have now learned how to get there, and my battles are finally over. All of us have heard the analogy that coming to know God is like peeling the layers off of an onion. As you uncover one layer, you find another layer of knowledge underneath. This information about these seven Names of God and the seven rooms of the soul was like uncovering that next layer.

Identifying the Needs

After the tragedy of Noah's flood, God singled out a man known as Abraham, and at a point of absolute desperation in Abraham's life, God revealed Himself as Jehovah-jireh. In other words, He was saying that He Himself would provide a sacrifice (Genesis 22:8). Later, when God saw the absolute misery of physical human suffering amongst the Children of Israel, God revealed to Moses that if mankind would carefully walk before Him, He would be Jehovah-raphah to us. In such a statement, He was truly giving us some incredible news—that He would be our healer (Exodus 15:26). A short while later, when Israel was about to be overcome by their enemies, God revealed to Moses and Joshua that He desired to be Jehovah-nissi to them. He wanted to be their banner in all of life's battles (Exodus 17:15). During the time of the Judges, when Gideon was in deep soul turmoil because he had seen God face to face, the Lord reassured him that he would not die, and identified Himself as Jehovah-shalom. This means "the LORD is peace" (Judges 6:24). Finally, in Psalm 23:1, the Lord identified Himself personally to David as Jehovah-ra'ah, meaning "the LORD is our Shepherd," the One who promised to guide him throughout his life's journey.

At a very dark time in Israel's history, Jeremiah was overwhelmed by the filthiness and disobedience that he saw all around him, but God again revealed Himself in a brand new way as Jehovah-tsidkenu. This meant that "the Lord is our Righteousness" (Jeremiah 23:6). It is to Him that we must turn to be cleansed from those things that war against our soul. At a later date, Ezekiel was shown that God would forever abide over His people. At that moment, He identified Himself to Ezekiel as our ever-present companion Jehovah-shammah (Ezekiel 48:35). The meaning of this name is "the LORD is Present."

These seven incredible revelations about God, set forth by Scofield (Bible Reference Notes, 1917), need to become a part of the foundational understanding of every Christian.

Keeping Our Rooms Filled

The idea of seven soul rooms gains further credence from the story that Jesus told us in Luke 11:24-26. He reveals that a displaced devil would try and reinvade his original home. If he was successful, he would bring in seven other wicked companions more evil than himself. He would be the administrator, and assign one demon to lock down each room of the man's soul. I also find it fascinating that Mary Magdalene was delivered from seven devils. Is it possible that each room in her soul was locked down by the enemy, and she needed some strong help from Christ to come free? She was wise, and stayed close to the Lord after that so that the enemy would have no chance to re-invade her soul.

In my previously-mentioned early morning meeting, the Lord also began to reveal the richness of the treasure that He desired to place within the rooms of our soul. Our ability to meet with Him and get our prayers answered was treasure enough; but now He began to connect His redemptive names and the rooms of our soul together. For example, if we have need of provision, then we must meet with Him in the room called Jehovah-jireh. As we commune with Him there, discussing His promises about our needs, He answers our requests. As He does this on a consistent basis, a pillar of confidence surrounding His Name would be reinforced in us. In John 15:7, Jesus states, "If you abide in Me (in the soul room), and My words abide in you (you've studied to show yourself approved), you shall ask what you will (your requests), and it will be done unto you" (His answer).

What an incredible revelation! He identifies the location of the Secret Place of the Most High, gives these rooms His seven names, and then reveals how His seven pillars of confidence are built in us.

100% God's Will

As I was going through my all-too-frequent bouts of depression, I had to squarely face a great controversy that rocks the Christian Church. I had to settle in my mind that it was 100% God's will to heal the inwardly-afflicted soul. Because I was going through such terrible inner blackness, it was necessary for me to be adamant about this. If I hadn't held on to this promise about inner healing, then I probably would have ended my life.

I knew that His Name was Jehovah-shalom, and I was not about to turn away from His mighty covenant Name. I kept meeting with Him in that soul room until His mighty pillar of peace was formed in me. I believe it also works for physical healing even though I haven't had as much experience with it. I did meet Him in the healing soul room when my son could hardly breathe, and when my wife was in serious labor difficulty with our first child. I poured out my heart to God, and reminded Him over and over of His healing promises, and in both cases, I received my answers.

I love how God brings all of the pieces of the puzzle together in Psalm 91. We know from Scripture that we are the temple of the Holy Ghost (1 Corinthians 6:19), a place where God and man meet together. But in this Psalm, God tells us that our soul rooms have a name…the "secret place of the Most High" (Psalm 91:1). He then tells us that He loves to answer our prayers for two very definite reasons. In verse 14, He states, "Because he has set his love upon Me, therefore will I deliver him; I will set him on high because he has known My Name."

The first reason about setting our love upon Him is exciting enough. He longs to answer our requests because we have taken the time to develop a love relationship with Him. But the second reason is even more exciting because it wraps up all of the ideas presented in this chapter into one package. He tells us that He will answer our requests because we have also taken the time to come to know His name. What an encouragement to our faith!

As I continued to study, I found more exciting information in Proverbs 8:34-35. There He states, "Blessed is the man who listens to Me, watching daily at My gates, waiting at the posts of My doors. For whoever finds Me finds life, and obtains favor of the LORD." Here He reveals that when we find Him in the Secret Place, we will also find the mysterious substance called "life." What an astounding mental health revelation!

People are frantically searching all over the face of the globe to find wiser counselors or better medications, and here, in one tiny verse, God tells us that we will find our answers in our intimate devotions as we meet with Him in the rooms of our soul. Thankfully, in the midst of my mental health crises, I had learned to turn to Him first, and I was able to prove the truth of this verse. We've been given the wonderful names of God, and as we search them out, we'll find all of the help that we could ever need. We just need to spend some time learning to understand the fullness of His names.

Even More Insights

As I was reflecting on these thoughts, the Lord began to give me some very personal information. He told me that even though I hadn't understood what He was doing in the midst of my depression struggles, my need for peace had been so intense that He had been carrying me as I met with Him in the room called Jehovah-shalom. He startled me by saying that many other Christians that were also depressed had failed to obtain their peace because they were trying to find their answers in this world, and in their haste had not spent time in this soul room.

He further encouraged me that when I had turned to Him with such desperation in Sechelt when I had run out of finances, He had met with me in the room called Jehovah-jireh. It was there that He provided for our financial needs, and gave us the many things that we needed for our struggling family. He also showed me that when I had depended on Him with my whole heart during the dangerous delivery of our first baby, I had been pouring out my heart to Him in the room called Jehovah-raphah. It was there that He had saved my wife's life, and placed a beautiful baby daughter into my arms.

Before I close this section, it's important to see how a soul room is established in the life of a Christian. God said that if a person feels a headache or a cough coming on, and they turn to Him first in intimate devotion, then they have started to construct this soul room. But if their immediate action is to discuss their symptoms, and always run to the medicine chest, then they don't give Him a chance to build the soul room called Jehovah-raphah. If this continues year after year, then they may have given mental assent to healing, but this room remains poorly constructed in them.

Things may go well for them for a long time because of the wonders of modern medications, and the person may escape all inconvenience and pain. But when something comes upon their life that doctors or medications can't cure, they haven't built confidence in His Name, and become desperate to find relief. If they still don't learn about the miracles hidden in His Name, it's possible that their lives could be greatly hindered or even shortened.

Go to Your Room

Although I didn't know all of the things in the past that I know today, I had learned one thing that has always kept me in time of trial: I took God at His word. If He said that He would do a certain thing, then I wouldn't let go of Him until I saw something happen. I'm certain that this is the reason that I received these valuable truths and I'm walking depression-free today. Whenever I was in distress, I would take the promises of God that applied to my particular need, and in my youthful zeal, I would try to overwhelm the Lord with them. He had lots of patience with my lack of understanding, and He seemed to love that I was always turning to Him first for my solutions.

At that time I didn't know that I was meeting Him in the Secret Place of the Most High, but while these meetings were occurring, He was forming His mighty soul pillars in me. In the natural world, we know that pillars are designed to bear great weight. It's exactly the same in the spiritual. Because of my frequent meetings with Him in these rooms, my inner strength and confidence were now greatly increasing.

This early morning revelation also added another dimension to my life. I saw that I couldn't just live off of the testimony of encouraging men of faith like Jimmy Swaggart, Kenneth Copeland, or Kenneth Hagin, and expect to see results. They had already spent their "room time" with the Lord. I had to go to the room myself, and work with God so He could build up these soul pillars in me. Confessing God's promises alone just doesn't get the job done. I see so many people running around and loudly quoting the Word of God. They firmly declare that they have faith, but without room time, it seems to always fall short.

Room #1: Jehovah-Jireh—The Lord will provide Himself a sacrifice (Genesis 22:8).

The obstacle: Many people think of themselves as independent, and it is often hard for human beings to bow the knee, and admit that they need help.

Over the years, I have seen that many have a very narrow view of the Lord. They see Him as the One who listens to their prayers and meets their needs—but they stop there. If we approach God this way, we miss the fullness of each name of God, and we won't grasp the Scriptural circumstances that brought each name to us. The implication of the Name given to Abraham was that the Lord Himself would provide our sacrifice. Several thousand years later, Calvary gave us the right to this redemptive Name of our God so that we might have our needs fully met by Christ. If we go into that room with a clear understanding of what it cost the Lord to give us this particular revelation of Himself, then we can have great confidence. As we learn more about the price He paid, His depth of sacrifice should make us very thankful indeed.

How well I remember those early days of ministry when we went to Sechelt, B.C. to open a struggling Christian school. We had very little income, and I was learning to live by faith. We put every cent we had, and then some, into getting the church and school doors open. When the tuitions did finally begin rolling in, they were barely enough to pay the bills, and there was almost nothing left over for our income. I still remember the day I stood praying over a late tuition, crying out to the Lord for His help. Without warning, the parent walked in and put the tuition payment on my desk. I was shocked to say the least. In the midst of my desperate circumstances, the pillar Jehovah-jireh was being reinforced in my soul.

As our family grew, we became tired of renting, and cried out for a home of our own. We scoured the town of Sechelt for a suitable house, but there was none to be found in our price range. Just as we gave up trying, the Lord gave a word through a visiting preacher. He said, "There is a couple here who have been looking for a home. I want them to relax and let Me put it in their hand." We obeyed this directive, and about six months later, a congregation member came to us and asked if we were interested in purchasing her parents' fixer-upper house before it went on the market. The price was manageable, and we jumped at the chance. It was so exciting to see Jehovah-jireh at work answering our prayer. Needless to say, there were other desperate financial needs along the way, but as we prayed, God just kept meeting those needs. On another occasion, we had reached an all-time low just before Christmas. Things looked somewhat bleak, but once again the hand of the Lord was there to provide for our needs. The Government of both Canada and B.C. decided to markedly increase the benefits to children in struggling families. All of a sudden, our family allowance tripled, and in the same month a mysterious check arrived in the mail from a friend for $1,500. I was somewhat overwhelmed by the generosity of this friend and of the government, but behind it all I saw the wonderful countenance of Jehovah-jireh. When it came time to move to Chilliwack, we found ourselves in another difficult situation. We had purchased a house there, but hadn't been able to sell our house in Sechelt. We were facing a very difficult financial situation as our moving day approached. It looked like we were going to have to take out a "bridge mortgage" which had the potential of becoming very awkward and expensive. Trying to manage two houses in different towns is difficult indeed. The day we packed up and left for Chilliwack, we were informed that we had an offer on our Sechelt house, and the moment we arrived at our new home, the phone rang. It was our real estate agent informing us that our Sechelt home had sold. Talk about perfect timing! Through these and so many other blessings, the Name Jehovah-jireh was forever carved into one of the rooms of my soul.

Room #2: Jehovah-raphah—"The LORD that healeth" (Exodus 15:26 KJV).

The Obstacle: The Lord reveals some serious requirements in order for mature Christians to receive healing. These involve our growth in faith, and our commitment to "study to shew [ourselves] approved unto God" (2 Timothy 2:15 KJV).

This Name of God is thrown about freely in our day, and some think that all they have to do is repeatedly quote "by His stripes we are healed" (Isaiah 53:5). While it is true that faith in His Word heals us, God also wants us to learn how to grow in our faith, and to grow in our love for His Word. In my years of experience, I have seen the new Christian receive His healing more easily; whereas the mature Christian is expected to have studied the Word of God so they might have some understanding about His healing, and show diligence in obeying His words.

Although I have had several serious operations during my lifetime for certain maladies, I have lived relatively free of sickness. Several years ago, my son came down with a nagging cough. I didn't pay much attention to this malady at first, but one night, it seemed that the Lord woke me up as he was coughing and gagging. I was alarmed at the sound, so I tarried many hours during the night praying for him, earnestly calling on the name Jehovah-raphah. At last the cough broke, but I learned firsthand what it meant to stay in this room with God until something tangible happened.

I certainly had some very troubled moments surrounding the birth of our first daughter. My wife's water broke on Thursday late afternoon, but as the hours dragged into Friday, nothing more happened. When the danger of infection started to become much more serious, they emergency-airlifted her into Vancouver where a specialist took over. That's when I fervently entered this soul room, and I really began to pray with my whole heart. I sensed that the Lord was building His strength into me throughout this ordeal, and He gave me full assurance that everything was going to be okay. But there was a further lesson to be learned because when I arrived at the hospital room in Vancouver, I laid hands on my wife's womb and began commanding the baby to come out—but still to no avail. Finally, the specialist felt that natural birth was no longer an option. My wife's life was now in serious danger. They rushed her in for an emergency C-section, and a beautiful baby girl was soon placed in my arms. The specialist told me that the cord was wrapped around the child's neck, and if she had been delivered by natural means, as I had prayed, she wouldn't have survived. I felt the gentle rebuke of the Lord that if I was to help people to gain their healing, I also needed to listen to His instructions.

Presumption is also a big destroyer of Christians, and I leaned a very uncomfortable lesson about it at this time. It was 2:00 a.m., and my sister-in-law and I were hurriedly following the medical procession to the operating room. I presumed that I could go in and see the birth of my first child. The "sergeant-major head nurse" took one look at me and yelled, "Get out of this operating room! You're not gowned-up!" I quickly retreated out the door like a whipped dog with my tail between my legs.

Moments later, this same nurse appeared pushing my baby daughter in a maternity cart, and said that we were to accompany her up to the nursery. I was nervously standing back because of her previous strong outburst. She suddenly smiled and said, "You can pick your daughter up. She's yours, you know." Although I didn't like all of the difficulties surrounding our first child's birth, I had been meeting Jesus in the healing room of my soul, and it was now my delight to be holding my first precious child in my arms.

Room #3: Jehovah-nissi—"The LORD our banner" (Exodus 17:15).

The Obstacle: It's not easy to win wars against our flesh. Some find studying the Word of God difficult, and others find it challenging to get up early to pray. In my own life, I have a real struggle with fasting. I enjoy my food.

The somewhat mysterious concept of spiritual warfare centers around this Name of God. When Israel came against Amalek (a type of our flesh), they were being defeated until the Lord showed them how to win this battle. Each time Moses overcame the weariness of his flesh and kept his arms raised to God, the Lord prevailed in the battle raging below him. But when he dropped his arms, the enemy began to prevail in the battle. Finally, two elders figured out a good solution, and held up his arms until the enemy was utterly routed. This example was designed to teach us that when we enter into this type of spiritual battle, it's not always agreeable to the flesh, but the results can be amazing if we prevail. In the same way, when we enter into this soul room, we don't always feel like fighting with our flesh, but as we do, we see great things accomplished in our lives.

The Name Jehovah-nissi was given to us because the enemy of our souls is a deadly foe. If we're ever going to win our life's battles, we need much divine help and clear guidance. Some people presumptuously enter into battle with the enemy having no knowledge of this Name of God, and they're beaten badly. The most glaring example is described by Paul when the seven sons of Sceva tried to copy his work. When they tried to cast some devils out of a man, they almost got themselves killed (Acts 19:11-20). They hadn't spent time in this soul room with God, and had no idea how the enemy operated. Taking the time to learn our lessons in this room can make a huge difference in the success of our Christian life.

In my previous book, I described how the administration in the town of Gibsons was overwhelming me with their demands that I pack up the Christian school, and move it out of an un-zoned location. But we had absolutely nowhere to go. Even though we were consulting a lawyer, and he had their attention with his fierce arguments, I knew it was only a matter of time before the school would be destroyed. As a consequence, they were forcing me, as well as our church congregation, to spend a lot of knee time in this soul room; and after a season of earnest prayer, the school lived to see another day. Another wearying experience over the years has been with difficult students, contrary parents, and frustrated staff members that were under my direction. On one particular occasion everything seemed to come to a head all at once in a parent meeting. Some real disrespect was thrown at the pastor and myself, and I felt my strength failing under this onslaught. In fact, it got so bad for awhile that I didn't even want to leave my office. Even though I was exhausted and emotionally overwhelmed by their display of anger, I went back to the soul room where I absolutely poured out my heart to God.

I didn't know exactly how God would answer this pressing need, but answer He did in a most unusual way. The school suddenly ran out of money. While we were battling through this financial crisis, one teacher stepped down, and the other decided to leave at the end of the year and seek other employment. When June came, they moved on in their lives, and we moved on with the school. Once everything was equitably settled, the enrollments and finances bounced right back again. Jehovah-nissi had heard our earnest cries, and answered once again in a most unusual fashion.

Room #4: Jehovah-Shalom—"The LORD Our Peace" (Judges 6:24).

The Obstacle: One of the most difficult things for people to do is to humble themselves and admit that they need help. But lasting peace only comes as God shows up on the scene; it can't be created otherwise.

Poor Gideon had a really rough time in the early part of his life. The Amalekites had been invading the land for seven consecutive years, every year at harvest time. This was because Israel had turned their backs on the Lord. So most people barely had enough food to eat. One day, he was threshing grain in a hidden place for fear of the enemy. Without warning, the Angel of the Lord appeared to Him, and told him that God would use him to deliver Israel. His lack of faith could have gotten him into serious trouble, but God had mercy. When Gideon realized that he'd seen God, he was alarmed, but the Lord declared over him that He was Jehovah-shalom, and that Gideon was not going to die (Judges 6:1-24).

Even though God promises His peace as part of our covenant blessings, mental and emotional problems continue to be rampant in our society. I became aware of this soul room and this particular name of God out of sheer necessity. My fight with serious soul issues was the ongoing battle of my life. But the confidence that God has now given to me as a result of these many desperate meetings formed a very strong pillar in my soul. Because of my severe depression problems, I had to learn to meet with Him in this soul room often, and His frequent deliverances in my life were nothing short of miraculous. How well I remember the repeated times when I would pour out my heart to Him with hot tears streaming down my face, and feel His strengthening touch.

In our modern day society, mental health problems seem to be increasing dramatically; and suicides, even in the younger generation, have reached alarming levels. At this time, the need in society for help in the mental health area is becoming so great that psychiatrists' schedules are completely filled, expensive medications have become the norm, and provincial mental health budgets have increased almost to the breaking point. Tragically, when faced with these kinds of frightening inner problems, many don't receive the strength and guidance that they need because they know nothing about this mighty name of God. I love to tell people of the incredible help that I received in this room of my soul, and remind them how Psalm 91:14 declares that people will receive all of the help that they need "because they know [His] Name."

How well I remember the hours spent before the Lord pouring out my heart to Him about all of my many internal problems. One of my most memorable experiences was the time when I was blanketed by fear. I had struggled with intermittent nagging fears all of my life, but at this time, it seemed to magnify itself in me with the intent of destroying my soul. As I poured out my heart in sheer desperation, the Lord reminded me that "perfect love casts out fear" (1 John 4:18). I thanked Him for the insight, but I also told Him that I needed more.

That's when He told me to seek Him for a deeper revelation of His "fear-destroying" love. So I began to fast and pray for it, and it seemed that three days came and went very quickly. But I still had received nothing. That night, I went to bed greatly troubled, but was suddenly awakened from my sleep about 4:00 a.m. with liquid love pouring right through me, and all over me. In fact, the revelation of His love was so strong that it washed every trace of fear out of me, and it has not been able to return because the memory of that experience remains strong in my heart. In this desperate time, I came to know Him as Jehovah-shalom.

Many years ago, our senior pastor, Reg Layzell, had shared with us how devastated he was over the sudden death of his wife. Even though he had been instrumental in bringing forth the praise revival that has now swept though this land, he wasn't prepared for anything like this. He said that black feelings of despair and hopelessness had gripped his soul. Even though he had taught for many years about the different types of praise, it was the hardest thing for him to fall to his knees and now offer the sacrifice of praise. But as he obeyed, contrary to all his feelings, the power of God came upon him, and gave him an amazing touch of inner peace and strength. This mighty touch from Jehovah-shalom enabled him to continue for several more years in his very fruitful ministry. Through his desperate praise, He had met with Jehovah-shalom, and was greatly strengthened.

Room #5: Jehovah-ra'ah—"The Lord is my Shepherd" (Psalm 23:1)

The Obstacle: David had gone through some difficult experiences as a shepherd, but through them, he saw that God was watching over him, and leading him.

Because of my terrible bouts of depression, my life was anything but pleasant or easy. But now, as I look back, I see that it was God's intention all along to lead me out of "the valley of the shadow of death" (Psalm 23:4). It just took me a long time to get really desperate and connect with His deliverance plan. I now understand that when God says that He will never allow us to be tested in a manner greater than we can bear (1 Corinthians 10:13), He is serious about that promise. The problem is that most of us don't turn to Him in our time of great need; so without His help and the Holy Spirit's guidance, the testing can most certainly overwhelm us.

One of my sons is quite reserved, and was having real difficulty finding the type of job that he wanted. It seemed that every time he would get an electrical job, he would be the first to be laid off when the work slowed down because he had been the last to be hired. He had been offered a chance to go out onto the pipelines of Alberta, but after some prayer, we didn't think that this was the best choice for him. He was even thinking of going into another line of work, when all of a sudden, God opened the exact door that he needed. As I look back now, I see that God works with our personalities. Even though he didn't have the aggressive nature to go and seize the type of job that he wanted, God was still leading him, and at the right time, opened the door for the perfect job. The Lord was proving to both my wife and I that He's not only our personal Shepherd, but also the guiding Shepherd of our children.

Some people struggle with the idea of believers receiving prophetic words, or the idea that God truly desires to speak to us personally. Nevertheless, I received accurate direction in a "laying on of hands" experience (Hebrews 6:1-2) from the presbytery of our church. The Lord identified my previous dilemma with depression, and told me what type of problems I would face concerning mental health issues in the future. He then gave some very helpful directions how I was to overcome it. As I look back many years later, I see that the guidance I received at that time was sharp and clear, and it enabled me to do the correct things to defeat the depression.

As a consequence, I am now on the other side of the depression, and able to craft this manuscript. I fully realize that it is the Lord's desire to lead us through life, and to bring us home safely. To assist me, He has met with me often in this room, and I have felt His gentle hand of shepherding.

Room #6: Jehovah-tsidkenu—"The Lord our righteousness" (Jeremiah 23:6)

The Obstacle: Jeremiah was overwhelmed by the filthiness of his generation. But God has purposed that we can all become pure by modeling our lives after Jesus Christ, and seeking cleansing through the power of His blood.

During one difficult experience, I had been struggling with the blackness of hell in my soul, and I didn't know how to break out of it. I had told the Lord that I would fast until I died if necessary, but I wouldn't take my own life. At one of my lowest ebbs, the Lord spoke clearly to my spirit. He said, "When you awaken tomorrow, I want you to praise Me, and don't stop." I knew that it was the voice of the Lord, and I purposed to obey Him. So the next morning when I arose, I began to praise in earnest even though the powers of darkness were just about crushing me. After a few hours of aggressive praise, suddenly it happened. It was like all of Heaven came down on my soul, and I was cleansed from this blackness. In a moment, I had met with Jehovah-tsidkenu, and I was set free. When a person has suffered from a previous time of abuse, it seems that some very unclean spirits can get a hand hold of the victim's soul. Tragically, there are counselees who spend all of their days in counseling or on medications just trying to get some relief from the invisible pressure of their past abuse. When I was fighting this same battle, I knew that I wasn't making headway against the uncleanness, so I cried out to the Lord, and asked what I should do.

He told me that the roots of abuse were still active in my soul, and were drawing up some very real poison from my soul into my mind. He encouraged me to lay my hands on my own head, and ask the Holy Spirit to cauterize these darkened roots. As I did, I sensed that the connections were finally being broken. Then the Lord guided me in asking the Holy Spirit to create His new roots in place of the old ones. As I returned to this soul room, I once again saw the power of Jehovah-tsidkenu at work, changing things in me.

If ever there was a day that we need cleansing, it's in our present generation. The glut of visual and auditory pollution is almost overwhelming. In fact, some people are so heavily addicted that they spend hours every day just looking at various types of pornography on the computer. But God isn't taken aback by this. He has given us the power of His name to use, and He wants to set us free. But we must go into our soul room so that He can show us His strength in the area of our greatest need. He will rarely erase things from our minds; instead, He puts His strength and substance inside of us so that the things of this world lose their power. This enables us to begin to turn away from things that are unclean.

As we place the Word of God inside of us, we will finally see the fulfillment of Scriptures like, "Each of you should know how to possess his own vessel in sanctification and honor" (1 Thessalonians 4:4), and "How can a young man cleanse his way? By taking heed according to Your word" (Psalm 119:9). Then as we learn to dwell in this room, we will have success coming clean, even though many around us continue to struggle. The Name Jehovah-tsidkenu is not some idle concept; it has been given as a gift so we might live a clean and holy life.

Room #7: Jehovah-shammah—"the LORD is present" (Ezekiel 48:35).

The Obstacle: Ezekiel had seen the pollution that the priests had caused; but God showed him a temple "not made with hands" a holy city in which the Lord wanted to dwell. We are the New Jerusalem, the bride of Christ, and God will forever reside within us.

Sometimes God can shock us in ways that we don't like. My wife and I have a good marriage, but one time I had a bee in my bonnet about something insignificant, and I wasn't being very nice. Finally, the Lord had heard enough, and He spoke to my spirit. He said, "Son, marriage is a practice session where you're learning to be married to Me. When you married Sherron, you committed yourself to this, and I'm really not happy how you're treating her." I was so shocked that I went straight to my wife and apologized for my insensitivity. Since that time I have been much more careful realizing that the Lord truly is Jehovah-shammah. He is present everywhere, watching the evil and the good.

When my daughter was with her missions group in Tibet, they went on a tour of one of the monasteries. Suddenly the monks gathered around the young people and began to loudly chant over them. At first they were afraid, but the missionary reminded them of the power of the blood of Christ, and that God was there with them. He told them that after the monks had finished their chanting, they were going to sing *Amazing Grace* back to the monks. They did just that, and to their delight, Jehovah-shammah came down on that little monastery in great power. Everyone was crying, including the people and the monks waiting outside of the monastery gate. My daughter also learned first-hand about the awesome power of the name Jehovah-shammah.

We see in Herod's day that Jehovah-shammah was not a name to be trifled with. Herod had given the Church a very bad time, and was feeling more and more confident in his own power and abilities. On a special occasion, he gave an oration to a visiting delegation, and they began to proclaim his might and majesty. He accepted their praises that he was a god, and not a man. It shocked me to see that the Lord struck him, and he was soon eaten up with worms (Acts 12:20-23). Herod learned to his horror that the Lord was present. As we move into the last days, and Satan proclaims himself to be more and more powerful, we will learn to go to this soul room often, and see Jehovah-shammah at work to protect and deliver us.

In Conclusion

Scofield (1917) identifies seven distinct names of God. It is their purpose to reveal to us the mighty work that God has done for the people of faith in the past. Each name also applies to today because God declares, "I am the LORD, I do not change" (Malachi 3:6). These names identify our most frequent areas of need during our life's walk with Him. In a very unusual revelation, the Lord linked together His seven redemptive names with the seven rooms of my soul.

Over the years, because of my desperate inner needs, I learned to frequently meet with God in these seven specific soul rooms. In fact, it was in these rooms that He saved my sanity again and again by answering my many desperate requests. As He did this, strong pillars of confidence and strength were formed deep within me. This pillar-creating has been a lifelong process, but it most certainly changed me inside. If you're facing difficulties, it's never too late to begin learning more about these rooms and the names of our God.

Chapter 5
A Fighting Soul: Its Seven Parts

About fifteen years ago in the southwestern states, there had been a rash of home invasions. The favorite target of this particular criminal was seniors who couldn't defend themselves. In the San Francisco area, this very nasty home invader was not only robbing seniors, but often beating them up so badly that many died from their injuries. But he eventually tangled with the wrong senior. He thought the man would be an easy target. Little did he know that this elderly man was an army veteran, and his assigned task had been weaponry. He had registered his service revolver when he retired, and kept it at the ready for any emergencies.

When this violent man came smashing through his front door, the elderly man was sitting in his rocking chair facing the doorway. Because of the many break-ins in his neighborhood, he had his service revolver in his lap, and fully loaded. As the guy raced across the living room toward him with a baseball bat in his hands, the elderly gentleman calmly lifted the revolver and placed three slugs in the shocked man's chest. He died on the spot, and the police commended him for doing a great service to the many seniors in that area.

If we put a spiritual twist on this story, I doubt that Satan could do all of the terrible damage that he's currently doing to mankind if we had the weapons of our warfare on hand and were skilled in their use.

> *For we do not wrestle against flesh and blood, but against principalities, against powers, against the rulers of the darkness of this age, against spiritual hosts of wickedness in the heavenly places.*
> *Ephesians 6:12*

It drives me nuts when people are too empathetic with people who are having struggles. This short Scriptural passage clearly warns us that we're in a life and death struggle with demonic foes and that we're going to have to show some real determination and guts. When I deal with people who are depressed, I first talk about consistency of personal devotions, intimacy with God, and the importance of engrafting the Word of God into themselves. But not long after, I'm talking about wrestling and the battle we all must face to overcome. I quickly stress that it will take some effort and commitment to fill up their soul, and to regain their mental health. When I was dealing with one depressed fellow at a banquet, I wasn't being very sympathetic with his plight…for very good reasons. He was acting completely helpless, and I wanted to show him that he must learn to stand against these ongoing thoughts of suicide using worship, prayer, and the Word of God. I have recently learned that he has responded to the counsel of many, and is now in a more stable mental condition.

All Christians, without exception, must learn how to fight well, and how to defend themselves if they desire to see the clearly-promised abundant life. At another 4:30 a.m. meeting, the Lord continued to increase my understanding about the needs of the human soul. He told me that if I desired to live a long and useful life as a Christian, then it was time to learn more about my spiritual armor and weaponry.

To my complete surprise, He revealed that our offensive and defensive weaponry was also made up of seven pieces. I asked the Lord if He minded if I counted them because I was certain that there were only six. He must have been amused by this because He reminded me before I started counting that the fervent prayers coming out of the Christian's mouth were the seventh piece, and that they were the most powerful weapon of all. It is the prayers of the saints and the Word of God that strikes terror into the heart of every demonic foe.

Having a Reality Check

If we've been listening to too much to this world's philosophies, then we need a reality check. We live in a world filled with people who think that no one should suffer pain; but that's not real life. Some short times of discomfort can make us sit up and take notice…and can also bring about genuine soul changes. In fact, God warns us in Proverbs 20:30 that "blows that hurt cleanse away evil." In my case, my terrible battles with depression caused me to become serious about the condition of my soul.

But I wasn't the only one to get disciplined. When Miriam and Aaron spoke foolishly against Moses, the Lord struck Miriam with leprosy. Aaron then pleaded, "Please don't let her be as one dead, whose flesh is half consumed when he comes out of his mother's womb" (Numbers 12:12). But the Lord was unmoved. He told them that she would feel the sting of suffering for seven days before He'd heal her. In our day, it's no different. Children need to feel pain of a good spanking if they are defiant, and criminals need to feel pain if they are to change their ways.

On the African savannah, if a pride of lions bring down a wildebeest or a giraffe, they will sometimes start devouring the guts and back end of the victim while it's still alive. It's the same in the spiritual. The enemy of our souls does this to people in our day…we can hear them screaming out in pain as they're being devoured by the enemy. In 1 Peter 5:8, the Lord warns us "be sober, be vigilant; because your adversary the devil walks about like a roaring lion, seeking whom he may devour." If we don't know what protects us, then we're in danger. As I look back on the nightmare of my depression days, I can identify with this description completely. The Lord saw my intense pain, and wanted to do something about it; but if I hadn't become serious about seeking Him, I would have been torn apart by the combined forces of depression, anxiety, and fear.

Thankfully, the story doesn't need to end in defeat. When we're struggling with heaviness in our soul, we're told to put on "the garment of praise" (Isaiah 61:3). This doesn't mean repeating over and over, "I put on my garment of praise. I put on my garment of praise." It means that we begin to praise the Lord with everything within us. When I was told by the Lord in the midst of a terrible bout of depression to praise the Lord the next morning, and not to stop, I did it fervently with all of my heart. Several hours later the heaviness was broken off of my life in a mighty visitation from the Holy One, and I was set free. If I hadn't obeyed, I could have eventually been torn apart by my inner struggles.

In the same way, when we're told by God to put on our spiritual armor, it doesn't mean that we quote Ephesians 6 over and over. It means that we're required by God to do certain specific things. These may include getting His truths into us until they come out of our pores, or learning about our faith so that it becomes useful to us.

Have Your Weapons Ready

A number of years ago, a group of seniors were playing Bingo in our local games center. Without warning, in burst a group of thieves with masks in place, and guns drawn. They quickly lightened everyone's pocketbooks, and proceeded to empty the safe of $15,000. Before anyone could recover from this shock, these bold thieves had headed out the door, and disappeared into the night. I often think how different the results might have been if the bandits had known that each person in the Bingo Hall had a weapon, and were skilled in its use. I am certain that the thieves would not be quite so bold. In the spiritual, it is the same. The terrible atrocities that Satan commits against the human soul could not be done if we were more skilled in the placement of armor, and the use of our weapons.

Some Christians wonder why such terrible things happen to the people all around them. But there's a constant invisible battle going on, and we need to become very serious in our study of the Word of God. A number of years ago, I had a great desire to end my own life, because I could no longer stand the very painful hits of blackness against my soul. I was puzzled when the Holy Spirit quickened the Scripture that Jesus had come into this world to bring abundant life. I certainly wasn't experiencing it at all! But He didn't leave me without hope. He encouraged me to read the full verse so that I might understand the exact source of these black pressures. I soon realized that if I was facing an enemy whose sole desire was to "steal, kill, and destroy" (John 10:10), then I had better learn how to protect my soul from his black pressures.

I quickly found that I was not alone in my ignorance about weaponry. Over the years, I have met many Christians who talked about armor and weapons, and quoted Ephesians 6:12-18 day by day; yet they had no idea what these verses actually meant. I was certain that there had to be much more to this passage than what I was hearing, so I asked the Holy Spirit for His help. I had experienced great success when I used these verses against the administrators in the town of Gibsons who were so fiercely opposed to our un-zoned Christian School. Now, as I studied these verses in more detail, they began to make much more sense. I realized that God wanted me to become more skilled in the use of each piece.

The Life of a Soldier

In Ephesians 6, Paul uses the armor and weapons of the standard Roman foot soldier to describe our own spiritual weaponry. He teaches us the basic facts that we all must know if we want to be effective in our battles. The skill and armor of the Romans permitted them to sweep through and conquer the entire known world; but this armor is heavy, and it is no mistake that Paul's first command to the Christian is to build up spiritual strength. In hand-to-hand combat, the battles were long-lasting and intense, so many times only the strongest and most skilled soldiers would be left standing at the end of the skirmish.

If we're feeling battle weary, then Isaiah's famous passage in Isaiah 40:31 about the renewal of our strength will be helpful. There he declares to all generations of soldiers that if we'll wait upon the Lord, our inner strength will be renewed, and we'll live to fight another day. If we learn the Holy Spirit's fighting techniques, we'll win; but if we ignore His voice, then we may get taken out by the enemy many years before our time. If we're foolish enough to fight the enemy without proper protection, we'll be hurt. I first learned that if I put on my armor properly, and became skilled in its use, then I need not fear the enemy. But if I became careless, then the enemy could do me great damage. On many occasions, I had such trouble with depression because I was unskilled in the use of my sword, and I didn't understand how the armor was designed to protect me. It was only by the grace of God that I survived my battles.

Preparing the Soldier

The world in which we live can be a wonderful blessing, or it can be horribly cruel. Our success or failure against depression and fear depends on our skill in handling our spiritual weapons, and our ability to wear our armor correctly. Whenever a Roman soldier took up his armor, he had to know how to properly place each piece on his body, and he had to be skillful in the use of his sword. During times between hostilities, he needed to build up his muscles because wielding his sword took great strength, and any weakness might mean that he might not survive his next battle. During his recreation time, a good soldier was not idle at all…he was preparing himself for future conflicts.

I sometimes get frustrated speaking with people who have no clue about any surrounding spiritual battle, and who continually say, "The Lord's will be done." I can see immediately by their situation that the Lord's will is not being done at all. Yet they have no clue that they must participate in the battle if they are to keep their health and sanity. Thankfully, I'm learning to be much more patient with people because it wasn't until the Lord opened my eyes that I really saw the scope of the spiritual battle that was raging around me. As I now look back from the other side of hell, I see the value of being a prepared soldier.

Summarizing the Passage

The Lord gives some important warnings to us before He begins speaking in more detail about our armor and weapons. First, He tells us that we are engaging in a spiritual battle, so it's imperative that we build up our inner strength by waiting on Him. Then He adds that we need to increase our spiritual skill by becoming more intimate with the Master. But that's still not enough. He warns that wearing incomplete armor is a dangerous idea because our adversary is very tricky.

Paul then gives us some inside information about our enemy. First He reveals that the terrible things happening to people are not a result of flesh and blood activities. They are spiritual in nature. He also shows that there are four main types of spiritual forces…some much harder to defeat than others. In the final verse of the preamble, He warns that the battle may be long-lasting, so we need to build up our endurance. He also reveals that we must stand courageously until the enemy falls back. Only then does He discuss our armor and weaponry.

The Whole Armor of God

I always cringe when a preacher at a funeral says, "We don't really know why the Lord took this individual home so early. God must have some special purpose for them in Heaven." It's true that God has a very special purpose for the person in Heaven, but we're first called to be fruitful here on Earth. We are also warned by Hosea that "My people are destroyed for lack of knowledge" (Hosea 4:6). I believe that one of the greatest lacks in our Christian world is the knowledge of the armor and weaponry that God has given to protect our souls.

If we don't think the battle is real, just look around at some of the things that people do to escape from their pain and suffering. Even though God has guaranteed to send us all of the help that we need, that help must come according to definite principles that He has set forth in the Word of God. The Lord is not skimpy in His help, but we're the ones who need to learn His principles. I often use the analogy that getting your healing for the mature Christian can be likened to an electric circuit. When all parts are in their proper place, the light will come on. I love the tenacity of Thomas Edison—he knew an electric light was a possibility—but it took much perseverance to achieve that dream.

Learning to Stand

We all need protection as we walk through this life. As a school teacher for many years, I have seen some of my students fall away into sin, and the lives of others end tragically. Yet when I look into the Word of God, I see clear promises of divine protection. My only conclusion is that divine protection is somewhat like an insurance policy: if you're fully paid up and meeting all of the requirements, then you have it; but if you're careless with your payments, then your policy is void, or intermittent. If disaster strikes, you have little recourse with the company. It seems a bit harsh, but that's also how it works both in the business world and in the spiritual world.

It's even worse when it comes to paying your income taxes. The governments of countries give lots of information about saving money from the tax man, but if you never read the information sheets, then you just don't get your benefits. It's your responsibility to know them, so it's a good idea to get help with your taxes from someone who is informed about tax rights and privileges. In the spiritual world, God's ways may seem harsh to the unlearned person, but they're just. He allowed His Son to go to the cross of Calvary on our behalf, and is planning to accept us as an eternal bride for His Son.

In turn, He asks us to develop a love relationship with Him, and demands that we become highly informed about the knowledge of God so freely offered to us in His Word. In doing so, we learn about our rights and privileges. When He states that we must "study to shew [ourselves] approved unto God, a workman that needeth not to be ashamed" (2 Timothy 2:15 KJV), He isn't kidding. It's on our shoulders to learn our responsibilities well.

Describing the Battle: A Practical Example

One of the most common spiritual pressures that come against us is "a spirit of rejection." It tends to create within a person the feeling that no one really likes them, and that no one really wants them around. Even though this is false, it's a very real pressure that must be actively resisted. When such feelings of rejection come against us, this is the time to step up and declare that we've been accepted by Christ, and that we're no longer giving in to this spiritual pressure. As we steadily resist it, and replace it with praise or thanksgiving, this feeling gradually loses its hold on our mind and emotions. But if we keep giving in to it, then these types of feelings tend to get much stronger in us.

In a physical sense, we also need to "get understanding" so that we can help ourselves and minister to other people more effectively. Too often we innocently ask a person how they're feeling, but that's the wrong question. We don't really need to know all about their feelings. We should be asking them about their "compete level" (their ability and desire to fight). I just about fell off my seat the other day when someone asked the person beside me if they were still suffering from their headaches. Their response was that they were still suffering, and they hoped that it wasn't going to turn in to a brain tumor. This person had no understanding that their words hold power, and their conversation could lead them into spiritual defeat.

Describing Our Adversary

> *For we do not wrestle against flesh and blood, but against principalities, against powers, against the rulers of the darkness of this age, against spiritual hosts of wickedness in the heavenly places.*
> *Ephesians 6:12*

Four types of spiritual adversaries are listed here, but it seems like our main enemies are the first two. "Flesh and blood" influence so many different things around us, and attempt to make us center our attention on fighting earthly things. But God wants us to quickly recognize the presence of these opposing spiritual forces, and learn to meet them head on. As I previously explained, when I was running a small Christian school, the administration of the town wanted to move us out of our building because of incorrect zoning. At first, I was so busy talking to lawyers and arguing my case with people that I failed to really see the spiritual side of the battle. The Lord finally warned our Church that this was a demonically-inspired effort to destroy our Christian school, and that we needed to get more serious with our prayer efforts. We finally did as He instructed us, and before long, the battle began to markedly change in our favor. All of us will be involved in intense spiritual battles from time to time, and we need to spend time with the Lord until we really see what is going on in the spiritual realm.

Item #1—The Girdle of Truth

> *Stand therefore, having girded*
> *your waist with truth...*
> *Ephesians 6:14*

It's amusing how language changes over the years. When we think of a girdle in our day, we tend to think of women's fashions. But a girdle has far greater use. In sports, it's worn in the form of compression shorts that hold everything in place, including the necessary padding. For the soldier, it was like a strongly-anchored waist belt that held the weapons.

When some are undergoing trials, they immediately think that they're being given a taste of Paul's thorn in the flesh, or experiencing some of Job's suffering. But those are specific cases with their own particular sets of circumstances. It's true that times of suffering do purify the soul, and make us very serious about seeking God; but it's also true that God wants to fully heal us, so He needs our cooperation.

When the Lord states that "you shall know the truth, and the truth shall make you free" (John 8:32), He is telling us that we need to bury ourselves in the Word of God like we never have before. This is when the Holy Spirit really begins to work deep within us. Tragically, many don't know enough truth from the Word of God for this to work for them. When I fully grasped that it was 100% the Lord's will to heal from depression, this truth greatly strengthened me, and definitely affected the way that I fought.

In the bank, the tellers don't spend a lot of time learning about counterfeits. They spend their training time handling lots of real money. Then when a counterfeit note does come along, they spot it right away because it doesn't look or feel quite right. It's the same in the spiritual. We need to spend lots of time in the Word of God, getting His promises firmly anchored into our hearts. Then, when Satan tries to deceive us, we speak the true Word of God right back to him. When Jesus was being tested in the wilderness (Matthew 4), Satan used the Word of God against Him, but Jesus was so familiar with the truth that He turned it right back on the enemy. After a time, the enemy left Him alone.

The truth that sets us free in the mental health area is knowing that it's not the Lord's will for us to continually live with ongoing mental or emotional afflictions. The crown of thorns was not fictional. It was jammed onto our Savior's skull so that through His suffering we might have peace of mind. This knowledge should aggressively lead us forward to search out what needs to be changed in us. In most cases, the truth will reveal that our soul is too weak to fight off the spiritual pressures that are coming against it, and it's going to take some time waiting before the Lord if we want to build up our inner strength. In mental health battles, the girdle of truth that supports us is knowing for certain that it is 100% God's will to heal us of our mental and emotional struggles.

Item #2—The Breastplate of Righteousness

Having put on the breastplate of righteousness...
Ephesians 6:14

Whenever the word "breast" is mentioned in our day, people immediately think of female anatomy. But that's not the intention of this passage of Scripture at all. A breastplate covered vital organs of soldiers' chests without limiting mobility. In our day, a bullet-proof vest has replaced this piece of armor. In the spiritual world, the breastplate of righteousness is a very important part of our protective armor because the enemy loves to target our heart and other vital organs. In particular, he stirs up thoughts of condemnation against us. These can do serious damage to any Christian.

Thankfully, this piece of armor is designed to teach us that our righteousness is a wonderful gift from Christ, and that we must never strive with God to make ourselves even more righteous. Those who are poorly taught in this area often take on a "religious spirit," and try to work fervently to earn their salvation. While exhausting themselves, they begin condemning those who don't live up their righteous standards. I still remember getting into a verbal tussle with a very religious man many years ago about our pastor's wife. You couldn't find a more godly woman anywhere, but this man was convinced that she was going to hell because her hair and makeup didn't meet his rigid religious standards. Twenty years later, she's still fervently serving the Lord, and he's long gone.

I still remember with great amusement visiting a very "holy" church one Sunday. We got to know the people and chatted with the pastor. I even explained how I had taught in Christian schools for many years. But I guess our outward appearance didn't meet all of the necessary criteria, so at the end of all our discussions and visiting, we were given some information on how to get saved. I still chuckle because I know that the people loved the Lord very much, but they couldn't fully grasp the importance of holiness in the heart, and were stuck into thinking that holiness was portrayed by outward dress. As we understand our place in Christ, we will find inner rest; otherwise, the enemy of our souls will overwhelm us with condemnation. When Satan tries to tell you that you're no good, simply acknowledge that your righteousness is not obtained from the many things that you may have accomplished. It comes from Christ alone.

I experienced this during my terrible days of blackness. I kept condemning myself, and repeatedly asking the Lord what I was doing wrong. He encouraged me that my inner issues had nothing to do with sin. In fact, He told me that I was a pleasure to Him, and that He loved me deeply. In a firm but gentle rebuke, He told me that it was my depression that was making me run too fast through life. At that time, He encouraged me to slow down my life and learn to wait upon Him so that I could build up inner strength. This was a great relief to me because I'd been struggling so hard to gain His love and acceptance.

In the natural world, our chest was designed to contain some very vital and vulnerable organs; so during times of battle, they need to be covered by strong, protective armor. For example, in the game of hockey, the puck can be a formidable missile indeed. If a hockey puck strikes a player in an unpadded part of their chest, it can either knock the breath out of them, or it can actually stop their heart. In battle, fainting from an unexpected blow to the chest could prove fatal because we must remain alert at all times. Thankfully, the breastplate of righteousness provides that kind of chest protection.

Whenever the enemy tries to get us focused on earning our salvation, this piece of armor is designed to remind us that although we'll certainly be rewarded for good works, we're also reminded that the righteousness that brings forth our salvation is not from what we do, but it's only awarded to us because of Christ's shed blood.

I have often had to counsel young Christians about the mechanics of their salvation. On one occasion, a person was very worried that they had lost their salvation, so we discussed this concern in great depth. Soon they realized that it was a faith issue, because they had never had any doubts about salvation until they were genuinely saved. I showed how their right standing with Christ was based on His sacrifice. I also explained about spiritual warfare, how the enemy of our souls tries to get us focused on our unworthiness, and not on Christ's love, power, and grace.

With others, I've had to explain that they must not mindlessly repeat, "I put on my breastplate of righteousness." Instead, I encourage them to have intimate devotions where they reflect on Christ's sacrifice on Calvary. During such times of reflection, we fall in love with Jesus all over again, and gain real confidence about our right standing before Him. This is when the breastplate of righteousness is most effective on us.

Item #3—Our Gospel Shoes of Peace

*And having shod your feet with the
preparation of the gospel of peace.
Ephesians 6:15*

One of the most annoying habits I've seen in people is when they cling onto others and continually strive to be accepted. They remind me of the anxious little cartoon character Odie in the Garfield comic strip series. He followed Garfield around until the cat would finally cuff him. When I was first saved, I remember spending my first few years doing the same thing to the ministry hoping to be noticed. Sometimes, they must have wanted to cuff me because I was so much in their face.

One Sunday night, I'd missed the evening service studying for my bus driver's exam. That was the time that the pastor chose to acknowledge my work in the Creation Science movement. My wife had to stand up and tell him in front of the congregation that I had another obligation that night. When I found out later, I was absolutely devastated. Now, when I look back at this incident, I chuckle because at that time, I knew so little about walking in the gospel shoes of peace.

As I moved on in my Christian life, I found that I wasn't the only one confused about this piece of armor. In fact, many people are in the bad habit of walking through life according to their day-to-day feelings. This "feelings-oriented" behavior doesn't please the Lord at all, so this particular piece of soul armor is designed by God to address this problem. One effective way to put on this piece of armor is to loudly declare when we arise in the morning, "This is the day the LORD has made; we will rejoice and be glad in it" (Psalm 118:24). As we go against our grumbly early morning feelings, we are stepping forward in our gospel shoes of peace, and in time our feelings will shift upward. God has intended that each one of us should learn how to walk in His peace throughout our lives. In fact, everywhere we travel, it's God's intention that we share the news about the wonderful peace and joy that He has given to us. If we're continually battling with inner mental health issues, then we can't complete this important assignment. In some of my worst times, I still remember quoting, "Thou wilt keep him in perfect peace, whose mind is stayed on thee" (Isaiah 26:3 KJV). Although this fervent daily confession didn't cause any dramatic instant changes in the way I felt, over a period of time, those inner changes did come. As I've now matured in the faith, I'm able to walk about in victory with my gospel shoes fully in place.

Item #4—Shield of Faith

> *Above all, taking the shield of faith with which you will be able to quench all the fiery darts of the wicked one.*
> *Ephesians 6:16*

Early in our Christian life, we're given a large lump of rock-like faith, and God wants our immature faith to undergo a period of change as we grow and mature in our Christianity. Before this change, a new convert's faith is often sharp and harsh where they may tell a grieving person that it wasn't God's will for their loved one to die. Thankfully, intermediate Christians are a little more sensitive where they can accept that there are some occurrences that we may not fully understand. Seasoned Christians have much more patience and endurance, where their faith has been softened by a lifetime of trials. In hard cases, they'll comfort people and point them toward the Master rather than trying to explain everything. They have finally learned to work with God to help others find peace.

Our shield of faith strongly develops in us as we grasp the understanding that God will never allow us to be tested in a manner greater than we can bear (1 Corinthians 10:13). We have learned that life is full of trials, but if our shield of faith is properly in place, we won't panic because we know God will always bring us through to the answer. For example, I recently had a serious hernia operation. The doctor warned me that the thing they had to watch for were signs of inner infection. If it got too far, he warned that they'd have to pull the netting out of my belly, and do the operation all over again. Every time I got a pain after that comment, the thought would come that an infection was starting, so I had to put my shield of faith in place, and start fervently declaring all of the good things that God had in store for me. As I did this, the pain would soon subside, and I would be fine once again.

A good friend of mine had learned how to walk with his shield of faith continually surrounding him. On one occasion, he was working with young people in a pool hall, and realized that he was going to have to remove the druggies from amongst the other teenagers. He gave the offending teens notices that they were not welcome back into the pool hall because of their ongoing drug habits. One young man, high on acid, became infuriated. He pulled out his knife and tried to stab my friend in the back. This druggie later told the psychiatric nurse that every time he tried to use his knife, some invisible force grabbed his wrist and prevented him from doing harm. In this case, the invisible shield of faith was surrounding my friend and protecting him from serious danger. In these types of situations, we can see that there is a huge difference between raw presumption and true faith.

I have been through many trials and deliverances in my 40 years as a Christian. These have matured me to the place where I realize how important it is to knit our faith with God. As I reflect back on my early days of panic in the mental health area, I realize that my shield of faith came into full operation as God spoke to me at my most difficult times, and calmed my troubled waters. During my intimate devotions, He began revealing that He was going to take me through a process where He would build up my soul, and steer me toward permanent peace. As I look back now, I see that it happened exactly as He said. Thankfully, my shield of faith was able to develop through this hard process, and remains in place because I now understand the process that brought me to this place of rest.

Item #5—Helmet of Salvation

And take the helmet of salvation...
Ephesians 6:17

Satan's greatest attack against us is in the area of our minds. For this reason, God has designed an awesome piece of armor to protect this part of our soul. As we spend time learning more about His salvation, we'll see that the Lord did some incredible things for us on Calvary. He wants to continually unfold more of His plans throughout the remainder of our lives, and then well into Eternity. One of my favorite Scriptures is "And to him who orders his conduct aright I will show the salvation of God" (Psalm 50:23).

The wonderful salvation that we once received at the altar was only meant to be an open door into all the wonders that God has to offer to us. It is now our turn to press into Christ so that He might reveal the depths of His salvation. As these kinds of thoughts and challenges filled my mind, I discovered that many of my mental and emotional issues were squeezed out.

At one time, I had been very fearful that I would pass on my mental health problems to my children. I had been concerned by the Scripture that the blessings go to a thousand generations to those who love Him, but the curses travel down three to four generations to those who hate Him (Exodus 20:5-6). So I was naturally thinking that my descendants were going to have trouble for four generations. I took this to the Lord because it really upset me.

But the Lord told me to read the full Scripture to Him a number of times. I couldn't grasp what He was trying to tell me, so He finally He asked me whether I loved Him or hated Him. I told Him that I loved Him with all of my heart. At that point, He firmly told me to only cling to the love part of the promise if I wanted my children to remain free, because the second part was only designed for those that hated Him. What a relief! I now keep my helmet of salvation firmly in place regarding this issue. I won't allow any contrary thoughts to take over my mind.

To protect our minds from mental pressures, God has designed a strategy of continuous revelation. It's His plan that we should keep up our level of excitement in this life by hungering after a deeper knowledge of God. Tragically, many get saved and try to camp on that truth for the rest of their lives. Eventually, they get bored with their salvation, and start looking for other things to stimulate them. They don't realize that it's God stirring us up to search after more of Him, not go searching after the things of this world.

If we'll meditate on His salvation, He will reveal more about the amazing work that He's done on our behalf. This protects us from a whole host of mental health issues, because as our mind is filled with the beauty of Christ and the wonders of salvation, the more we are freed from the terrible pressures of emptiness and loneliness.

Item #6—The Sword of the Spirit

And the sword of the Spirit, which is the word of God...
Ephesians 6:17

When a person struggles with heavy black thoughts, a worldly counselor will advise them to refocus on something else such as the cat, or the television. This worked for a time for me, but all of a sudden my mental dam would break, and I would start drowning in blackness once again. The Word of God tells us how important it is to use praise and the principles and the promises of God's Word as a mighty weapon against the enemy. By doing this, we're still refocusing our mind, but now we're focusing on something that has great spiritual power. As we learn to use God's Word, we'll discover that it will slice apart spiritual pressures, and we'll come free from those oppressive black thoughts.

If you reflect on the sword-fighting portrayed in the Old Testament, you'll see that it was a nasty business indeed. After some battles, tens of thousands would lay dead or dying on the battlefield. Your best defense in these types of battles would be to have others watch your back, and your best offense would be to become extremely skilled in the use of your weapons. When we go forth in our Christian lives, it's the same. When you feel sickness or black thoughts coming against you, it's important to ask for prayer. At the same time you must protect yourself by filling your mind with praise, and with the Word of God. If you have been steady in your intimate devotions, and you understand God's will about the issues of life, you're going to win every time. Sometimes you may have to stand and endure—just as I had to do against those who tried to shut down our Christian school—but as you swing your sword, things will change around you.

I love to hear stories about the many miracles that occur in Israel, and how God has protected them over and over. He has also given them a fierce, fighting nature. One of the reasons that they survive today is that they won't tolerate those who are aggressive against them. If missiles are sent their way by the enemy, then they send twice as many missiles right back. They also don't hesitate to make preemptive strikes against real threats. So it is with evil coming against our lives. If we know that it has the intent of destroying us and our loved ones, then we need to use our sword to destroy it before it breaks free.

When I was going through my worst times with depression, the Lord showed me how to refocus my mind on His mighty promises. As I look back now, it was the hope of these promises that kept me going. I just knew that God was going to fulfill them, so I used His words as a two-edged sword. One side was reminding God that His promises couldn't fail, and the other side was cutting apart the hopelessness that the enemy was trying to sow into me. I also found that as I engrafted His words into my heart, His promises filled me and became like a sword that my spirit could wield. Even though the actual words of Scripture belonged to God, as I put them into active use, it now became the sword of my spirit. With it, I was able to cut apart all of the black pressures of the enemy. As I did this year by year, and saw the effect, I grew mightily in strength.

Item #7—The Prayers of the Saints

> *Praying always with all prayer and supplication in the Spirit, being watchful to this end with all perseverance and supplication for all the saints...*
> Ephesians 6:18

Many people are mad at the police when they seem too hard on lawbreakers; but, at times, strong force is necessary. Those who willingly do evil won't go away on their own...they need to be soundly defeated. In the same way, depression and disease won't just go away on their own. There needs to be some definite touches by the Lord to change the situation. When we're putting the correct spiritual forces to work, we're actually crossing border lines in the spirit, and rooting out the enemy. In fact, James encourages us that "The effective, fervent prayer of a righteous man avails much" (James 5:16).

Sometimes I wish I was better tuned in to hearing words of knowledge from the Lord. A beautiful young lady that I had taught many years previously on the Sunshine Coast was staying in Victoria with some college friends. During the night, a candle tipped over in their living room, and the house caught on fire. The blaze spread so fast that she and another girl were trapped by the fire and thick smoke in an upstairs bedroom. There was no escape route for them, so they both perished. I sometimes grieve that if I had only been more tuned in hearing words from the Lord, I could have prayed for her to escape this tragic early death.

Prayer is one of the most powerful things that we can do. With it, we can make such a huge difference in our life, and the lives of others. Many think that they're living this life so that they can make it through their personal trials to Heaven's shore. But we have a huge assignment from the Lord in the above verse, and we must take it very seriously. When Spirit-filled prayers come out of our mouths, the enemy trembles in fear.

Many years ago, a lady fled to a Christian retreat center in the Fraser Valley to escape from her angry and aggressive husband. Somehow he found out where she was, so he came after her. When he saw her, he ran at her with an axe upraised. She screamed out the name of Jesus, and the most amazing thing happened. His muscles froze, and he was left standing with the axe raised high in the air. When the police came to take him away, he was still frozen in exactly the same spot. She proved once again that the prayers that cross our lips are extremely powerful and effective.

In Conclusion

Let me bring this section to a close with this illustration. I sometimes really enjoy watching the old western movies. I'm amazed at how cold and cruel the gunfighters were. In these gun battles, you could have no mercy on your opponent. If you hesitated, even for a fraction of a second, you could be the next addition to "Boot Hill" (the local cemetery). But even if you were the fastest gun in the West, your reputation would precede you, and there would always be another hothead trying to show that he was even faster than you.

Thankfully, with the weaponry that the Holy Spirit provides for us in Scripture, this isn't the case. If your six-guns are loaded and ready, you could have the world's best swordsman coming at you, but it would be no contest. Your weapons are far superior, and if you're skilled in their use, you'll win every time. This "seven pieces revelation" about our armor and weaponry was given to us for our use, so it's vital that we carefully prepare ourselves for all present and future conflicts.

Chapter 6
A Growing Soul: Its Seven Additions
One Complete Book

I had long been resistant to the idea of bringing all my material together into a book because I knew I still didn't have a complete message. Nevertheless, I set aside my own plans to write more daily devotionals, and obeyed Him by faith. Because of this surrender, I knew the Lord was about to give even more soul construction secrets. As time progressed, He certainly didn't disappoint me. Each time He unlocked His treasure chest of mental health secrets, it opened up yet another vast field of learning, and I was really getting excited.

In an unexpected early morning meeting, the Lord revealed that He hadn't stopped His soul building program with seven pillars, seven rooms, and seven pieces of armor; He also desired to make seven additions to the human soul of every person. This would enable them to fulfill the high calling that He had planned for their lives. This new information on soul additions became so comprehensive that I was able to form it into yet another full chapter.

When I was a very small child, I still remember the excitement that my parents felt as they planned out some new additions for our family home. Our house had been just the right size for two adults, but now that children had come along, it was definitely time for an expansion. The carpenter spent much time and effort with my parents to plan out this enlargement, and it was exciting indeed when it was all completed, and we were able to move in. My brother and I could hardly believe how much room had been added to our play area. And so it is with the human soul: when God enlarges us, we'll be amazed at the plans He has for us, and the things that He wants to build into us.

When we're first saved, our soul is like a newborn infant, but God has great plans for its growth and expansion. Salvation is the first critical step in the life of the Christian, but we're never expected to camp there. The Lord wants to add so much more to us, but that requires our willing cooperation. When a child is born, parents have great expectations for their infant. If it's a boy, the father may see the child as a football player, or a bank president. If it's a girl, the mother might see her as a figure skater, or as a woman of influence. We also know that as soon as they're born, children need good food and exercise if they're to grow in both height and weight. We must also take them to school and enroll them in various sports programs if they're to develop their knowledge and skills. This is where inner troubles can really start because some people stop with the first two additions. Many fail to see that there is a third very important mental and emotional component to our ongoing growth and development. Our Heavenly Father has great expectations for each child born into His Kingdom. In fact, He's like an excited parent who sees us as a future teacher, a missionary, or even a college president. But to reach these achievements, He knows that He has to make many timely additions to our soul.

The growth and development of any Christian begins with their love for the Word of God, and their desire to have intimate devotions with the Master. As these things are done, God causes spiritual growth, and the soul begins to take on size and strength. It was at this point that the Lord unveiled another critical soul construction secret. Just as the body and mind grow in size and capacity, our soul must also grow. If the person never finds Christ as Savior, or if they're careless with their salvation, a spiritual vacuum is gradually being created inside of them. Year by year, their other parts have been growing, and the spiritual space opening up in them must now be filled with something. If it's not, there is spiritual trouble ahead.

In this early morning meeting, God was revealing that the space in our ever-growing soul can be filled with things that are either good or bad depending on our choices. As we look at mental health problems, we don't have to search very far to realize that this space is too often filled with the spiritual forces of fear and anxiety. When the 9-11 disaster happened in 2001, psychiatrist's offices were filled to overflowing with badly frightened people. The problem was not the acts of terrorism; the real problem was the lack of the proper spiritual substances in the human soul. If Christ had been permitted to make His additions to those individuals, they would never have been overcome with such gut-wrenching fear during such times of crisis. To prevent this, we need to consider the following passage of Scripture very carefully:

> *But also for this very reason, giving all diligence, add to your faith virtue, to virtue knowledge, to knowledge self-control, to self-control perseverance, to perseverance godliness, to godliness brotherly kindness, and to brotherly kindness love. For if these things are yours and abound, you will be neither barren nor unfruitful in the knowledge of our Lord Jesus Christ.*
> 2 Peter 1:5-8

Note the phrase "giving all diligence." The growth and development of our soul is important to the Lord, and critical in the building up of our mental health.

When the Lord informed me that He wanted to use this passage to make His seven additions to my soul, I was certain this time that there were only six. So once again, I checked it out, and again, I was wrong. There were indeed seven additions. I was really starting to get excited because I knew that seven was often taught as God's number of completeness, and after all of my battles, I certainly wanted my soul to be complete. As I considered this passage of Scripture, I could see that God wanted our spirit and soul to grow mightily throughout the course of our lives. Here He reveals that the building up of faith in our lives is our basic house with its solid foundations. But the soul additions that He desires to make are what convert our tiny bungalow into a large family home.

But these seven soul additions are not automatic. Christ charges each one of us with the responsibility to go after them and build them onto our faith. In this opening passage of Scripture, He reveals that once these soul structures are set into place, we will never stumble in our faith. But we're also warned that these items aren't a reward for the careless Christian. In fact, He states that those who ignore Him and fail to make these additions, are blind and shortsighted (verse 9).

I see often in Scriptures that those who don't respond after much dealing are eventually replaced with others who will listen to God's voice. God has purposed that we should enter Eternity with a fully-developed soul, fully alert to the Master. It's His plan that we all blend together with others and become a smoothly-functioning body of believers.

Although I was excited by this seven additions revelation, I still felt that there was much more to it; so I asked the Lord how this section was to fit with this manuscript on the health of the human soul. He told me that He had never designed us to be isolated individuals. He's building a strong, connected body of believers, and if I wanted to be numbered in that group and have a soul that is strong, then I needed this vital information. Those who isolate themselves from His body were missing a core part of their soul-strengthening program, and would be in danger of stumbling in the days ahead. He sums up this idea in the following Scripture:

> *For by one Spirit we were all baptized into one body—whether Jews of Greeks, whether slaves or free— and have all been made to drink into one Spirit. For in fact the body is not one member, but many.*
> *1 Corinthians 12:13-14*

Our God is an experienced builder, and He tells us in Psalm 133:1 that He loves unity and wants to cement every brick together into a solid, unbreakable wall. When joined together in unity, they become strong and unmovable in the face of any storm. He knows that isolated souls are weak and in danger of falling away, so these seven additions become like the mortar that binds us together into this tight unified body. It's His plan that each individual soul should lend its strength to others so that the body of Christ becomes strong and complete.

Whenever things of great value are discussed, it's not uncommon to repeat the most important things near the end of the speech. In this particular passage, God wants to remind us about the importance of building up and strengthening the human soul. Several of the key items He mentions re-emphasize the fruits of the Spirit. These include goodness, brotherly kindness, self-control and love. So let's break down this passage piece by piece, and discover more about His construction secrets that will prepare us both for this life, and for all of Eternity.

As we dissect this passage, we see that He prefaces His statement by declaring that He wants everyone to escape the corruption that is in the world through the dangers posed by lust. He emphatically states in 2 Peter 1:5, "For this very reason, giving all diligence, add to your faith…" So He's telling us that our soul is incomplete and in danger of falling if we don't make these particular additions to our faith's foundation. He also reveals that it's going to take great effort to build up our soul, and to connect ourselves with others in His body. Many never escape from their inner problems because they don't understand the opening phrase, "giving all diligence." It's going to require great, diligent effort to make the necessary changes and soul additions.

Add To Your Faith

> *For this very reason, make every effort to add to your faith...*
> *2 Peter 1:5 (NIV)*

Faith is the critical foundation of every soul, and God is highly displeased when people lack it (Hebrews 11:6). We have to look no further than the Children of Israel. Even though He had rescued them from the cruel hand of Pharaoh with many mighty miracles, these people had no clue that they were supposed to pray and respond to God in love when they had a need, or when things didn't go smoothly. Instead, they yielded to their cravings and fears, and made malicious accusations against the Lord and His servants. Many even wanted to return to Egypt; so after ten attempts to get them to respond in faith, the Lord finally lowered the boom. We're told that all of the rebels died before the Lord, and their carcasses littered the wilderness (Numbers 14:29). So when speaking about soul additions, it's assumed that we love the Lord, and already have this faith issue settled in our lives.

Adding Goodness

> *For this very reason, make every effort to add to your faith goodness...*
> *2 Peter 1:5 (NIV)*

Several years ago, we were getting apples from a farmer up in the Okanogan Valley. I was helping him to load our box of fruit when he rebuked me. He told me that I was handling the apples far too roughly, and that I was going to bruise them. He said that these bruises would soon spread through the whole box, and cause them to quickly deteriorate in quality, or to rot. He also informed me that if I desired to store these apples for any length of time before eating, then they must be kept cool, and carefully maintained away from the elements.

What a parallel to what God is doing with our souls! He knows that if we're to be in close quarters for all of eternity, then our souls must be carefully maintained, and filled with His goodness. To do this, God has given us the clear example of Jesus Christ. He's the model that we must fashion our lives after. To help us respond to Him, He gives us a choice. We can study the Word of God and let its thoughts permeate our being, or we can continually feed on a diet of worldly things such as television programs where much of the programming is about criminals, sexual lust, and evil.

If we obey Paul's statement "whatsoever things are true…if there be any virtue, and if there be any praise, think on these things" (Philippians 4:8 KJV), then we'll maintain our level of goodness. But if we feed on the world's garbage, our soul will eventually break down.

A parent of a Grade One student was telling us how her little girl had been sent home from school. When they inquired further, they found that she had committed a serious crime in the school's eyes…she had been singing Sunday School songs on the playground, and telling her classmates about Jesus. The parents of the little girl were furious, and confronted the school administration. In spite of all of their protests, the day and a half suspension stood. The parents promptly withdrew their child, and placed her in a Christian school.

Unknown to this ungodly public school administration, this child was spreading a message of goodness in her classroom, the very recipe that was needed to make an excellent school. In fact, a key reason for education is not so we can know more things about this natural world, but so that we can better communicate the Gospel of Jesus Christ to this dying world. Take away this driving purpose from education, and the school system begins to undergo the type of struggles we currently see happening. As we minister the Gospel to every creature, we must let them know not only about the goodness, but the severity of God (Romans 11:22).

When we are adding goodness to our soul, we must be careful that we have the definition correct. Any goodness we possess is through the life, death, and resurrection of our Savior, the Lord Jesus Christ, and His Spirit dwelling in us. From the excellent quality of His life and death, we can build these same character qualities and sacrifices in our own lives, and then demonstrate them to many others. Throughout the ages of Eternity, our sacrifices of goodness and good works will be part of the glue that strengthens our soul, and binds us all together into a tight-knit unit with other believers.

Adding Knowledge

> *For this very reason, make every effort to add…to goodness, knowledge…*
> *2 Peter 1:5 (NIV)*

When the Lord tells us that He wants us to add knowledge to our inner man, He's not referring to the knowledge of natural things. He's referring to "the knowledge of God" (Proverbs 2:5). It's God's plan that the more we come to know our Savior, the closer we will bind together into a tightly-knit body. As the knowledge of God fills us, it will strengthen our mental health and keep out unforgiveness and hatred. This addition of the knowledge of God is important to our future success and I have spoken much about it in my writings. It all started in early Genesis where we are commanded to eat from the Tree of Life, and shun the knowledge that comes from the Tree of the Knowledge of Good and Evil. This first type of knowledge—the knowledge of God—greatly strengthens our soul whereas the second type—worldly knowledge—will weaken it. Ultimately, we choose what tree we will eat from, and in a sense determine our own destiny. One of the sections of Scripture that really startles me is Matthew 25:31-46. In this parable about the sheep and the goats, the Lord leaves no room for error. He demands that we have a very clear knowledge of His will when it comes to our fellow human beings. We're commanded to show love and kindness to them, and if we fail to do so, it means that we're refusing the basic knowledge that God has so carefully placed within us. In this passage, we see that those who trample on their fellow man, or who refuse to demonstrate genuine Christian love, will be sent into a Christless eternity. Much earlier in the Scriptures, we see that Cain was expected to know that his lack of love toward God and his brother would send him into a downward soul spiral—yet in his blind anger, he refused this knowledge.

I was recently talking to my neighbor who is an expert fisherman. I had been fishing for sockeye salmon with very little success, so he explained how he had been casting out as far as possible, and then letting his hooks travel through the right kind of water in a certain manner. When I saw the fish that he was bringing home, it taught me a real spiritual lesson. Knowledge of how to fish, and where the fish lie, can make all the difference between successful angling trips, or a series of frustrating "skunks." It's the same in life. Knowledge of spiritual things makes the difference whether our soul works as it was designed, or whether we fail in life. It is little wonder why God commands us to add knowledge if we desire to have a healthy soul.

Adding Self-Control

> *For this very reason, make every effort to add...to knowledge, self-control...*
> *2 Peter 1:5-6 (NIV)*

Some people have such a strange view of Heaven. They think that when they arrive there, all of their problems will be over. This may true in a sense, but I believe that if we've failed in parts of our training here, there will be a loss of rewards, and there may be some more training classes required in the future. God didn't design us to be robots. He has given us a will, and He will continue to demand that we practice self-restraint. Heaven is a controlled place with definite order, and a clear authority structure, so practicing restraint is a critical area of our daily training.

It's often hard for me to be fully self-controlled. In the early days of my life, I am certain that I would've been labeled as having ADHD. As a young lad, I attended a boy's private school, and I never knew until then that anyone could need the rod of correction as frequently as I did because I had no idea what self-control was. When an older student would ask me to go up behind a teacher, and say, "Hi, stupid," I'd do it. Of course, I would promptly get "six of the best" with a bamboo cane. Gradually, my sore bottom sent enough strong painful messages to my brain, and it caused me to practice more self-control. Even today, I still get laughed at for my silly jokes. For example, when they put hot-air hand-dryers in the church washrooms, someone tacked a note onto the air dryer, saying, "Push this button for a short message from your pastor." I would have put that note on the air dryer first if I had thought of it.

Self-control is one of the fruits of the Spirit, and is a very important part of the second pillar of discipline. As you search the Scriptures, you discover that Satan was an important cherub, and practiced self-control for a season. But when he saw the worship that God received, he slowly became filled with jealousy. After a time, he threw away all restraint, and craftily convinced one-third of the angels to leave their first estate, and follow after him in his rebellion against God. He is now attempting to get mankind to also follow him in his rebellion.

One of the most common examples we see where he is deceiving mankind is in the area of nudity. Even though God strongly commands mankind to cover their private parts, he's convincing people to reveal ever-increasing amounts of flesh. This stirs up ungodly lusts, particularly in men, and causes them to act in a very uncontrolled manner.

Our future in Heaven centers around our ability to restrain ourselves and to practice self-control. If God wants to add these things to us, we need to wake up and work with Him. Otherwise, one of the consequences may be fierce pain in our inner man. Hopefully, this type of painful stripe will get our attention, and cause us to mend our ways. Heaven suffered war because of a lack of self-control in Satan's day, and God has purposed that it should never happen again.

Adding Perseverance

For this very reason, make every effort to add... to self-control, perseverance...
2 Peter 1:5-6 (NIV)

To persevere means "to continue steadfastly with great determination." This is exactly what our Savior had to do in order to obtain salvation for us. Even though this salvation is offered as a free gift to us all, we will all be required to endure some difficult things in order to hold on to it. In fact, Jesus warned us that each one of us would undergo a tremendous fight of faith in order to reach the finish line. We need to give careful attention to His warning that "He who endures to the end shall be saved" (Matthew 24:13). In other words, as we endure trials of our faith, spiritual muscles are built up within us. But those who expect an easy ride in their walk with Christ are in for a rude awakening.

I always admire the stamina of those who participate in the Tour de France cycle race. This bike race is extremely grueling, and lasts over many days. It requires years of preparation just to reach competition level. Ryder Hesjedal, a cyclist from my home town of Victoria, began his preparations as a ten-year-old boy on the steep hillsides near his home. Over the years, he raced up and down those hillsides until he built up the extremely high levels of endurance necessary to compete effectively in the Tour de France. But perseverance is also a spiritual requirement, and a very important part of our salvation. Jesus Christ isn't planning to marry a weak, emaciated bride. He wants us to be strong and filled with a passionate fire for Him.

This is the exact thing that God was trying to infuse into the Children of Israel. But time and again, they rebelled at His testings, and complained bitterly against His servants. Each time, they refused to persevere and rose up with angry complaints against the Lord. All of us will most certainly be tested in the quality of our devotional lives because it's not easy to persevere in praying for others, or spend quality time engrafting the Word of God into our souls. The more we add these character qualities to our soul, the stronger we'll become in life.

Adding Godliness

> *For this very reason, make every effort to add…to perseverance, godliness…*
> *2 Peter 1:5-6 (NIV)*

The quality of godliness is very important, and the Lord demands that it be present in every soul. In fact, the Word of God declares that we must have "holiness, without which no one will see the Lord" (Hebrews 12:14). As we grow and mature, we're expected to become more and more like Him. I love the Scripture that states that "we shall be like Him, for we shall see Him as He is" (1 John 3:2). If we understand that the term godliness means becoming more like God, then we can see the high standard that God sets for each one of us. Then, as we spend time before the Lord in our intimate daily devotions, we know that we're being internally adjusted. Little by little, we can see the characteristics of His precious Son growing in us.

Over my 35 years of teaching in Christian schools, I have served the pastors of four different Churches. During that time, I've come to know many wonderful saints who love and serve God with all of their hearts. But I have also seen believers who repeatedly tore down the pastor, and who would often "bite and devour each other" (Galatians 5:15). This won't be happening in Heaven, so we must get this kind of ungodliness out of our system before we go there.One certain sign that ungodliness is at work is the large number of Church splits. Far too often, people start well on their Christian walk, but because they fail to press into Christ as they should, they begin seeing the flaws in their brethren, and ignore their own flaws. As their vision continues to deteriorate, they feel that the only way to solve the problem is to separate from the Church. Adding godliness to their soul would have solved this problem before it became a major issue.

I'm always amazed when I see an inheritance fight. The benefactors have gathered to pay their last respects to the deceased, but sometimes before the body is even in the ground, relatives begin fighting over his earthly possessions. This is a good time to know if we have become like God. To solve this dilemma, Christ encourages us that "godliness with contentment" (1 Timothy 6:6) is what He longs to see in each believer. If we press into Him, He will heal the troubled areas of our soul, and replace them with His nature. It may take a lot of work to become more like Jesus Christ, so we need to work on godliness immediately and consistently.

Adding Brotherly Kindness

Add to your godliness, brotherly kindness...
2 Peter 1:5, 7

I love God's sense of humor. He knows that we all struggle with selfishness, so instead of isolating us, He crams us really close together into a tightly-knit body so that we can learn to be kind one to another. Even though many walk away from families and churches because of offenses, the church and family were His idea, and we're expected to be intimately involved in both. He demands that we learn to display brotherly kindness, and will accept nothing less. It is a major character quality demanded of all Christians; and if it's not yet operating in us in full measure, then He will work with us until it is added to our soul. He won't allow offenses and bad attitudes to be present in Heaven.

Over the years, many have thought that they could serve Him independently by staying at home and watching TV evangelists. But these people are in for a surprise one day. God always has Heaven in mind, and He's preparing each one of us to submit to authority, demonstrate kindness, and learn to practice forgiveness. In my 40 years of serving the Lord, I've never seen a shortcut for learning these things. I've been challenged to my core on this very subject. In the past, I did some extra gardening. One client had one of the shortest fuses that I have ever seen. If I got his directions wrong, or didn't quite understand what he was saying, he became very upset, and would sharply raise his voice at me. I would return the favor by looking him straight in the eye and telling him to smarten up. This made him even more angry; so I had to work on brotherly kindness. I sincerely asked the Holy Spirit for a different strategy, but I never did seem to get this one right before he fired me.

My daughter had an eye-opening experience when she was on a missions trip in a distant foreign land. Their group found a lady collapsed and dehydrated near the side of a hiking trail. They partially revived her with their water, and carried her into the local village. There the town officials refused to help saying that only the priests and higher officials were worth something in the next life. The kids were shocked at their very bad attitude, and paid for her recovery with their own money. Later, the town mayor was so embarrassed at the poor response of his people that he gave them their money back. This was good for them to see because they had learned that brotherly kindness isn't a core element of all religions.

In daily life, we still need to sacrifice and show brotherly kindness whether we feel like it or not. If you're in a restaurant and get poor service, leave a tip anyway. Don't be mean. When I was a new convert, a brother in Christ took me out to lunch. He gave the waitresses a bad time, and had them in tears. What he was doing felt wrong, and I wish I had known this Scripture at that time. I would've told him to smarten up. Often, it isn't the waitress' fault that the food isn't exactly right, or that things aren't done quickly. There may be too few staff, or the cooks may be slow. We need to practice brotherly kindness. It adds real joy to life.

The Parable of the Sheep and Goats in Matthew 25:31-46 leaves us little wiggle room on the subject of brotherly kindness. Those who practiced common kindness got to go with the Lord; those who were cruel and obnoxious toward their brethren lost out with Christ, and were sent to a place designed for the devil and his angels. We're the ones who must smarten up. God knows that we all need this character quality, and He desires to add brotherly kindness to the soul of every person. It's no light matter in the Lord's eyes. Besides, it's a lot of fun to help others in need. I often slip some money or a gift card to a struggling widow in our church, or send an extra offering to certain missionaries. The look of appreciation, or the success stories of that missions program, is more than worth the labor that it took to earn that money.

Adding Love

> *Add to your...brotherly kindness love.*
> *2 Peter 1:5, 7 (NIV)*

Even though the addition of love to our soul is the last mentioned in this passage, it's certainly not the least. The Scriptures tell us that "God is love" (1 John 4:8). Therefore, love is the most important thing that we can add to our souls. If we ignore the need for this addition, we're very foolish indeed. As we search the Scriptures, we learn that God has much more to say on the subject of love. We are told that "God so loved this world that He gave His only begotten Son" (John 3:16) that we also might become a vital part of His kingdom. As this substance of love is added to us, and gradually fills our souls; it pushes out all other evil—including the very real fear of death.

I've always enjoyed the story of the chicken and the pig. One morning as they were walking about in the farmyard, and passed the kitchen window, the chicken said to the pig, "Let's really love on the farmer today and give him a nice breakfast of bacon and eggs." The pig replied, "Not so fast, chicken. Giving eggs may be your way of showing love to the farmer, but giving him my bacon is total commitment for me." We see from the life of Jesus that in order to demonstrate God's love, Jesus had to show us all what real commitment was; and now He expects the same kind of commitment from our lives. When the Twin Towers collapsed in 2001, some died because they refused to leave the building. They circulated around the towers helping the wounded, and leading others to safety. This kind of love is something that so fills the soul that it overcomes all sense of danger and forces out the fear of death. Self-giving love will be the oil that causes Heaven to run smoothly. In my home Church, a real love for the pastors and elders has been cultivated over the years. Now, if anyone speaks badly about them, they're confronted immediately by many different people. It will be exactly the same in Heaven. If anyone ever tries to operate in selfishness as Satan once did, it would become extremely obvious, and they'd have to give an immediate account of their actions.

Even though love is mentioned last on the list of soul additions, it's the most important soul substance that we could ever contain, and we must give all diligence to adding love to our soul throughout the course of our lives. As this spiritual substance fills us, it forces out all negative things, and has a huge effect on improving our mental and emotional health.

The End Result

> *For if you possess these qualities in increasing measure, they will keep you from being ineffective and unproductive in your knowledge of our Lord Jesus Christ. But whoever does not have them is near-sighted and blind forgetting that they have been cleansed from their past sins. Therefore, my brothers and sisters, make every effort to confirm your calling and election. For if you do these things, you will never stumble.*
> **2 Peter 1:8-10 (NIV)**

This final exhortation by Peter serves as an excellent conclusion for this chapter. He's presenting us with an "if–then" statement that's designed to challenge us very deeply. In this passage, he says that if we add these many things to our soul in increasing measure, then we'll never stumble in life. What an incredible promise! Here we have millions of people in society stumbling over the mental health rock; yet the Lord is telling us that this doesn't need to happen. If we're careful about making all of these necessary soul additions, our life will be considered a success as we stand before the Lord to receive our awards.

When I'm preparing for the next year of school, the administration asks for an annual plan. This plan is like a steering document that guides me through the whole year, and shows the administration that I'm covering the core curriculum. This passage of Scripture is like that annual plan. The Lord is saying that He doesn't want us to be unproductive or ineffective in our Christian lives. He identifies the tasks for us, and then tells us to "work out your own salvation with fear and trembling" (Philippians 2:12). He warns us to be very diligent in making our calling and election sure so that Heaven is a certainty for us (2 Peter 1:10). Christ had no joy in telling the man without a wedding garment that he was not fit for Heaven; nor the foolish virgins that He didn't know them. He weeps for those who miss out because He's not willing that any should ever be lost.

In Conclusion

To wrap up this chapter, we see that God is building His Body, and He demands that we have something of worth to contribute to the group. If we have selfishly lived our lives, we will not be a good fit in the Body of Christ. God's desire is that we should possess a soul that is full, and He makes is possible for us to achieve that in this life. These seven character additions are critical in the soul of every Christian, and it's important that we be diligent in adding these things to our inner man. The Lord sums up the soul additions in one powerful Scripture where He states in Revelation 22:12, "And behold, I am coming quickly, and My reward is with Me, to give to everyone according to his work." Let's not be deceived; mental health is found in a soul that is full. We all have much work to do, but the rewards are worth the effort.

Chapter 7
An Overcoming Soul: Its Seven Challenges
Turning Rocks into Riches

In my early college years, I worked at the world famous Butchart Gardens north of Victoria, BC, during the summer months. It was my job to help keep the gardens beautiful by walking along the many secluded trails constantly picking up paper and cigarette butts. But these colorful, breathtaking gardens weren't always world famous. In the early 1900s, the Butchart family bought a large piece of barren, rock-strewn land near Victoria to use as a granite rock quarry. Month by month, teams of men extracted tons of high-quality granite to erect many of the buildings in the nearby city of Victoria. After several years of surface mining, the men had removed most of the available granite, and moved on to another area. The surface of their property was left as an ugly scar on the landscape.

But Jenny Butchart was an overcomer. She loved things of beauty, particularly flowers and gardens. She had an idea that with the correct mix of landscaping, soil, trees, and flowers, the huge hole from which the granite had been extracted could become a thing of beauty. Many laughed at her crazy gardening idea, but with the blessing of her husband, she hired a team of landscapers and gardeners, and began to transform the ugly scar into something very different. As it took shape, those who had once been opposed began to bring friends from Victoria to see this ever-changing sunken garden. Little by little, this determined lady and her team continued their difficult work, and the ugly rock quarry and its surrounding area became transformed into one of the wonders of this modern world, the now world-famous Butchart Gardens.

We All Must Overcome

But the idea of overcoming didn't start with Jenny Butchart. She was merely one of millions who are confronted every day by very difficult problems. Thankfully, she didn't cave in to overwhelming circumstances; and she left us all the legacy of this now world famous garden. But it's no different in so many of our lives. Because of poor inheritance, abuse, or the storms of life, many face a totally barren and denuded mental and emotional landscape. Such people—and this once included myself—are faced every morning with a huge challenge just to overcome the black thoughts and feelings that rob the joy out of life. Because of the terrible confusion that surrounds inner problems, many troubled souls never climb out of their "rock quarry." They live lives of misery, never seeing the hope God has provided for us through Calvary.

I was headed for the same fate or worse. But the Lord revealed Himself to me in my early adult years, and gave me renewed hope where there seemed to be no hope. When I first turned to Him for help, I did an odd thing. I bargained with Him, and told Him that if He would remove my depression, then I'd serve Him for the rest of my life. He did just that for eight wonderful years. But then the depression returned in full force, and I was once again faced with a bleak, rock-strewn landscape. God required me to rise up just like Jenny Butchart, and develop into an overcomer.

But by this time I had learned to take His many mental health promises at face value. If He said He would do something in His Word, I would continue to respectfully remind Him about it until He actually did it. Year by year, I was given the strength and know-how to overcome my inner problems, and the hopeless mess of my sunken garden was transformed into a life that can bear witness to the healing and transforming power of Jesus Christ.

Because of my difficult background, the challenge to overcome in life is very real to me. So, when our Church began a series on "the seven overcoming Churches" in the book of Revelation, I listened carefully. I immediately heard the Lord's voice say that I was to pay close attention to this teaching series because He wanted to reveal more construction secrets about my soul. Even though I had gained much from these seven challenges presented to the seven Churches, I had never applied these teachings to the area of mental health. Now I was getting excited, because I saw that it was also a seven-part overcoming challenge that could be applied to the human soul. I realized that these overcoming challenges were universal, and applied not only to my life, but also to the lives of all mankind.

> *He who has an ear, let him hear*
> *what the Spirit says to the churches.*
> *To him who overcomes, I will give*
> *to eat from the tree of life, which is*
> *in the midst of the Paradise of God.*
> *Revelation 2:7*

This phrase "to him who overcomes" is repeated seven times in the early part of the book of Revelation. If we don't catch hold of this phrase, we're in danger because it's God's purpose to present His Son with an overcoming bride.

When I was very young, there was a popular TV show centering around the very comfortable life of a man called Riley. The misconception was that in the postwar years—and even in our present day—that society should be allowed to take it easy. But we see from these seven soul challenges that the Christian life was never designed to be like that. In fact, much of life seems to be about tests and trials, and it's God's plan that all of us should overcome those tests so that we might take our place in the Body of Christ. It's time to wake up and realize that either we properly connect with His soul development program, or we get left behind. Over the years, I've seen far too many set up their own comfortable image of what our Heavenly Father is like…but were soon in for a rude shock.

An even worse danger is the sense of entitlement (the concept that good things are owed to a person) that seems to fill the hearts of this present generation. This is totally opposite what the Word of God teaches. Good things come about as we wait upon the Lord, and we spend time in prayer (2 Chronicles 7:14). It is with a sad heart that I watch capable people spend their days in front of a TV screen or a computer console being entertained, and wondering when their next social assistance check will arrive. We need to wake up and hear these words of John in Revelation.

Put On Your Wedding Garments

For years I puzzled over the New Testament parable which talks about the man who was confronted by the Master because he failed to put on his wedding garments. But I now believe that this parable speaks of a man who was lukewarm during his life here on Earth. It appears that he did things his own way, and had little appreciation for his salvation. I was even more startled to see what happened to him…he was forcibly removed from the wedding banquet, and thrown into the outer darkness.

It reminded me once again of the Scripture, "Therefore consider the goodness and severity of God" (Romans 11:22). I am able to grasp the good side of God, but sometimes I have a difficult time grasping the severity of God—especially in Proverbs toward those who are complacent. Thankfully, as I grow in my Christianity, I can see that God doesn't abide fools lightly. He paid a very high and agonizing price to redeem us, so He demands that we will all "press toward the mark for the prize of the high calling of God in Christ Jesus" (Philippians 3:14 KJV).

Looking back, I see that this parable plays out in day-to-day life. I've seen so many become strong in the faith as they develop a passionate love for the Master, but others, who never really connect to the life of Christ, continue to do things their own way. They have their own view about life, and never seem to overcome the soul challenges that have been set before them. In time, they wither away, and finally disappear from the Church.

Each of us is given the life challenge of gaining wisdom and understanding, and storing up the knowledge of God. Obtaining these three elements is critical because hidden within them are the secrets that teach us how to build up our soul, establish our feet under us, and fill our soul to overflowing. If we're not serious about gaining these things, then we could be headed for spiritual disaster. Another glimpse of the severity of God can be seen in the seven soul challenges presented to us in the early part of Revelation. God is warning all believers that if we want His best, then He expects us to give all diligence to being "overcomers" in this life. The idea of being an "undergoer," so that we barely crawl through Heaven's gate is not what the Lord has in mind for any of us.

The God whom we love and serve has placed a fighting nature within each of us; so He continually loves to challenge our soul to fight for a deeper and more intimate relationship with Him. In Revelation, the Lord states seven times that only those souls that overcome will be given rewards in His future Kingdom. Then He lays down seven challenges for the believers in each type of Church…and these challenges must never be taken lightly. I am often concerned for those who take their Christianity casually. I don't believe that we should be walking on pins and needles…but what has been done for us is absolutely incredible, and we need to appreciate it. When Christ commanded us "to work out your own salvation with fear and trembling" (Philippians 2:12), He was definitely encouraging us to appreciate what we have been given, lest we become sluggish and neglect it.

The Life of David

God loved David, and declared that he was "a man after His own heart" (1 Samuel 13:14). In spite of this, David was human, and also needed to learn how to be an overcomer. We're told that "at the time when kings go out to battle" David stayed at home (2 Samuel 11:1). Satan chose this time to put before David one of his very serious temptations. As David was walking on the roof of His palace in the cool of the evening, a very attractive married woman was bathing in her courtyard below. As he gazed on her beautiful form, he was overcome with lust. It wasn't long before he was inviting her up to his palace to commit adultery. As time progressed, David received word that she was pregnant. To try and cover his sin, he called her husband home from the battle, got him roaring drunk, and tried to encourage him to go to his own bed and lay with her—so that when the child was born, he'd think it was his. When that didn't work, David arranged for his general Joab to have the husband killed in battle; then he took Bathsheba as his wife before the pregnancy could be noticed.

We see that even a great man like David didn't overcome in this instance. As his secret deeds were revealed, David was genuinely repentant. God forgave him for these acts of adultery and murder, and in so doing, gives us all hope for our future. But he didn't get away without punishment. The Lord declared that David wouldn't die for his sins, but warned him that "the sword shall never depart from your house" (2 Samuel 12:10). As the story progresses, we see that he paid dearly for these transgressions. Many of his children went through tremendous struggles, and from his desperate cries to the Lord in Psalm 51, we see that his soul took a real beating.

Learning to Number our Days

When I was recently in hospital for hernia surgery, my heart was troubled by what I saw. There were many hollow shells of people lying in the beds around me in the hospital ward. It seemed that they were just barely surviving from one day to the next. I tried to witness to a few, but was sternly rejected. These people hadn't overcome the obstacles in their lives, and now their days on this Earth were rapidly slipping away. It reminded me again that all of us are expected to grow in our faith, and become fruitful for the Master in our appointed time span. We only have a certain period to do this, and it caused the psalmist to cry out in earnest prayer, "teach us to number our days, that we may apply our hearts unto wisdom" (Psalm 90:12 KJV). If we neglect our salvation, our days will slip past us, and our opportunities will be gone forever.

So the seven challenges to overcome found in the book of Revelation aren't to be taken lightly. God demands a very high standard from those who would rule and reign with Him in Eternity, and He's absolutely determined to have a people who know their God. As we press into Christ and overcome in our lives, our souls will grow in strength and make us fit for the many challenges that lie ahead. So let's examine these seven challenges from the perspective of soul growth and development. These challenges provide yet another construction secret that will help to heal us of our soul troubles.

Ephesus—Challenge #1—Our First Love

> *You have left your first love.*
> *Revelation 2:4*

Many years ago, an elderly monk and his junior apprentice were walking through the monastery gardens. This junior monk had the annoying habit of pestering his elder until he got answers to his questions. On this day, he had decided to ask how we can really know if we love God, so as they were walking, he repeatedly asked the same question. The elderly monk looked frustrated and very pensive, but refused to answer his question. When they got to the water fountain at the center of the garden, the older monk got down on his hands and knees, and began to take a drink from the pool. The junior monk did the same. Suddenly, without warning, the older monk grabbed the younger man's head, and shoved it under the water. The younger man struggled, but the old monk would not let go. Finally, he released him. The young man came up sputtering and demanding to know why he had done such a strange thing. The elderly monk gently replied, "I was just answering your question about how to know if you really love God." "What do you mean?" shouted out the junior monk. "Well, when you want God as much as you wanted that next breath of fresh air, then you really love Him," replied the senior monk. From that point on, the junior man was more careful about pestering the old monk with questions.

The story about the monks helps us to grasp the magnitude of God's first challenge. Here the Lord reveals His expectation that we should love Him above all else, and He also shows that we must maintain that relationship throughout the rest of our lives. This challenge is not only important to the Churches, but also applies to our current mental health studies. It supports the teaching that our spirit must be filled with the right substances, and engaged in correct activities if it's to grow strong and remain healthy. From daily life, we understand that love is an action, but it's also much more. It's a spiritual filling substance. In 1 John 4:8 we are told that God is love, so it is God's expectation that we demonstrate love, and that we be filled to overflowing with this same love.

Valuing Our Salvation

I visualize salvation as being a transfer of our soul's ownership from the Kingdom of Darkness to the Kingdom of Light. As part of the terms of that transfer, we are willingly committing ourselves to love the Lord with all of our heart, our soul, our mind, and our strength. God has taken on the very difficult task of conforming us to the image of His Son (Romans 8:29) by adding in the component of love. This will mean challenging the person to take on a "first love" commitment, and maintaining that commitment throughout the full course of his life. Thankfully, one of the tasks of the Holy Spirit is to stir up love within the human heart (Romans 5:5). Without His presence, there's a danger that this critical process of changing our soul won't be satisfactorily completed. For good reason, the Lord charges us all that our "first love" relationship is to be carefully maintained.

From my own life, I saw that the open door of salvation was just the beginning of my soul-restructuring process. Even though I lagged a number of times in building up my first love, God was merciful to me. He sternly disciplined me on a number of occasions, and each time, He really got my attention. The last spiritual spanking was so severe that I stopped my running through life, and now purposed to work with Him until this cursed black hand of depression was gone forever. I had to learn the hard way how to build the right materials into my soul walls, and how to keep my soul filled with the correct spiritual substances. I also learned first-hand that wrong things will always be seeking to gain entrance into the human soul. Satan's strategy is to apply spiritual pressure to our lives in various ways, so the most effective resistance against his plan is to deflect these ongoing pressures by using this "first love" technique.

It's very common for a person to come to Christ, and love Him with all of their hearts during the first part of their exciting new salvation relationship. But the Parable of the Sower warns us that other activities will creep into our lives, and attempt to crowd out our first love. Those who are careless in this matter never really seem to obtain much depth of soil in their lives; so, when the heat of trial comes, they begin to wither and die (Matthew 13:20-22). Through this first soul challenge, we're shown that if we always want God the way that that junior monk wanted that next breath of air, then we have nothing to fear. We're challenged to guard and strengthen our first love relationship with Christ day by day. It will give a great boost to our mental health, and little by little, will cause it to grow ever stronger.

Smyrna—Challenge #2—Testing and Suffering

> *Do not be afraid of any of those*
> *things which you are about to suffer.*
> *Revelation 2:10*

Suffering is avoided by our comfort-seeking generation. Yet suffering is the very thing that shakes us out of our complacency and causes us to measure the value of eternal things. My area of suffering centered around some deep-seated mental and emotional problems. Thankfully, I was given permanent relief from my terrible afflictions, but one experience during my years of suffering is very significant. I had often fought with terrible dreams concerning the persecution of the Last Days. At times, the dreams would be so bad that I would wake up shaking and sweating. I cried out to God for revelation in this area also, and the touch of love that I received in answer to this desperate prayer rocked my world, and forever removed these bad dreams from my soul.

The power of His touch in answer to this prayer was so strong that it enabled me to see how the martyrs could give their lives. It also answered the question that I had about those being tortured in Hebrews 11. When this kind of love fills us, we're filled with boldness and will not back down from any devil-inspired persecutor. God says, "As your days, so shall your strength be" (Deuteronomy 33:25). He will empower us at the time that we need it.

This fight between good and evil now makes sense to me because the Lord tells us that His thoughts are not our thoughts (Isaiah 55:8). And this is also true in the area of suffering and pain. The legal price tag to buy us back from Satan's domain required a level of pain and suffering that no one could ever pay. So God paid the full price of our redemption by offering up His precious Son as a sacrifice for us all. To do this, the Father and Holy Spirit went through a time of very real suffering as they saw Jesus separated from them, and hang between Heaven and Earth to pay the price in full for the sins of mankind. Out of His suffering came blessing indeed. Mankind was offered the place of ruling and reigning with Christ, and the privilege of becoming a part of the Bride of Christ.

More Old Testament Examples

Many Old Testament examples are given that are designed to help us live more successfully in our day. The Tabernacle in the wilderness had a very plain outward covering of black animal skins. To the casual observer, it was extremely uninviting; but inside, it contained the glory of God. This is a spiritual type that reveals how it plays out with spiritual things such as suffering. It may not look inviting at all on the outside, but within there can be hidden some amazing benefits. I certainly didn't enjoy my many long years of hell as I suffered under the black hand of depression; but in the midst of my suffering, I met God in some very deep and unusual ways. At those times when I was the most desperate, I had no place to turn, so I cried out to Him with all of my heart. It was then that He revealed Himself to me, and gave me a much greater depth to my life.

I mentioned earlier that our inner health was lost the moment that Adam and Eve chose to disobey God. From that point in history, suffering became real, particularly in the area of mental and emotional health. It then became God's plan to return the soul back into its pre-Adamic state in those who were willing. But it was a very difficult route. The almost unbearable pain that Christ endured on the cross purchased our salvation, and forever changed the course of history for the believer. In the previous verse, Christ said, "Do not fear any of those things which you are about to suffer" because He promises us that our suffering won't become greater than we can bear. As we grasp the meaning of this truth through real life experiences, not only do we come to know God better, but it will take away all fear.

We live in a society that wants to spare people from suffering any pain. But this isn't God's view at all. He sees pain and suffering as a valuable tool that causes very real soul changes. In Proverbs 20:30 He informs us, "Blows that hurt cleanse away evil." Pain causes us to sit up and take notice of our present condition, and urges us to change those things that are lagging in our development. As I was fighting through the terrible pain of depression, I learned an amazing truth. The act of resisting soul pressures and pain that were coming against me had the benefit of building up my spiritual muscles.

Pergamos—Challenge #3—True and False Doctrine

> *But I have a few things against you, because you have there those who hold the doctrine of Balaam… you also have those who hold the doctrine of the Nicolaitans, which thing I hate.*
> *Revelation 2:14-15*

In weaving, the "warp and woof" are the crossing fibers that make up the foundational structure of any cloth or rug. The fibers can have various strengths; the stronger the fiber and the tighter the weaving, the more durable the garment becomes. So it is with the tapestry of our soul. God intended the Word of God and the Holy Spirit to be the warp and woof of our inner man. The more they are present and woven into the fabric of our being, the stronger our soul becomes. Mental health problems usually signify that there's a weakness in this inner tapestry, and that we need to return to intimacy in our devotions.

The Word of God is the fiber and substance of all things, both natural and spiritual, and the Holy Spirit is the binding thread that holds all things together. So it's vital that we make it an immediate priority to build our inner man on the strength of His Word. Tragically, we're in such a rushed society that our daily devotions are often the first thing we cut short. It's very common in our day that as a person gobbles down their breakfast, they'll snatch a quick verse from Our Daily Bread. In time, they wonder why their Christian life is losing its excitement. If this is happening to us, then we must slow our lives down and look carefully into the Scriptures. There we'll see

His challenge to engraft His words into our soul. Only then can our life become more exciting and fulfilled as our new soul contents guide our steps, and control our thinking. This third soul challenge urges us to become firmly grounded in the Scriptures. However, Satan will oppose any and all efforts by Christians to become anchored in the Word of God. He repeatedly attempts to turn mankind away from the truth of God's Word so that he can introduce his own false teachings. Satan's ideas may appeal to our fleshly desires, but only the Word of God has the effect of making us free deep within. People are searching the face of this world for their own solutions, but mental health is built and supported by the strength of the Spirit and the Word in us. If we give little time to engrafting and meditation, then our soul will be weak; it will also be subject to collapse, or even be tricked by Satanic deception.

When God speaks about the immoral woman in the Book of Proverbs, He has a twofold purpose. He's describing the natural pull of the flesh toward immorality, but He's also referring to the lure of the cults and today's popular do-it-yourself religion of "believe in God and live as you please." These unstable teachings, and their ability to appeal to the flesh, seduce vast multitudes of people. God is warning us about our need to be firmly anchored in the Word of God so that we might overcome the deception trap that faces all of us. If we look to the natural, we see that fishermen are most successful when they make their bait look as much like the real thing as possible. In the original deception, Satan didn't oppose Adam and Eve…he merely sugar-coated his words so that he could catch these two unwary souls off guard.

If false doctrine led people away from mental health, then the truth of God's Word will bring them back again. Those who are serious about their studies will prove the truth of the Scripture, "And you shall know the truth, and the truth shall make you free" (John 8:32).

Thyatira—Challenge #4—Control vs. Submission

*You tolerate that woman Jezebel,
who calls herself a prophet.
Revelation 2:20 (NIV)*

The major battle that all Christians face in their lives is the letting go of their own way and accepting God's ways. Elijah had overcome this spirit of control in his own life, and when he confronted the vicious, controlling spirit that ruled Queen Jezebel, he had some initial success against this dominant spirit. But later, when he was targeted by the spirit that drove this woman, he fled for his life. God wants to teach us all a valuable mental health lesson here. He warns us that many will choose to live with a spirit of control rather than to oppose it, but the results of such compromise can be hurtful for the future of that person because when they try to break free, and turn the reins of their lives over to God, they'll face opposition. Nevertheless, if we're to be strong both mentally and emotionally, we must get down on our face before God, and trust Him with the outcome of life's difficult situations.

The subject of rulership, authority, and control is very important in the eyes of God. It sticks in the throat of many Christians, but God makes it one of His seven soul challenges. He knows exactly how things should be ordered in His Kingdom, and He requires that we learn to submit to this order in spite of our contrary feelings. In Hebrews 13:17, we're warned, "Have confidence in your leaders and submit to their authority, because they keep watch over you as those who must give an account." Our willing submission here on Earth prepares us for our future in Heaven with Christ. There is a definite authority structure there, and we're expected to be submitted to it for all of Eternity. If we won't trust those that He has placed in a position of rulership here on Earth, then we'll have great difficulty accepting any kind of authority when we get to Heaven.

Marriage has been given to us to teach many practical lessons about the workings of spiritual things, especially in the area of control and submission. Just as we must learn to submit to Christ here on Earth, we must also learn to submit to our mates. Marriage was never designed for one person to rule the roost without regard for the feelings of their mate or for their children. In marriage, we must work hard to maintain the love that we have for our mate after the excitement of the honeymoon has worn off. It's the same in our relationship with Christ. In fact, God gives a warning in Hebrews 2:1-3 about the incredible value of our salvation, and the danger of us neglecting it.

An example of overcoming is provided for us by Joshua and Caleb. The Lord sent twelve spies into the Promised Land. But most of those spies cast off God's control, and came back with an evil report that they looked like grasshoppers in the sight of the enemy, and that the land was unconquerable. Their report quickly influenced the whole Israelite camp, and brought great despair. In time, it caused over one million people to die in a hot, barren wilderness. The only ones who accepted God's control were Joshua and Caleb. They realized that God was challenging them to do something that was much greater than their abilities. Tragically, the other ten spies were blind to the challenge, and openly spoke rebellion against God and Moses. In doing this, they sealed their own fate (see Numbers 13:1-33; 14:1-38).

Through these many examples, we learn that there is no wiggle room: either we learn to submit to God's control, or our mental health will suffer greatly. God is no respecter of persons. He often challenges every Christian to overcome their fears and to learn to trust in Him. Those who accept this challenge and allow God to rule will succeed; those who refuse to give up control will find that their lives on this Earth are greatly shortened.

Sardis—Challenge #5—Watching and Waiting

*Wake up! Strengthen what remains
and is about to die...
Revelation 3:2 (NIV)*

The Children of Israel found out the hard way that one of the most difficult tests that people face in this life is waiting for God's timing. When Moses was called up into Mt. Sinai, the whole camp awaited the outcome of this incredible meeting between man and God. But when Moses delayed in descending from the mountain, the people thought he must have died in the smoke and fire, and they began to complain. They pressured Aaron to make them a golden calf, and they soon fell into idolatry and hungered for lustful pleasures. In our day, Jesus has delayed His return from Heaven, and people are falling into exactly the same trap. They say, "My master is delaying his coming" (Matthew 24:48) and begin living for themselves. These people don't realize that we're supposed to learn from these previous lessons of Scripture. This same soul challenge to watch and to wait (Mark 13:35-36) is tailored to reach people of all generations; those who heed this call have a strong sense of purpose as this strong mental health pillar is built into their soul.

When we as teachers are on the playground watching the children at school, there's a danger of getting distracted and talking with other adults. If I fall into that trap, I suddenly recognize that I'm not able to fully focus on the needs and the safety of the children. In the same way, we're called to pay attention in life, and carefully observe what's happening around us. If we're careless in our watching and waiting, those things that God has entrusted to us can be stolen away. In fact, Jesus warned that in all generations, people would draw near to Him with their lips, but their hearts would remain far from Him (Matthew 15:8). Thankfully, the Lord speaks clearly to those who would accept this fifth overcoming challenge. He states in Proverbs 8:34-35, "Blessed is the man who listens to Me, watching daily at My gates, waiting at the posts of my doors. For whoever finds me finds life, and obtains favor from the LORD." Hidden in this challenge is yet another secret of vibrant mental health.

As I was pondering this, I realized that a huge part of my own mental health was built squarely on the idea of the greatness and mystery of our God. I am thrilled day by day in my Christian walk because I have discovered that there's no end to the exciting revelations that God wants to give to us. Just when I think I know something about an area, He reveals Himself to me in an entirely different way. In the midst of my long years of depression, I knew that there was no known cure. So I respectfully challenged the Lord to fulfill Jeremiah 33:3 in my life. There He states, "Call to Me, and I will answer you, and show you great and mighty things, which you do not know." I waited on that Scripture and wouldn't let go of God. And show me He did! This book comes from my watching and waiting upon God during that very difficult time of my life.

When the Lord tells us in Isaiah 40:31 that "those who wait on the LORD shall renew their strength," He's speaking to the mentally afflicted of all generations. Tragically, many fall short of this Scripture because God doesn't tell us how long we'll have to watch and wait. All I knew was that in my life, it took many years for my soul to run down, and it was going to take time and effort for God to rebuild it. The 98-pound weakling described by Charles Atlas didn't overcome the cruel beach bullies in one night. It took a season in the exercise room at the gymnasium before he was ready to return to the beach, kick sand in the face of his tormentors, and claim his girl back again. Charles Atlas swore that his beach story was true, and made this famous quote: "Nobody picks on a strong man." So it is with those who will accept the challenge to wait on the Lord.

When it comes to eternal things, many neglect their salvation. They think that they'll get more serious about spiritual things when the time for His return draws nearer. But the five foolish virgins discovered that this fifth overcoming challenge is not to be taken lightly. Jesus speaks to all generations, warning us to not treat His admonition to watch and wait carelessly. He states that there are a few names in Sardis who He considers worthy, and He will grant them the incredible reward of walking with Him in white. This fifth overcoming soul challenge is very important indeed, and it'll greatly fuel the mental and emotional health of those who accept it.

Philadelphia—Challenge #6—Endurance

> *Since you have kept My command*
> *to endure patiently...*
> *Revelation 3:10 (NIV)*

When God made the command to Israel, "Be holy, for I am holy" (Leviticus 11:45), He was very serious...yet some treated these commands lightly. We see that the sons of Aaron and of Eli—as well as leaders such as Korah, Dathan, and Abiram—all died before the Lord when they ignored God's warnings, and lived only to please their flesh. But they weren't the only ones to fail. Many in our generation are doing the same exact things. They live out their lives seeing only the things of this world, but have no eyes for the life that lies beyond. This challenge was embraced by the Patriarchs, as is made clear in Hebrews 11:13: "These all died in faith, not having received the promises, but having seen them afar off were assured of them, embraced them and confessed that they were strangers and pilgrims on the earth." Such people endured their trials patiently believing in God's promises. In so doing, they kept their mental health strong because they could clearly see the wonderful treasures that lay beyond this life. All of us are called to live a pure lifestyle. This means that we'll have to endure some hardships along our journey, and suffer patiently as a whole battery of evil things are thrown at us. As we resist the evil and endure, it builds up strong spiritual muscles and prepares us for eternity. One of the hardest things every parent suffers is to see their children battered around by evil things. I often stand before the Lord for my own children declaring that I didn't raise them for Christ just to have Satan come along and lure them away with his evil tricks.

Endurance Isn't Easy

Years back, I didn't know what I know now, so it was very difficult for me to endure my trials. I had to fight through my terrible black feelings of depression, knowing that there were no known answers. But as I patiently endured and refused to let go of God's promises, the Lord began to teach me how my mental health was designed to work, and also made clear the important mental health principles that supported it. At long last, I was rewarded for my endurance. I received a full and complete healing from my inner afflictions, and was given a burning passion to help others.

In my youth, I certainly gave my teachers a challenge. I would continually disturb the class, and finally the vice-principal took me into his office and warned me that they would not hesitate to begin applying the strap if I didn't grow up and act more like a man. They were becoming disgusted by my foolish and unrestrained behavior, and after many canings and warnings, wisdom finally reached my brain, and I began to change. In our Christian life, if we will patiently endure our times of suffering, and diligently engraft His words into our souls, we will see growth and change in our lives.

God expects each one of us to live a life on this Earth that honors Him. It's our task to patiently endure surrounding sinful attitudes, and to teach His holiness to an unclean generation. Even though God saved multitudes of people from Egypt, He still faced the huge challenge of getting the stain of impurity out of them. We saw from the Mount Sinai experience that it wasn't very long before the Children of Israel spurned God, and returned to their idols. Through times of testing in the desert, God was trying to build endurance in their souls, but the Scriptures tell us that they failed because they refused to respond to Him in the correct manner. This sixth overcoming challenge is very real even today. Those who accept it find a rich recipe for their mental health as they diligently prepare their souls for both time and eternity.

Laodicea—Challenge #7—Complacency

*I know your deeds, that you are
neither cold nor hot.
Revelation 3:15 (NIV)*

The Church at Laodicea had become very wealthy, but they weren't held in high regard by the Lord. Riches and wealth aren't bad when they're used to help and strengthen others; but in Laodicea, it caused many people to become lazy and very complacent in their faith. They had turned their eyes away from Christ, and were concentrating on the building up their own lands and houses.

In another passage of Scripture, the Lord said of one rich merchant, "Fool! This night your soul will be required of you" (Luke 12:20). This wealthy man was completely clueless about the value of time and the reality of Eternity. For these reasons, God gives us a strong challenge to focus every day on what is important. We must use time and riches as a blessing to do the work that we've been called to do; otherwise, soul-sleep sets in, and we become very complacent in our faith.

We must all realize that Christ's salvation is the first step into our future. It's the open door to incredible opportunities in this life. In addition, it leads to an amazing future where we're promised that we'll rule and reign with Jesus Christ. Tragically, many people get saved, but only make their salvation another part of their day-to-day routine. In God's eyes, they're neglecting their salvation, and He tells them that they're in danger of becoming lukewarm. The act of living carelessly leaves much room in their souls for Satan to enter, and this can result in mental and emotional suffering. If we desire to close those doors, we must live every day with a keen hunger to know Christ.

One of the greatest dangers for every human soul is loss of spiritual focus. In the case of the Laodicean Church, their souls had gone to sleep within them. In our modern-day Christianity, this same drowsiness continues until a major crisis occurs. At that time, people find themselves unprepared for these troubles, and enter into major soul difficulties, including depression and fear. We all need to be on guard, lest we come against spiritual pressures that have the strength to overcome unprepared souls. Two of the most notable Bible characters caught by this deadly trap of complacency were Solomon and Samson. In Solomon's case, the easy availability of finances and the lure of women—and in Samson's case, simply the lure of women—caused them to turn their eyes away from the Lord, and pursue their fleshly lusts. At first, everything seemed great, but they didn't see the dark times lurking around the corner. So when things fell apart, they both ended up in great depression and despair.

Although each man apparently repented before he died, we see that the sum of their lives was only a mere shadow of what God had intended. It'll be exactly the same story in our lives if we allow complacency to settle in.

Christ's "overcoming" challenge to the Laodicean Church is not out of reach for anyone. He warns us all to awaken out of our spiritual complacency so that we might regain our focus. When He told the Laodicean Church that they were neither cold nor hot, He was speaking to them about spiritual passion because He has no intention of living throughout eternity with a bride that's lukewarm. The Father is now preparing a fervent bride for His Son. We must love Christ passionately, and allow ourselves to increase in inward strength. The challenge to every Church and every individual throughout all of the ages is to wait upon Him so that they continually build up their strength, their fervency, and their eternal passion.

In Conclusion

The "overcoming" challenges presented to the seven Churches were meant to give us a wake-up call. God has set Himself a monumental task by desiring to provide a high-quality, loving bride for His Son. To do this, He must repair our souls and make us whole. We are to be of the highest character, so this leaves no room for resistant attitudes or for complacency. If we want to reign with Christ, there is much work to be done, and those who hear these seven challenges are well on their way to succeeding in life. As their success grows, they'll also learn how to overcome any mental health problems that they may face along the way. The revelations that God wants to give to us are a secret reward for drawing close to Him and submitting to His authority; they are called "hidden manna" (Revelation 2:17). Those who find it will enjoy vibrant mental health in this life, and adopt a real vision for the years to come. The thing that startles me the most is that I could have missed these things. I discovered to my great surprise that you don't see truth until you hunger after it, and press into it. Then it's revealed to you …so much so that you then wonder why others can't see the same things that you see.

Through these seven "overcoming" challenges, God warns us that an improper attitude toward spiritual things can lead to serious mental and emotional difficulties; so we must wake up and heartily accept what He sets before us. In the process of meeting these seven "overcoming" challenges, our soul will grow mightily in strength, and we'll be well on our way to finding the perfect peace that God so clearly promises in Isaiah 26:3. But overcoming doesn't come easily. It will take great effort to lay down our lives, and pick up the new life of giving and sacrifice that Christ sets before us. As I close this chapter, let me stress again the importance of love and mercy as we attempt to show people the importance of this "seven challenges" truth.

Section III
Foundations and Substances of the Soul

I'm always very concerned when I hear of the many people starving in East Africa—especially when I hear on the news that some of the much-needed food that was destined for these helpless women and children was appearing for sale in the black markets of the larger East African cities. I asked the Lord what I could do about this terrible situation, and He responded, "If the foundations are destroyed, what can the righteous do?" (Psalm 11:3). He encouraged me that the things that I had done in the past and am doing now to help widows and orphans wasn't going unnoticed, but He was redirecting my attention back to the mental health area. He explained that whenever foundations are destroyed, He assigns His people the task of rebuilding those foundations through the vehicle of His Church. It was my main task to help rebuild the foundations in my assigned area of mental health, and He would appoint others to the task of re-building shattered foundations in East Africa. In the same way, we can be running all over the place trying to find things and people to help heal our troubled souls, but if we'll concentrate on building our foundations, and give diligence to building up our inner contents, we'll grow in strength, and find our peace at long last.

*If the foundations are destroyed,
what can the righteous do?
Psalm 11:3*

Chapter 8
Building a Basic Soul and The Wise Builder Parable
Setting the Scene

Scientists, psychiatrists, and worldly philosophers have a difficult time describing what's happening inside of a man when he's anxious, fearful, or afraid. But the Lord has no such limitations. He uses all manner of descriptions to teach us about the inner workings of our spirit and soul so that we can better understand how our mental health has been designed. I particularly like the analogy of house-building used frequently in the Scriptures. Two of the most powerful are Proverbs 24:3-4 and Matthew 7:24. Proverbs states: "Through wisdom a house is built, and by understanding it is established; by knowledge the rooms are filled with all precious and pleasant riches." Matthew's description is similar, and gives us this snapshot: "Therefore whoever hears these sayings of Mine, and does them, I will liken him to a wise man who built his house on a rock…"

We see here that our house (soul/spirit combination) is constructed out of a substance called wisdom, and our passion to obtain it will determine whether we are strong or weak inside. As I was studying this in more detail, I realized that it was the Lord's eternal plan that a spiritual substance known as the knowledge of God should cover our inner walls and fill our rooms. When it is there in full measure together with a host of other spiritual substances, we're able to experience the type of joy and peace that the Lord had originally planned for every person. But if it should be lacking, then all manner of other things become a part of our inner house, and life may not be so pleasant. In 2 Timothy 1:7, one of these non-approved substances is better described. We are told, "For God has not given us a spirit of fear, but of power and of love and of a sound mind." Instead of the knowledge of God being the primary filler in that house, a spirit of fear has muscled in and taken over.

Something to Consider

If we expand this previous thought, then we see that the things that we give ourselves to become a significant part of our internal makeup, and they have a definite voice in how we think and feel inside. If we've allowed drugs, alcohol, nicotine, pornography, materialism, or a whole host of other things to get a grip on us, we can try as hard as humanly possible to come free, but we may be fighting a losing battle. It's my opinion that these things actually become attached to the walls, floors and ceiling of our soul in such a way that only the Holy Spirit can cleanse them from us. If we try to get rid of them in our own strength, we leave a soul space, and our inner man craves for those missing substances to be returned.

Thankfully, there's good news: God's remedy is to give us brand new spiritual substances that completely change and rearrange us inside. Romans 12:2 declares, "And do not be conformed to this world, but be transformed by the renewing of your mind…" It is God's desire to give us spiritual building materials for our house that replace the hurtful substances with something much better and much more satisfying.

From my own difficult experiences it seemed like depression became a part of my inner man, and I couldn't break free of it by natural means. In fact, it had such a grip on my soul that my thinking and feelings were dominated by it. No matter what I did in the natural, it was tightly woven into my soul, and it wasn't about to move. Thankfully, as I became ever more intimate with the Lord Jesus Christ, the Holy Spirit took over, and began to restructure me and then fill me up deep inside. In the rest of this chapter, I'd like to better describe how this inner transformation takes place, and how the Lord makes our inner temple a place to be desired, and to be lived in.

A Sad Heart

It really grieves my heart to see people struggling year after year to overcome a life-choking addiction or some grievous ongoing affliction. Yet many go to the grave with their problems untouched. This is really sad, because this present revelation about God's passionate desire to build His own spiritual house inside of them might have changed all of that. As we search through the pages of Scripture, we see that it's the Lord's desire is to not only prepare a home for us in Heaven, but also to build His house in our hearts right here on this Earth (Luke 17:20-21). If we truly get hold of this revelation, it will completely alter the way that we think and feel inside. This change will come as we understand that we have a definite part in this house-building process, and learn how to work closely with the Lord in its day-by-day construction.

As I did this, I became ever stronger within, and finally saw my lifetime bouts of fear, anxiety, and depression begin to fade away. To my great delight, the peace that I had searched after for so long gradually took hold of my heart, and I walked in a new freedom. It also raised the questions in me, "Isn't it time to admit that we're crafted in the image of God?" And, "Isn't it long past time that we understand that our soul and spirit (our inner house) is the core of our mental and emotional health?" To my excitement, I found that the stronger my soul and spirit became, the less opportunity the enemy had to break through my soul barrier, and trouble me. That's why Proverbs 4:10 states, "Hear, my son, and receive my saying, and the years of your life will be many." Powerful scriptural declarations like these caused me to look again at the book of Proverbs through a very different set of glasses. At last, I could see that it wasn't just a book containing many wise nuggets. It's an amazing set of blueprints carefully advising us how to build the kind of inner house that the Lord desires to see in each human heart. That's why He speaks so graphically in Proverbs 1 against those who ignore His building plans. To my shock, as I read the second half of Proverbs 1, I could almost hear my own cries as these individuals loudly screamed for help. I discovered that assistance was available for me personally because I allowed the Spirit to guide me onto a new pathway. But those who refuse these instructions find themselves in a very difficult place indeed. If they continue refusing to turn, their screams will become ever louder as their poorly-constructed house (soul/spirit combination) begins to collapse.

A Startling House-Building Revelation

Proverbs 1:7 warns, "The fear of the LORD is the beginning of knowledge, but fools despise wisdom and instruction." The Lord makes it very clear throughout the Scriptures that He's building His eternal home in each one of our hearts, and the core of His building program is our willing obedience to hear His instructions, and put them into effect in our lives. In 1 Peter 2:5, the Lord reveals that our particular "living stone" is to be a vital part of His eternal temple, and it must fit snugly into the place that He has prepared for it.

Therefore we need to listen carefully to the instructions described above, and carefully walk in them. Our eternal purpose is further described in 1 Peter 2:5: "you also, as living stones are being built up a spiritual house, a holy priesthood, to offer up spiritual sacrifices acceptable to God through Jesus Christ." I discovered to my great delight that if I would allow God to build up my temple (inner house) according to His directions, then as a wonderful side-benefit, my mental health would also become very strong.

Some Personal House Renovations

When I was first married, my wife inherited a large three-story home from her father. Everything in it was either run-down or very much out-of-date. This meant that all parts of it needed to either be changed or upgraded. At first, the task seemed enormous, but we tackled it with great gusto. We tore off the old lath and plaster walls, strengthened the sagging floors and ceilings, pulled out the old insulation, re-wired and re-plumbed the structure, re-carpeted it, and painted absolutely every visible surface. When we finally finished all these changes, our pocket-books had taken a beating, but the made-over house didn't look too bad.

But I wasn't done yet. In my youthful zeal, I decided that I'd work in the basement to reset the walls so that I could make proper rooms, and put in necessary insulation. In my haste, I didn't take the time to learn about the function of bearing walls, and I almost caused a disaster. As I was pounding away on some 2x4s, it seemed that the house was shuddering every time I knocked out another stud. I suddenly realized that I was taking out the main undergirding supports for the house, and if I continued on this foolish course, the whole structure would collapse. I replaced the bearing pieces, and breathed a sigh of relief when it all seemed secure once again. This taught me that I must also give attention to the proper construction and internal support of my own soul.

Removing Christ from Counseling

But this foolish act is not only restricted to my misguided building activities. In our society, misinformed men thought that they could remove the Lord Jesus Christ and His tried and true supports from counseling. They then attempted to set in place their own man-made counseling philosophies. Their teaching may have helped some with obvious surface problems, but the methodology of this world is not able to heal those with deeper inner pain. The counseling and strong medications may give them some hope for a time, but you can't heal serious spiritual problems with natural solutions. As a consequence, in our day, many are standing around in utter confusion, crying out for help. Thankfully, the Lord stands before us still offering His remedy for our mental and emotional health.

As we search the pages of Scripture, we see that the Lord is also a house builder, and He uses the analogy of building construction to instruct men how their mental and emotional health should be set in place. Thankfully, the Lord builds according to knowledge—not hit and miss like my own feeble attempts. One of the first building Scriptures that really caught my attention is found in Proverbs 9:1. It states, "Wisdom has built her house, she has hewn out her seven pillars…" I understood that Wisdom was referring to Jesus Christ Himself, and I could see that He wanted to place seven strong pillars in the human soul. For this to happen, I could see that we had a responsibility to gather the necessary wisdom so that He could begin His pillar-forming activities.

As we discuss "building according to knowledge," there's a tendency for all of us to be overwhelmed by the world's mental health literature. Their libraries are full of books in which they attempt to teach men how to address the complex problems that face mankind. Because they have rejected Christ, they have no strong foundation for their studies. Hence, they don't recognize that these human problems are only surface symptoms caused by the incorrect functioning of the soul and spirit. When people use the world's literature to find help, they discover to their dismay that they're opening up a maze of rabbit trails that often cause even greater confusion.

Placing the Lord Back in the Equation

We already know that He is the Author of the human soul, so let's return to His mental health steering statement in Proverbs 24:3-4. "Through wisdom a house is built, and by understanding it is established; by knowledge its rooms are filled with all precious and pleasant riches." Here He pushes aside all of the mental health teachings of this world, and in their place He offers us His own concise mini-summary of man's mental health. No wonder Paul said so emphatically in 2 Corinthians 11:3, "But I fear, lest somehow, as the serpent deceived Eve by his craftiness, so your minds may be corrupted from the simplicity that is in Christ." According to these Scriptures, mental health solutions should be simple to understand, and apply...not the nightmare that we currently see in our present-day world.

A Different Set of Glasses

So let's now put on a different set of glasses, and examine man's mental health from the Lord's point of view. For the sake of moving forward quickly in these counseling studies, let's declare up front that Freud was wrong. By doing this, we're accepting that man's innards are not made up of some strange consciousness, neither are they made up of the id, ego, and super-ego. In fact, the Scriptures clearly reveal in Genesis 1 that we're all crafted after the image of our God. Genesis 2:7 (KJV) further adds, "And the LORD God formed man of the dust of the ground, and breathed into his nostrils the breath of life; and man became a living soul." It appears that God had set up the soul/body framework, but it wasn't truly alive until God actually breathed His Spirit into Adam—then things really started happening. This is significant in mental health studies, because without the Spirit of God, man will wander about endlessly on the face of this planet like a lost soul without purpose or direction.

Paul confirms in 1 Thessalonians 5:23 that we're all comprised of a spirit, soul, and body. When our original architecture was wrecked by Adam's disobedience, serious mental health problems entered the human race. Thankfully, God promised that a Savior would be born who would provide us with an exact building model, and that He'd destroy Satan and his cruel schemes. From that point onward, we see that it's the certain plan of God to restore man's mind, and bring him once again into peace and fellowship with Himself. To do that, He lays out in Scripture the history of bringing man back into the image of Jesus Christ.

An Amazing House Construction Secret

To bring us back into a much-clearer focus regarding the body, soul, and spirit, let's think of the exterior walls as being the body, the interior construction and furnishings as being the soul, and the life in the house as the spirit. When all three work together, it makes the house into a well-functioning home. If we look at the same set-up as a modern-day computer, we see the body as the outer metal frame, the soul as the many wires and circuit-boards, and the spirit as the battery, electrical current, and programming.

Having these visual templates helps us to see more clearly that the soul and spirit combination is the place where our thoughts and feelings originate. Hence, we can understand that they must be the seat of our mental and emotional health. With this clear reference point, we can then grasp that the condition of our soul and spirit will have a huge bearing on how we think and feel inside. If our thoughts and feelings are bad, it makes sense that we would work on the strength of these two items…not spend our days chasing down perceived problems.

In Genesis 3, we're given a clue into the nature of the spiritual pressure the devil applies against us. Eve lacked understanding about how things worked in the spiritual realm, and was utterly deceived by Satan when he applied some strong pressure against her soul. Of course, she rounded up Adam, and then both of them collapsed inwardly. It then became the Lord's extended task to show mankind through the pages of Scripture how damaged souls might be rebuilt into the image of the Lord Jesus Christ. As I climbed into this same healing cycle, the Lord finally revealed to me that my soul was too weak or damaged to effectively resist these serious spiritual pressures, and what I was feeling as depression, fear, and anxiety was actually the work of these spirits. When a man is weak or damaged inwardly, then he'll often feel these pressures as an internal crushing.

The Lord Builds the House

The Lord is not overcome by the constant work of demons against the human race. In fact, we see in Matthew 12:43-45 that He gets quite upset if we don't work closely with Him to build up and fill up our spiritual house. He states, "When an unclean spirit goes out of a man, he goes through dry places, seeking rest, and he finds none. Then he says, 'I will return to my house from which I came.' And when he comes, he finds it empty, swept and put in order. Then he takes with him seven other spirits more wicked than himself, and they enter and dwell there, and the last state of that man is worse than the first."

The Scriptures often refer to our inner man as a house that can be occupied by the Holy Spirit, by useless chaff, or by demonic spirits. In this case, the man had been cleansed of demonic spirits and filled with godly substances. It was the Lord's expectation that this man would not neglect his salvation, and would continue to keep himself filled with the right materials. Such was not the case, and over a period of time, the man used up the spiritual substances that he had been given. Consequently, he was leaving his house empty and unguarded, and the enemy took full advantage by re-occupying his house and locking it down.

Some of our missionaries from Brazil were explaining how they had recently bought a large piece of property on the Xingu River. Our Church was helping them to raise funds to put up fences around the property. In that culture, if you leave your land unfenced and unguarded, squatters have the right to come in, and after a season of time, claim a right to your property. Hence they set to work right away to be certain that their area was properly cleared, and fully occupied by the Church. This previous verse gives strong warning that the same thing happens in the spiritual world. If demonic squatters are given the opportunity, they will always seek to occupy that soul that they previously had a grip on.

People Will Laugh

In our community of Chilliwack, a large lot was cleared, and a fairly expensive cement building was erected on that site. When complete, it looked really nice, but then the owners went bankrupt. As the months went past, no one stepped forward to occupy the new building. More time passed, and the unoccupied building began to deteriorate. Finally, the bank tried to reclaim their losses by selling the lot to a well-known restaurant chain. The never-occupied building was torn down, and a new restaurant was constructed on that same site.

This principle is explained to us in Luke 14:28-30, which states, "For which of you, intending to build a tower does not sit down first and count the cost, whether he has enough to finish it—lest after he has laid the foundation and is not able to finish, all who see it begin to mock him, saying 'This man began to build but was not able to finish'?" I believe the Lord is telling us that if we want to have a successful life, then we need to take advantage of the soul-building opportunities and work with Him toward the completion of our house. Otherwise, our life may fail, and others would have an opportunity to speak lightly of the Lord.

In Psalm 127:1 we're told, "Unless the LORD builds the house, they labor in vain who build it..." We see a world filled with self-help instructions, and many try to make a success of their own lives; but the Lord warns that He must be at the helm, or our life will become a shipwreck. Building up a soul correctly is a difficult and detailed operation, and we need to be very careful to work closely with the Holy Spirit. Once we do, the rewards are incredible, and a great stability will come into our thoughts and feelings.

The Parable of the Wise & Foolish Builders

The activity of soul-building is not some fancy sidebar with the Lord. His driving passion to reform us back into the image of Jesus Christ. That's why 1 Peter 2:5 declares that "you also, as living stones, are being built up a spiritual house, a holy priesthood, to offer up spiritual sacrifices acceptable to God through Christ Jesus." He tells us that He is not only the Author of our eternal salvation, but He is also the Author and the Finisher of our faith (Hebrews 12:2). These things are of high importance to Him, and throughout the Scriptures, we see Him actively engaged in house-building. The Scriptures are a life history of those who have allowed Him to build their houses successfully, contrasted with those who haven't allowed Him to restructure their inner architecture.

So it should not surprise us to see in Matthew 7 that He gives us some personal soul-building instructions. In the Parable of the Wise and Foolish Builders, He contrasts two very different kinds of Christians. The wise Christian is described in vs. 24-25, which states, "Therefore, whoever hears these sayings of Mine, and does them, I will liken him to a wise man who built his house on the rock; and the rain descended, the floods came, and the winds blew, and beat on that house; and it did not fall for it was founded on the rock."

This man didn't treat the condition of his soul lightly, and knew that it had to be firmly anchored on the salvation that Christ was offering to him. He knew that He needed to not only engraft the words of God into his soul, but he needed to carefully obey them, and make them the reference point and road map for his life. God highly commends this type of man because he allowed the Lord to build his soul into an eternal home.

In the next portion of Matthew 7, the Lord doesn't sugarcoat His words. In vs. 26-27, He describes a man who appears to undergo a full nervous breakdown. Jesus states, "But everyone who hears these sayings of Mine, and does not do them will be like a foolish man who built his house on the sand: and the rain descended, the floods came, and the winds blew and beat on that house; and it fell. And great was its fall." There is a definite judgment that falls on people who hear the words of the Lord but choose to reject them. In a sense, this man has turned away from the Tree of Life, and has chosen the Tree of the Knowledge of Good and Evil as his main feeding ground. This foolish man treats the necessary building-up of his soul far too lightly, and when serious troubles come upon him, he comes unglued both mentally and emotionally.

From personal experience, I found that this condition doesn't have to be the end of the road. Even though I had failed in my earthly attempts to find lasting peace, when I finally turned to the Lord wholeheartedly and adopted His building plan, everything changed. The Lord took my troubled soul in His hands, and began to speak to me. He told me that if I would draw close to Him, listen for His words, and obey His instructions, then He'd re-structure me internally. As He did, He promised that I'd find the permanent inner peace that I had sought my whole life. I want to tell you that I'm here today writing these words of encouragement because that's exactly what happened to me. He was true to His promise.

Psalm 127:1 declares "Unless the LORD builds the house, they labor in vain who build it." This means we must listen carefully for His specific guiding in our lives. Many are chasing after self-help instructions, and others try to rebuild their damaged lives, but the Lord warns that He must be at the helm giving directions, or our life will become a shipwreck. Building up and re-structuring the architecture of the human soul is a difficult and detailed operation worthy of the Holy Spirit's ability, and we must work closely with Him. If we do, stability will come at last into our thought life.

The Human Soul Is Delicate

In the early days of Canada, the making of maple syrup was a fine art. Buckets of thin maple sap were obtained from the individual trees, and poured into a large cauldron boiling away over a hot fire. As the flame and boiling time was carefully managed, a rich, sweet essence was formed in the pot. When conditions were just right, the sap was removed from the fire, packaged, and sold to eagerly waiting families. It then became a highly-sought-after sweet treat.

The power that fills our soul is like that delicate maple syrup. It's formed from the words of God abiding within it, and as our soul (the pot containing God's Spirit and words) is refined by life's circumstances, the treasure inside us becomes a rich, sweet essence that we call "wisdom." This is the strength of our human soul, and reveals to us why God claims that wisdom is the most valuable substance that we can obtain.

The Soul Must Be Treated With Utmost Respect

The Lord encourages us in Scripture that our house (soul) is constructed from His wisdom, founded on understanding, and filled with the knowledge of God (Proverbs 24:3-4). When we turn to the book of Proverbs, we also see that the soul is a delicate structure, and can be seriously damaged by such things as sexual activity outside of marriage. By observation, we also see that those who meddle with the occult, abuse drugs, or become filled with pride are also in real danger of soul collapse unless they repent.

The temple or house that God desires to build in us is no light matter. In fact, God warns us in 1 Corinthians 3:16-17, "Do you not know that you are the temple of God, and that the Spirit of God dwells in you? If anyone defiles the temple of God, God will destroy him. For the temple of God is holy, which temple you are." Here we see that God is not only building a house in us, but He is building His temple in our hearts so that He might live there forever. We need to be committed to this task if we desire our mental and emotional health to remain strong.

In Conclusion

I believe that the collapse of man's inner health occurred when man disobeyed the Lord, and his inner architecture was wrecked. Thankfully, the Lord didn't leave mankind in that place. He declared that He would send a Savior into the human race (Genesis 3:15). Before that happened, He prepared the way by forming a blueprint of excellence in the pages of Scripture, and He commanded that all men should follow it. Century by century, as the Lord's building plan is carried out, one benefit is the restoration of our inner health.

In a final building statement, Jesus encourages us by stating in Matthew 16:18, "On this rock I will build my church, and the gates of Hades shall not prevail against it." So let's cooperate in this building program, and permit Him to build a house in us that will stand against any demon, or any of life's many storms.

Chapter 9
The Soul's Foundation and Pathway

*Forsake foolishness and live, and go
in the way of understanding.
Proverbs 9:6*

*Through wisdom a house is built,
and by understanding it is established... Proverbs 24:3*

A Double Description

When I was completing my Master's degree at the University of Manitoba, I had a hair-raising experience. My project was to examine plankton growth and development year-round on a pre-selected lake. So in late November, the guide and myself were about to proceed out to the sampling station in the middle of the lake. Just before we headed out on the ice, he mentioned that it was still a bit thin in spots, and if we should break through the ice, then I was to jump sideways away from the skidoo. This put some real fear into me, and all the way out to the sampling station and back, I was on my tip toes ready to make an "Olympic-style" leap to safety. Thankfully, we made it there and back without incident, but the thought of not having a secure pathway under my feet still gives me the shudders. Later that winter, the guide did go through the ice, and it was only by the grace of God that he lived to tell the tale.

In the two opening Scriptures we see that Solomon is telling us the exact same thing. Firstly, we're told that understanding is a secure pathway set in front of every Christian. To walk on any other pathway through life is sheer foolishness. He warns that we all need to become well-established in our walk before the Lord, and encourages us all that this amazing spiritual substance called "understanding" will set us firmly in place. I have walked with the Lord for almost 40 years, and in that time, I have seen so many come into the Church, contend with other Christians and the ministry, and then fall away again. They didn't stay around long enough to "get understanding." Hence, they never really understood God's ways, so their walk never became established. In time, they became an easy prey for the enemy.

The Need for Solid Foundations

A tragic event occurred many years ago that shook my small hometown on the Sunshine Coast. It was so terrible and dramatic that it caused me to think very deeply about the whole subject of life's foundations. Late one evening, two teenagers had gone onto private property, jumped several barrier fences, ignored the warning signs, and climbed onto some huge sand piles near our home. There was only one major problem. They may have wanted to spend a relaxing evening looking at the stars and enjoying themselves on top of the sand piles, but unknown to them, these sand piles were soon to be loaded onto a nearby barge for transport into Vancouver.

Without warning, the gates on the conveyor belts underneath the piles opened, and the sand collapsed downward. The boys were quickly sucked down into the center of the descending cone, and smothered under many tons of sand. Their bodies were later found buried underneath the sand piles because they were blocking the grating onto the conveyor belt. These lads may have been peaceful and secure in the quiet night time, but when their foundations were removed, there was nothing to grab onto, and no way that they could save themselves.

It can be this way in our daily lives. We may have a reasonable level of mental health at this time, but if we haven't paid much attention to the foundations of our lives, we may find ourselves in serious difficulty when a sudden trial comes upon us. Others may try to help us by their counsel and support, but if we haven't sunk our roots deep into Christ (consistent devotions and prayer times, touches, revelations, and experiences with Him), then we may find ourselves overwhelmed if the bottom should suddenly drop from underneath us. As we move through this chapter, I want to show that God delights to build solid foundations under us as we come to know Him intimately.

In previous chapters, I've talked much about inner soul support, the soul's rooms, its armor, and the life purpose that God gives to every person. But now it's important to discuss our soul's foundations, and the pathway that God has provided for each person throughout their life. In His wisdom, the Lord has set down a clear walking trail for every individual, and this route is only to be found in the tried and true principles of Scripture. It's His plan that His Spirit should light this pathway, and the many thousands of principles found in His Word should provide the paving stones for our feet.

But I fear, lest somehow, as the serpent deceived Eve by his craftiness, so your minds may be corrupted from the simplicity that is in Christ (2 Corinthians 11:3).

Poor mental and emotional health shouldn't be a mystery to the Christian; its major cause is a result of running too fast through life. God has designed our spirit and soul to be like a battery that can only be recharged by Him, so if we continue to run too quickly through our days, or take on too much responsibility, we'll soon be neglecting our daily devotional times. Feelings of inner distress are the predictable result as the enemy moves in to take advantage of this weakness. God's promise given below is just as meaningful now as it was when it was first given.

He gives power to the weak; and to those who have no might He increases strength. Even the youths shall faint and be weary, and the young men shall utterly fall, but those who wait on the LORD shall renew their strength; they shall mount up with wings like eagles, they shall run and not be weary, they shall walk and not faint (Isaiah 40:29-31).

We see that weakness of soul is common to all men, but far too many Christians reject this incredible battery-recharging promise because God refuses to tell us how long it will take to recharge us. Although we may want a quick charge because we feel so unstable, the Lord prefers to use a "trickle-charger" that builds us up little by little. Thankfully, I waited, and week by week, I could tell that things were changing inside of me. And in time I was fully restored.

Defining the Pathway

In the book of Proverbs, we're warned to leave our selfish trails, and follow God's pathways of understanding. It's His plan that this route will become easy to follow as we earnestly seek Him. In fact, Solomon tells us that God has laid down an individual trail in front of every person. This is helpful for finding our way, but even with Solomon's strong warnings, we have to be careful. He was doing great in his own walk with the Lord, until he allowed his wives to turn his heart after other gods.

Once he began going in the wrong direction, he soon found himself in great confusion. This is clearly portrayed in the book of Ecclesiastes. Solomon speaks as a man depressed, and the warning is clear that those who choose their own route will find themselves in the same miry quicksand. We must turn from our own rabbit trails and follow the pathway that understanding will so clearly set before us.

By this time, I understood that the many paving stones that make up this pathway could be discovered in the principles from Genesis through Revelation. I was becoming ever more convinced that their purpose was to build up and strengthen our mental and emotional health. An even greater personal reward came as I took the time to understand these principles; and as I grew in them, I discovered that they removed all fear from my life. The pathway out of my valley of depression seemed like such a long and winding trail, but thankfully, these principles guided my way, and solidly established my feet under me.

My Desire to Teach

As I understood these principles, they began to make a huge difference in my life. I became so confident with them that I told the Lord that I really wanted an opportunity to teach them to others. For many years, I tried to assemble them into a clear pathway that would be easy for everyone to follow, but time and time again, I ended up in great frustration. Finally I said to the Lord, "If I'm going to teach these principles, You'll have to bring them together for me in a way that's easy for people to understand, and that makes sense." To my surprise, the Lord said, "Son, you don't have to reinvent the wheel. Start from Genesis 1:1, and proceed forward from there."

I was startled by His simple response, but as I began to examine what He had said, I saw that it made perfect sense. I now had the direction that I needed to set down a clear trail. But before I do, let's look at our personal responsibility. Coming to understand these principles, and then setting them solidly in our hearts, is not an easy task. It takes a high level of involvement. But we shouldn't be too surprised, because the life of the Christian is like that. If we consider Christ's salvation to be precious, then we'll begin to set aside less important things, and go after the knowledge of God with everything in us. As His words enter our hearts, God will begin to speak inside our spirit using these same words. He delights to reveal secrets that change us internally, and His promises give hope for the future.

Starting at the Beginning

Let's begin our study of these mental health paving stones with Genesis 1:1. It states, "In the beginning, God created the heavens and the earth." As we dissect this opening Scripture, we will see that a vast number of early Genesis principles fall into a definite order, and lead us step by step toward a much greater knowledge of the Master. In a previous discussion about "understanding," I introduced the concept of a pathway formed from these life-stabilizing principles. I will review the first five paving stones from Genesis 1:1, and then proceed to Genesis 1:2.

As you move forward along this well-marked pathway, you can observe that the opening verses and their many principles assemble into a commonsense trail that is complex enough to challenge even the greatest scholar, yet easy enough for a child to follow. Solomon encourages us in the passage below, saying that as you gain more information about the Master, the pathway becomes ever brighter. But foolish people aren't so fortunate. Their walk through life can be a nightmare, and they don't know what is causing them to fall and to be so badly hurt.

> But the path of the just is like the shining sun, that shines ever brighter unto the perfect day. The way of the wicked is like darkness; they do not know what makes them stumble.
> Proverbs 4:18-19

Defining the Paving Stones From Genesis: The Great Creator

Genesis 1:1 declares, "In the beginning, God created the heavens and the earth." This is God's great "Hello" to all mankind. Some receive His greeting heartily, others with reservation, and many with contempt. But let's be like the first group, and look at this amazing Scripture to know Him better. In it, we discover that the first and greatest principle is the existence of our mighty Creator. He's the reason that everything else around us makes sense. Exclude Him, and you get millions of philosophers down through the centuries endlessly debating the meaning of life. As well, you find millions of people desperately searching for a reason just to live one more day. This Creator principle reveals that God is the cause of everything, and it opens our thinking to ask the question "Why were we created?"

We were not built to wander lifelessly around this planet with an empty heart. John 3:16 clearly explains that God desires to pour out His love upon us; so our first paving stone is solidly set in place under our feet as we allow our heart to swell with love for our Creator. As we apply this principle to the mental health area, it means that when we have an inner problem, it honors God if we will turn to Him first. We see immediately that He designed and built the human soul, and He's the only one truly qualified to give us counsel. We greatly dishonor Him if we ignore His guidance and then scour the face of the planet for our own answers.

Creationism and Intelligent Design (Genesis 1:1 cont'd)

Let's review Genesis 1:1 again. It declares, "In the beginning, God created the heavens and the earth." I never heard anything about this in my high school biology classes, in my seven years of university training, or in the Fisheries Department. This principle certainly challenges the thinking of our modern era. Most have been taught from the earliest days in school that there's no design in the world around us, that all of this incredible beauty was brought about by time, chance, and natural selection.

Ignorant people spurn the concept of an Intelligent Designer, and insist that mankind descended from the apes; yet in this one short verse, God sweeps aside all of man's futile ideas, and tells us that He is the One responsible for all of the beauty and design that we see in the world. As I meditated on this, I remembered that one footprint on Robinson Crusoe's island was enough to convince him that he must get prepared to defend himself from the cannibals. He knew he had company, and perhaps he was to be the dinner guest. God has left millions of unmistakable footprints and fingerprints in the world around us. They can be as simple as the smile of a tiny infant, as indescribable as the radar system of a bat, as complex as the human eye, as amazing as the return of a salmon to the exact place it was birthed, or as incredibly beautiful as the blazing star systems. Intelligent design is clearly displayed in so many ways in His majestic Creation that God doesn't even stop to debate the subject with the evolutionists. He calls them foolish, and tells us that His signature is very obvious, and no one will be able to offer any credible excuse on Judgment Day (Romans 1:20). A correct belief system about our origins is the second mighty paving stone for our soul.

Purpose and Destiny (Genesis 1:1 cont'd)

As I took my first steps along this well-marked pathway of life, I was shocked at the deception that I had submitted to during my seven long years of university training. I shudder as I think how I could have stood before the Lord on Judgment Day trying to explain why I refused His Son's great sacrifice. In fact, how can any of us say that there's no evidence of intelligent design? Thankfully, I did accept Him, and as I did, the two critical stepping stones of purpose and design came clearly into view.

We know from this first verse of Scripture that God didn't create this universe in vain. He has such great plans for mankind, plans that give us a destiny and a future, and a keen sense of purpose for living each day. But it's also His plan that we should become the Bride of Christ so that we may rule together with Him for all of Eternity. So, in a few short steps, He has brought life into our soul, taken away its emptiness, and given us a future. In His great wisdom, God has given us a very strong foundation for our inner health…and the Genesis journey has only just begun!

Systems of Order (Genesis 1:1 cont'd)

We don't have to look very far to discover the next stepping stone. By direct observation, we see that God has set everything around us into cleverly-designed systems. This means that the tiniest atom and the greatest galaxy all respond to His invisible principles of order; otherwise, they would quickly blow apart. When we examine the human body, we see that it's exactly the same: every system of our physical body functions together as an intelligently-designed unit.

In our hidden spiritual parts, the same invisible systems were also set into a carefully-designed order so that we might experience His perfect peace. If we're struggling with mental health issues, it means that one or more of our inner systems has broken down, and now needs repairs. Knowing this takes some of the mystery and fear away from things like depression, because we can see that our inner man can be set into order once again using the tried and true principles of the Word of God. But this is only a first step; we still must spend time in the Scriptures, as well as "knee time" with God to get some words of knowledge, and some specific touches for our own particular affliction.

Divine Health (Genesis 1:1 cont'd)

One of the things that drove me into depression was the terrible sickness and suffering that I saw in others all around me. Thankfully, the fifth paving stone speaks to that problem. When God first created His universe, it was His plan that everything should work together in perfect harmony. But sin soon changed that. It completely wrecked God's perfect order, and brought about the terrible suffering that we now see. But we can take heart, because it's God's intent to restore order once again by giving health to our bodies and creating peace in our minds. The path to receiving those things may not always be easy, but He has given us everything that we need to overcome in this life, and it's His eternal plan that all people should be able to enjoy the benefits that He has purchased for us at Calvary with His own blood. As we proceed along this pathway, we'll see that mental health issues, cancers, and incurable diseases can be identified as spiritual pressures targeting both the body and soul of man; and it's God's plan to build us to the point where these things no longer penetrate our defenses.

Paving Stones Found in Genesis 1:2: Introducing Genesis 1:2

Now that we've laid down our first set of paving stones, let's direct our feet toward the next set of foundational principles found in Genesis 1:2. This verse states, "The earth was without form and void; and darkness was on the face of the deep. And the Spirit of God was hovering over the face of the waters." Although I won't go into a detailed debate at this point, many Christians believe that there is a large gap of time between Genesis 1:1 and Genesis 1:2. They find that this interpretation reconciles the apparent great age of the Earth with the later account of a more recent Creation given in the rest of Genesis 1.

According to this line of reasoning, during the time between verses 1 and 2, Satan was cast down from Heaven to the Earth. The result of the upheaval that followed was a colossal destruction of the things that God had first created. It appears that in Genesis 1:2, God is now restoring order. Discussing the pros and cons of this interpretation at this time, however, would lead away from the main topic of regaining our mental health. Such debates can sharpen our thinking, but would detract us from our main purpose in this book.

The Paving Stone of Oppression (Genesis 1:2 cont'd)

As we study the Scriptures within the framework of this interpretation, we find our next important paving stone embedded in this verse. It brings to light a key fact that is largely unknown to worldly counselors—that demonic beings do exist, and that they create negative pressures against every human soul. Thankfully, the Scriptures also reveal that we have been given power and authority to rule over these dark pressures through the death and the resurrection of Jesus Christ (Luke 10:17-19; Hebrews 2:14). Those who understand this place of authority are well on their way to finding rich and fulfilling mental health. During the difficult times of life, these black pressures will exert themselves against the human soul in cruel and painful ways. That's why I have been stressing that we must give strong attention to build up our soul while things are quiet in our lives. Jesus warns us that those who give no attention to building up their inner man are in great danger of leaving their soul empty. This is the spiritual condition that serves as an open invitation for the enemy to return and once again exert his black pressures. If people still don't learn from their negligence, and ignore the need to build themselves up, then these unrestrained pressures can do some real damage. For this reason, when I counsel those suffering from depression, my first question always centers around the strength of the person's devotional life.

Death and Decay (Genesis 1:2 cont'd)

We can identify the sin of Adam and Eve as the exact point where mental and emotional problems first attacked the human race. It was then that humanity's inner architecture was corrupted. Also, at that time, the whole universe became subject to a terrible curse of death and decay (Romans 8:20-21). The carefully-designed systems that our Creator had put in place had now been thrown into utter chaos by this one act of disobedience.

Thankfully, when God sacrificed His own Son, He put a repair strategy in place that fully paid for the sinful acts of mankind. Those who accept the Lordship of Jesus Christ are given an umbrella of protection from the terrible ongoing effects of the Adamic curse in spite of contrary demonic pressures. If we will spend the time and effort to discover what spiritual benefits belong to us as a result of Christ's sacrifice, we will not be torpedoed by the death and decay principle, and we will find our route back to mental and emotional wholeness.

"Without Form and Void" (Genesis 1:2 cont'd)

When a person is depressed or discouraged, they often feel "without form and void" in their soul. I remember how, during my long periods of depression, every hopeless thought could just go right through me. After a time, I felt in such a helpless state because there seemed to be no way to stop these black thoughts. This was compounded by empty and lonely feelings that racked my soul year after year. Even as a Christian, I still experienced some of these awful things, but as I became more and more desperate, I purposed to understand the incredible provisions of my salvation. As I did, I learned how to connect with the Savior, and little by little, the revelations and touches that He gave filled the empty places in my soul. Those awful feelings of being "without form and void" in my soul are now just a distant memory. The excitement of Christ's love, and the wonderful things that He has planned for my future, now fill my soul completely.

The "Hovering Over" Paving Stone (Genesis 1:2 cont'd)

The "hovering over" principle is one of my favorites because the proper understanding of it can mean the difference between life and death. Throughout every stage of life, the Spirit of God hovers over individuals, just waiting to repair those areas in them where the enemy has caused soul damage. These verses reveal to us a powerful Bible truth: the Spirit of God did nothing until the Father spoke authoritative commands to Him. As these words were spoken, He sprang into action and the tasks were accomplished. In the same way, He hovers over our lives, but will do nothing until we speak God's words to Him. At that point, He springs into action, and does those things that we ask of Him. That's why it's so important to spend time taking in the Word of God, and crying out for greater understanding. As we do, an improvement of our inner health is certain to follow.

The "Spirit of God" Paving Stone (Genesis 1:2 cont'd)

In the natural world, the level of the water table is critical for the life and growth of plants. It's the same in the spiritual world. If we desire to experience life, then we must have an abundant supply of water gushing through our spirit and soul. When

I first came to the Lord, I joined a worshipping and praising Church, so I quickly learned about the Holy Spirit and His offer of spiritual water. I was also taught that God had given a method of bringing water to those who were thirsty for it—praying in a Heavenly language. As I entered into these things, I found them very helpful because they brought rest to my troubled soul. As I worshipped and spoke in my Heavenly language, I knew that there was a strengthening occurring deep within me. It seemed as if my inner water table was being gently raised, and it was causing great growth in my spiritual life.

The "Face of the Waters" (Genesis 1:2 cont'd)

When I was at Boy Scout camp many years ago, we didn't have all of the modern conveniences that we use so frequently today. The water we needed was deep underground, so we had to use a hand pump, and do some very hard work to bring up water from many meters below our feet.

It's similar in our spiritual lives. We first use worship, praise, and thanksgiving to raise the water table in our souls; then, as we come together on Sunday mornings, and enter into a corporate worship service, the water in each one spills over and soon becomes like "rivers of living water" (John 7:38). Those who come to these praise services with a low water table spend their time building up its inner level, and therefore fail to experience the fullness of the living water that God has to offer. These two paving stones that speak about inner water are important because the level of spiritual water hidden deep within our souls has a huge bearing on our soul strength.

The "Waters Above/Waters Below" (Genesis 1:2 cont'd)

In some desert areas, the ground remains dry and dormant until the waters pour down from above during a thunderstorm. At that moment, the faceless desert springs to life, and greenery and insects suddenly appear where there was only dry, barren sand a few days before. It's similar in our spiritual lives. When the Holy Spirit in the atmosphere connects with the water table of our soul, there's an explosion of growth, and our faith comes alive deep within us. As we use this faith year by year, we gradually grow from a small sapling into a large fruit-bearing tree. This kind of gradual growth and development is expected in all Christians, and is what Jesus meant when He stated that He'd come to bring each one of us into abundant life. It doesn't happen overnight.

The Paving Stones Hidden in Genesis 1:3: Introducing Genesis 1:3

Genesis 1:3 is extremely significant because it's God's first recorded words to all mankind, and defines the first pillar of the human soul. It says, "Then God said, 'Let there be light': and there was light." God revealed a wealth of dynamic mental health principles in this verse. As I meditated on them, I recognized that light is an amazing creation of our God. It springs forth from the Father, and fuels the life that He has placed on this natural world. This first recorded phrase that God speaks beautifully describe His nature and character. He wasn't about to let darkness reign over His universe any longer, so He filled Creation with His own amazing light. As we looked at the process of photosynthesis in the Seven Pillars chapter, we also saw that light was the critical foundation stone that supported all life on this Earth, so we need to learn all that we can about it.

Light vs. Darkness (Genesis 1:3 cont'd)

When there's complete darkness, we can easily stumble or lose our way, because we can't see a thing. It's the same in the spiritual. Darkness in this realm speaks of a lack of understanding of spiritual principles, and an ignorance of how they're designed to work in our lives. I discovered that it was extremely difficult to recover from inner afflictions if I had no clue what was going on inside of me. That's why depression and fear can go on endlessly in a human life. But when God spoke, "Let there be light," He immediately changed the world. Everything became visible in the natural. And in the spiritual, He opened the way for us to learn how His secret things were designed to work, and challenged us all that it was "the glory of kings" to search out His hidden truths (Proverbs 25:2)—and we are all God's royal heirs.

So the more understanding of spiritual things that we obtain, the less we're going to be tripped up by the afflictions so common in our day. If we desire to set this paving stone solidly under our feet, then we must be serious in gaining understanding. But there's a problem for the casual Christian because light isn't given automatically. It shines on us and in us during our intimate devotional times with the Lord. When this precious light is given, the causes of long-time afflictions are going to be exposed, and we're going to be set free.

The Faith Foundation Stone (Genesis 1:3 cont'd)

We all have an abundance of natural faith. We get up in the morning believing that the floor will hold our weight; we eat food believing that our body will digest it; and we turn the ignition key believing that our car will start. But God wants to bring us all to a much higher level. In Genesis 1:3, He spoke words of faith over His unformed universe proving that the language of Heaven is designed to bring things into order. When the Father spoke, He knew that the Holy Spirit would do those things that were respectfully commanded of Him.

Then He gave us His precious words so that we might also use them. It's important to realize that the things that the Father asked of the Holy Spirit didn't exist at the time they were requested; so as He was speaking to the Holy Spirit, He was also teaching us how faith is designed to work. When we're in proper relationship with God, we can have the same confidence in God's words as we do in that ignition key when we turn it. Our faith gives us a steady walk with Christ because we know that God will not fail us. Step by step, as we learn to use our faith correctly, it can restore our mental and emotional health.

The Words You Say (Genesis 1:3 cont'd)

Some people speak so carelessly about life and their circumstances. They think it really doesn't matter how they speak, or even what they say, because, after all, they're "just words." But it most certainly does. God used carefully chosen words to set spiritual forces into action that framed this universe. In Proverbs 18:21, Solomon warns, "Death and life are in the power of the tongue, and those who love it will eat its fruit." In a spiritual sense, the things that we say can either set the Holy Spirit to work, or they can open the way for demons to war against us.

In the midst of my hellish bouts of depression, I would remind the Lord that I wasn't going by how I felt. His Word declared that He would build His strength in us (Isaiah 40:31) and I wasn't about to give up on that promise. I simply refused to quit until I got it. It was a terrific fight of faith, but, in time, I got in full measure exactly what I was saying, and what I had tenaciously believed for.

The "Light of the World" (Genesis 1:3 cont'd)

When I began my difficult journey to find a cure for my mental health afflictions, I knew very little of what I now know. The information that I'm passing on was given by direct revelation from the Holy Spirit. After all, who could know the construction secrets of the human soul unless God revealed them? It all started when I received a "laying on of hands" from the elders of our church (1 Timothy 4:14). At that time, information was given to me that would have meant little to anyone else… but it mapped out the course of my life. God gave me exactly what I needed in order to find my answers, and also revealed the information that I needed to get through some very difficult years.

Through all of this, Jesus was giving light or revelation so that I might succeed. The world may hold their thousands of volumes of information in high regard, but we have the "light of the world" (John 1:9) to speak to us, and give the information that we need to bring us out of the darkness, and lead us successfully through this life. Those who are struggling with mental health issues will find great assistance as they learn to take hold of this wonderful gift.

The "Prayer and Rulership" Paving Stone (Genesis 1:3 cont'd)

As a young lad, I attended a private school for boys in Victoria. With help from the often-administered cane of the headmaster, I learned how to rule over my very foolish impulses. When I later attended university, I was in danger of failing my first year until I determined to take charge of my poor study habits. It's the same in day-to-day life. We're all expected to mature, and take on ever-increasing levels of responsibility. In the spiritual world, God expects us to learn how to rule over sickness and depression, or anything else that the enemy might send our way. To do this, He has given us powerful tools, including prayer and a wealth of promises found in the Word of God. With them in our arsenal, we can change things that this world has resigned themselves to accepting. But each one of us needs to go through a period of schooling to learn to use the Word and prayer correctly.

Genesis 1:4 and Beyond: Introducing the Remainder of Genesis 1

God has laid a powerful foundation for our mental and emotional health in the first three verses of Genesis 1. It shouldn't surprise us that this is the part of Scripture that the enemy has attacked the most throughout the past centuries. In fact, it's so bad now that if you should go into the world's hallowed halls of learning, and try to share these wonderful foundational truths of mental health, they'd probably laugh you right out of the door. In the rest of the chapter of Genesis 1, God continues to share an amazing series of foundation stones with us that will make a very secure pathway underneath our feet.

The "Essence of Life" (Genesis 1:4 and beyond)

"Life" is a mysterious substance that the whole world desperately seeks after. In the spiritual world, it's God's antidote for mental health problems. In the natural world, many try to find it through unrestrained pleasure, alcohol, or drugs; but these artificial stimulants lead toward terrible disappointment, and so often to an early death. True life began when God breathed into Adam's nostrils "the breath of life," and man became a living soul (Genesis 2:7). But this wonderful breath is consumable, so it was always God's plan that we should be given additional breaths of His amazing life as we earnestly sought after Him. I have shown in different ways throughout this manuscript that true life can't be discovered by ordinary means. It's formed by God in us as we seek God. In fact, the strength of the life that resides in us is in direct proportion to the intimacy and strength of relationship that we have with our God. Life is also a spiritual substance that grows deep within our own spirit as we feed on the words of God. In fact, it is the substance that God uses to push depression and fear out of the human soul. The more we have life, the less we experience death.

The Foundation Stone of Salvation (Genesis 1:4 and beyond)

To prevent mankind from being snared permanently by Satan's trickery, the Lord prepared a legal contract that would enable people to regain a proper righteous standing before God. This contract came with a very high price tag: it cost Jesus Christ His life, but it forever settled the question of man's sin. When we ask God for forgiveness for our transgressions, it can now be granted to each one based on the work of Calvary, not on our own efforts. Salvation is the critical foundation stone for all mental health studies, and as we closely examine the Scriptures, we see that although mental health was lost at the point of man's disobedience, it was fully regained through Christ's willing obedience. It's our responsibility to learn the terms and conditions of that salvation contract so that we might walk forward into a brand new life.

The Separation Foundation Stone (Genesis 1:4 and beyond)

Natural light allows us to see and enjoy God's amazing Creation, whereas spiritual light allows us to see beyond this natural realm, and into God's invisible world. David said in Psalm 119:105, "Your word is a lamp to my feet and a light to my path." He was stressing that light allowed him to see the path in front of him both naturally and spiritually. Darkness takes away our ability to see anything in the world around us. More specifically, spiritual darkness removes our ability to see or understand God, and will eventually bring us into depression and fear. In Genesis 1, God's first action was to separate light from darkness so that we might have an opportunity to come to know Him. It's now God's expectation that we'll remain in the light, and keep ourselves separated from the darkness. Peter puts it far more bluntly, warning people to not be like a dog that returns to devour its own vomit (2 Peter 2:21-22).

The Firmament Paving Stone (Genesis 1:4 and beyond)

I heard a true, humorous story about a fellow and his wife living in a townhouse complex. At night, they were sure that they could hear the muffled sounds of people above them, but they knew that it wasn't possible. One night as they were sleeping, however, there was a terrific crash, and a shower of dust and gyproc. When they recovered from the initial shock, they realized that someone had fallen through the roof onto their bed. The police came and discovered that a number of illegal immigrants had been housed in the attic upstairs, and one of the squatters had missed his footing and fallen right through the roof. This describes our society so perfectly. People are looking for a stable footing and a safe place to live, but don't know where to find it.

The thing that afflicted people seem to need the most is the sense that they have something solid in their lives, and under their feet. When I was going through my terrible bouts of depression, I longed for an intimate friend who could really understand my difficulties. Thankfully, I found that intimacy in Jesus Christ, and I finally understood that He valued me, and deeply cared for my soul. In our society, people are looking everywhere for this kind of intimacy, but many are looking in the wrong places. As I found true intimacy with Christ, I also found that solid ground; and as more time passed, I became ever more stable within.

The Paving Stone of Division (Genesis 1:4 and beyond)

As we search through the Scriptures, we see that God frequently divides things. For example, He divides between light and darkness, between Jacob and Esau, between the saved and the unsaved, and between the wise and the foolish virgins. Invariably, one group is considered wise, and the other foolish. In our quest for inner strength, there are two ways that we can go: toward God, or away from Him. Those who run hard after God find that their lives get stronger and their footsteps more certain (Psalm 63:8). Those who draw away from Him find that life loses its meaning, and they go on a frantic search for something that satisfies. God wants to give us a clear purpose for living. Hence, God wants to divide us from those terrible feelings of emptiness and failure, and add into us His sense of fullness and life.

The "Replacement" Paving Stone (Genesis 1:4 and beyond)

At the time of Creation, God took shapeless things and replaced them with useful, functioning substances. Gradually, the formless mass of His Creation took on beauty and order, and caused Him to declare that the things that He had made were very good. He does exactly the same things in the soul of damaged human beings. He replaces that which is bruised or broken with something that functions well. But God needs our ongoing permission to succeed in this. He offered good things to Cain and Saul, but they refused His ways, and turned to their own devices. In the life of David, He took an imperfect shepherd boy, and fashioned him into a man after His own heart. In the same way, He wants to take the heart in us that may be damaged and depressed, and to fill it with His life, and His new spiritual substances. He longs to draw us into intimate relationship with Him and to fill the emptiness of our hearts.

The Foundation Stone Called "Seed in You" (Genesis 1:4 and beyond)

We understand through the Parable of the Sower (Mark 4) that the seed represents not only the word of salvation, but the many precepts and promises found in the Word of God. It is God's plan that these eternal principles will take root and grow to maturity in the human heart. But we have a great responsibility to provide the Lord with a soft heart; otherwise, those precious seeds will merely rest on our head, and will eventually shrivel and die. I know that I'm alive and functioning today because when I was presented with the claims of Christ, I believed His promises, and gave God no rest until I saw them fulfilled in my own life. His promises became fertile seeds in me that grew into a mighty oak of peace and rest. One day we must give an answer what we have done with His precious seeds; those who have used them well will find that they have strong, vibrant mental health growing in them.

The story about the dreams of the butler and the baker in Joseph's day (Genesis 40) is insightful. They were both arrested and cast into prison. But in time, the butler was released, and once again put wine goblets in Pharaoh's hand. But the baker wasn't so fortunate. We learn that in his dream he was unable to deliver the bread to Pharaoh. The bread had been picked off his head by the birds; it was not in his heart. We see that the seed must not be loosely sprinkled on our heads where the devourer can consume it. It must be engrafted into our heart where it can be the main conversation piece between us and the Holy Spirit. If we're careless with the seed (the Word of God) we'll eventually be picked apart and die.

The "According to Kind" Paving Stone (Genesis 1:4 and beyond)

Those who take God seriously will discover that we're not some random Creation. He has made us in His own image. This is very significant in our mental health studies. If we take time to discover a little about the image of God, then we'll learn some important things about our own makeup. We know that no matter what our outward appearance is, we've been accepted by the Lord because of our faith in Christ. It's this revelation that God can use to enable us to overcome all manner of negative spiritual pressures, especially rejection and inadequacy. When worldly counselors try to discover the reason for the life-threatening problems of a client, they have some general principles to work from, but because they've been given wrong information about man's inner makeup, they can't help their client deflect the terrible pressures that Satan has directed toward their soul. With correct information, however, the soul of the counselee can be built up.

The "Image of God" Foundation Stone (Genesis 1:4 and beyond—cont'd)

If we're to serve God well, and overcome the problems that come our way, then we need a pattern that will allow us to see God's heart, and a clear model that will allow us to live out our lives in the correct manner. When Adam chose to rebel against God, he was immediately cut off from the Tree of Life so that he didn't continue eternally in his rebellion. At first, God seemed to hide the Tree of Life, but then we see it resurface in Proverbs in the form of wisdom. God still wanted to reveal Himself to mankind through His words. Throughout history we see that those who cling to Him are accepted; those who refuse Him are condemned. In fact, rejection of God became so bad in Noah's day that only eight souls were saved from the raging floodwaters.

At an appointed time in history, God set His precious Son before all mankind to serve as His model of righteousness. Everyone was then given a clear choice that would determine their eternal destiny: if they received Christ's forgiveness and accepted His righteousness, they were saved; then, as they lived in Him, they embraced this model of Christ. Then they could work back toward the image of God and "make themselves pure, just as He is pure."

The Marriage Covenant (Genesis 1:4 and beyond)

Even though people are getting divorced everywhere, the idea of marriage and life commitment is God's idea. When I was having some minor troubles in my own marriage, the Lord spoke firmly to my heart. He stated that in my marriage, I was practicing to be married to Him, and I needed to apologize to my wife for the way I was behaving. I quickly made things right. I saw that God didn't just create human beings to populate this Earth; He had a definite purpose in mind. It was His plan that mankind should form a loving bride for His Son; her eternal purpose would be to rule and reign together with Christ throughout all of eternity. This is an extremely high calling, and it gives a great sense of purpose to those who accept it. In my mental health teachings, I show that the more we're filled with things that give us meaning and purpose, the less room the enemy has to move against us, and to afflict us. The Bride of Christ has access to the things that belong to her husband such as peace, healing, and wholeness.

The "Ruling Over" Paving Stone (Genesis 1:4 and beyond)

God expects us to learn from the examples of others so that we might rule over those things that would try to destroy us. In recent days, we lost yet another fisherman in the deep, swift waters of the Fraser River. Three men were so intent on catching fish that they ignored the need for life jackets, and were wearing only chest waders. As they attempted to wade out to an ideal fishing island, all three were swept away. Two were miraculously rescued, but the third was sucked under the water by the currents, and not seen again. It's the same in our daily lives. The danger of mental health problems is very real for every human being, and God expects us to exercise discipline so that we might rule over those things that would pull us away from our devotional times. We'll always face negative spiritual pressures in this life, and God expects us to make the choice to rule over them. Those who choose correctly will reign with Christ for all of Eternity.

In 1 Corinthians 10:6 Paul states, "Now these things became our examples, to the intent that we should not lust after evil things as they also lusted." The Children of Israel, the inhabitants of Sodom, and the people of Noah's day were clueless about life. They lived their lives in such a reckless manner that their whole generations had to be wiped off the face of the Earth. But it wasn't to end in complete tragedy. God uses these stories to warn us all that our lives are designed to serve as an example so that we might live differently. If we shun the evil and accept the model that God has placed before us, then we'll rule over our sinful desires and be accepted before the Throne of Grace.

The Paving Stone of Nutrition (Genesis 1:4 and beyond)

Through my own poor nutritional habits, I'm learning that if my body is to become really healthy, then I must fill it with the proper selection of nutritious foods. In this natural world, we see that it's not the Lord's responsibility to open up our mouths and place the food in. He has lovingly provided all of the nutrition that we'll ever need, but He has also given us the task of selecting the right foods, and then preparing them. It remains our responsibility to chew, swallow, and digest our food. In the spiritual world, God has given us His Word and His Spirit to feed and strengthen our inner man. But it's our responsibility to slow down our lives, spend time mediating on His words, and engrafting them deep within our soul. As we learn to become intimate with Him in our daily devotions, we'll come to know Him in a deep and meaningful way.

The "Very Good" Paving Stone (Genesis 1:4 and beyond)

Everything that God does is very good, so when things aren't good around us, we must wait upon Him until things change. Even the winter periods of life can be good if we'll recognize that they're preparing us for the spring that is soon to follow. It's during these dark rest periods that we must slow down our lives, so that we can become even more fruitful for Him in the next season of life. The Children of Israel responded poorly with murmurings and complaints against God whenever things weren't good. This is very significant, because we're told that the things that happened to them were designed to serve as a teaching example for us today. Their poor responses caused them to be cut off from the Lord, and we're told that their carcasses littered the wilderness. If inner blackness strikes, it isn't time to murmur against the Lord. We must diligently seek the Master until things become "very good" once again.

Summarizing Genesis 1

This chapter has described some of the paving stones that God desires to place under the feet of every Christian. Yet it's only the beginning of a very long pathway. As we move on into Genesis 2, we'll see that the Word of God continues to provide a rich treasure house of solid foundations, wall-building material, and secure paving stones. It's through careful use of these building materials that our soul becomes established, and we gain a deep sense of confidence in the Lord. When Nehemiah was called to Jerusalem, it wasn't to engage the enemy in battle. It was his task to secure Jerusalem by reconstructing its wall and gates. His activities infuriated the enemy, but as He listened to the Lord's instructions, the city again became a safe citadel for all of its inhabitants. When Jerusalem was fully secured, Nehemiah then set about organizing its inhabitants, and demanding a greater purity in the way that they lived and conducted themselves. In this way, they were once again drawing closer to the Lord and preparing themselves for an uncertain future. Consequently, the next chapter describes yet another vital soul construction secret…that we must slow down our lives, draw near to Him, and put effort into seeking after the knowledge of God.

CHAPTER 10
Filling the Soul: A Top Ten Shopping List

Introducing the Concept

Several years ago, I heard a most unusual story on the evening news. An elderly lady and her husband had been hoarding junk in a large home. One day, the gentleman came home to find his wife nowhere in sight. They had a bit of a distant relationship, so he thought that she had gone off to visit her relatives. Several days later, after hearing nothing, he began to get concerned so he started searching for her all through the house, and eventually discovered her body in a back basement buried under a mountain of heavy stuff. Apparently she had been rummaging through piles of hoarded things when the whole wall of unstable material collapsed onto her killing her instantly.

When we draw a spiritual lesson from this, we see that God doesn't wants us to hoard the things of this world, but He does want us to wisely store up His precious substances of wisdom, knowledge, and understanding. Thankfully, He has ways of safely storing these contents within us. If we'll fill our house (soul) with the correct things, far from killing us, they'll make our lives much richer, and actually lengthen our days.

> *By knowledge the rooms are filled
> with all precious and pleasant
> riches. Proverbs 24:4*

As I spent time reflecting on my mental health, I realized that the concept of being filled or being empty is a very important one indeed. I had to learn the hard way that when my soul was filled with the wrong contents, life didn't go well for me. After a lifetime of trials, I knew exactly what the Lord meant when He described a people who were smothered by the hopelessness of their inner problems: "In the morning you shall say, 'Oh that it were evening.' And at evening, you shall say, 'Oh that it were morning' because of the fear which terrifies your heart" (Deuteronomy 28:67). This is exactly how I felt, and my life seemed so very empty. I searched endlessly for answers, but no one seemed to know much about soul contents, and it seemed that even less was known about the continuous need of the human soul for fuel.

Looking around, we can also see this problem in natural things as well. Over the years, I've had to learn the hard way that it's not a good idea to drive my vehicle to the point where the gas needle registers empty. Because of my inattention to this important detail, I've been stranded on the side of the road on more than one occasion with no fuel in my tank. And as we all know, my car wouldn't start until it was given a fresh supply of gasoline. Spiritually, it's the same. Many break down on the roadside of life because they have no time to tank up with intimate devotions. Yet, if they repent of their too-busy lifestyle and wait upon the Lord, He will fill their soul once again.

I had to learn the hard way, because I returned to the same running pattern; and yet again I found my spiritual fuel needle on empty. I noticed that the final warning before my spiritual fuel ran out was a return to the previous panic attacks and black feelings. Thankfully, I responded to the Lord and got very serious with Him concerning the condition of my soul. But tragically, when many people experience these, their lives simply come to an abrupt halt. If they still don't do anything about their low spiritual reserves, then they're too often medicated, and some will remain under a black cloud of oppression for the rest of their lives. But it's still not too late. If they will learn to "kiss the Son" (Psalm 2:12) even at this late date, God in His mercy will give them their strength back once again.

The Stories of Aesop

Aesop's famous fable about the ant and the grasshopper can teach us a very valuable mental health lesson. The foolish grasshopper is like so many Christians in our day who waste a lot of time during the good times of life. They become so busy with activities and enjoying life that they have little time for intimate devotional times; hence, they store away few inner supplies. When spiritual storms come against them, they're in immediate trouble because they have no rooting system, nor do they have any gas in their tank.

Both Aesop and Solomon teach us that we can learn much wisdom from the lowly ant. While the grasshopper is wasting time when the weather is good, the ants are busy. They may not have a leader, but each one instinctively knows that tough times are just ahead. They remain busy all through the growing season building up their colony, and laying in an abundant store of supplies. When winter finally comes, their larders are full, and their tunnels—strategically placed far underground—are warm and protected. This enables them to survive through even the coldest of winters.

As we dissect this story, we see that there's an amazing parallel between the grasshopper and the five foolish virgins. Both were left without food (or oil) during the dark times of life, and both were refused by the wise. The ants and wise virgins weren't being cruel by retaining their precious supplies; they had no choice. The ants also would perish in the cold days ahead if the winter was prolonged, and the virgins would run out of oil themselves if they gave their oil away.

The Ten Virgins

As we now look at soul supplies in greater detail, there's no better place to start than the Parable of the Ten Virgins. In this story, we're told that five were wise, and five were foolish. Those whom God considered to be wise spent their days living to serve Christ, and listening to the Spirit of God. As a result, their hearts were filled with a rich abundance of anointing oil. The foolish virgins were Christians, but were like Aesop's grasshopper—so busy with their affairs that they didn't respect the need for this anointing oil. When dark times came, one group had the inner fuel to make it through a time of trouble; the other group didn't. In Bible days, the task of laying in adequate provisions for an impending battle, or a prolonged siege, was not an assignment that was to be taken lightly. It meant life or death for the inhabitants of that city. I was amazed when I read the story about Hezekiah's unusual water tunnel. He knew the importance of a steady supply of water in such times, so he prepared the city for an impending siege from the Assyrians by constructing a 533-meter long hidden tunnel underneath the streets of Jerusalem. It channeled the waters of the Gihon Spring, located outside of the walls of Jerusalem, directly to the Pool of Siloam situated well inside the city. With this constant supply, they were able to withstand the Assyrians for a long season. But when the people of Jerusalem rejected the Lord, no amount of food or water could save them.

The Tragedy of Selfishness

It's the same in our lives. If we're to withstand the assaults of a very vicious enemy against our souls, we'll need adequate supplies of water and provisions. I previously spoke of the foolish presumptions of both Napoleon and Hitler as they sent their armies out onto the steppes of Russia without adequate supplies. The results were disastrous. Christ describes another type of foolish man who had gathered many tons of food and supplies, but his intent was to use these things for his own pleasure, and give no thought to the desperate needs of his brethren (Luke 12:16-21). This man parallels the antics of those in this rich and hoarding generation. Many start well in Christ; but in their busy lives, they neglect their devotional times, and either fail to resupply themselves, or they use their supplies for their own pleasures. Neither group is pleasing to the Lord.

The Traveling Corpse

An unusual story about inner supplies centers around two ladies who were taking their elderly father to a resort town somewhere in Germany. To their utter dismay, he suddenly died far from their home, and they were now faced with the huge transport cost of bringing his corpse back home. As they reflected on their dilemma, they had an idea. They propped him up in a wheelchair, buckled him in, and fixed up his appearance with a hat, sunglasses, and a scarf. The customs officers asked if he was okay because he seemed a little pale and sickly. The ladies assured them that he just needed a little more fresh air and sunshine. The officer became suspicious and upon closer examination, discovered that he was dead. The ladies were immediately arrested and detained until the police fully understood the story, and realized that the man had died from natural causes. This is an unusual story, yet we see it happening all of the time in our Christian churches. People are dressed well, and they appear normal; but something is wrong. Upon closer examination, we see that their walk with God is not providing them with the inner life that they need to function correctly. They're filled with inner problems, and the abundant life is a far distant concept. At one time, they excitedly embraced the idea of Christianity; but now the idea of dying to self and filling themselves with Christ doesn't fit their busy lifestyle. After a time, they completely consume their former spiritual supplies, and began running even faster to keep themselves at peace. But they're in danger of becoming like the elderly man in the wheelchair.

Empty, Swept, and Garnished

As we speak about inner contents, we also need to give careful attention to the words of Jesus Christ. He warns that any soul cleansed by Him that is left empty is in a dangerous spiritual condition. At salvation, He gives us a wonderful cleansing. But then, He expects us to appreciate this mighty salvation by drawing close to Him, and fulfilling Proverbs 8:17: "I love those who love me, and those who seek me diligently will find me." But if we're not continually being filled with good spiritual things, the enemy will set about to deceive us, and fill our inner vacuum with some very troubling things. Those who wish to avoid trouble and receive an abundant entrance into Heaven (2 Peter 1:11) are those who set their hearts on knowing more about Christ, and fulfilling His mission for them on this Earth.

In my teaching and counseling, I have seen countless Christians have a glorious salvation experience, and set people on fire around them. But years later, they're nowhere to be found, leaving everyone wondering why they'd fallen away from the Lord. But if we grasp this need for constant refilling, we can firmly take hold of yet another soul construction secret that may assist our own inner growth. In Proverbs 8:34-35 we're encouraged: "Blessed is the man who listens to me, watching daily at my gates, waiting at the posts of my doors. For whoever finds me finds life, and obtains favor from the LORD." If we want our lives to be filled with vibrant mental health, we must go after the things that sustain life. These materials are extremely valuable, and are explained in much greater detail in the remainder of this chapter. But due to space limitations, we'll only consider the first ten.

Soul Substance #1—Father God

In the very first verse of Genesis 1, we're introduced to God the Father, and told that He's responsible for creating all things. We can glean information about the Father's nature from everyday life. My thoughts immediately shift to the many reasons that parents desire to have a family. First John 4:16 tells us that God is love itself. If we extend this thought, then the more we allow this substance of love to grow and mature in our hearts, the more we're filled with the Father. As we apply this to mental health, we know that the Father doesn't suffer from inner afflictions; so the more we embrace the Father and seek to understand His love nature, the stronger we'll become internally.

One of the most profound statements about Father God is found in John 3:16 (NIV). We're told that "God so loved the world that he gave his one and only Son..." I can hardly imagine the agony that He endured as He made the decision to provide this love offering for mankind. But He did it, and then He tells us, "I love those who love me, and those who seek me diligently will find me" (Proverbs 8:17). This verse rocked me out of my selfish black depression, and helped me to realize that I had a part to play in my own recovery. When I responded correctly in the midst of my own terrible trials, I found the Father; and I when I did, I also found the incredible soul-filling substance called love. That's when everything started to change for the better.

I also discovered that this essence of love flowing from the Father's heart was never designed to be kept for very long—it must be given away. Some have mistakenly felt that once they were filled, they could live lives of ease from then on where they became spiritually fat, full, and flourishing. But the Father doesn't fill us with His love for that reason. He wants His love to be the catalyst that causes us to reach out to a dying world and show them His love. In so doing, we're filled with a great sense of purpose. In fact, it could be our testimony of His love that brings another soul into His Kingdom. Mark 12:30-31 gives us a twofold command. It tells us that we must love the Lord our God with all our heart, soul, mind, and strength; and then we must love our neighbor as ourselves. Many of Jesus' followers did this freely, whereas many Pharisees were cruel and heartless. The reasons for this dramatic difference are illustrated in the following story.

The Sea of Galilee is the jewel of all Israel. It receives huge amounts of fresh water from the snow-capped peaks of Mt. Hermon, but that water doesn't stay in the basin for very long. It's used to water the land of Israel as it flows down the Jordan River into the salt-encrusted Dead Sea. This water is trapped in a deep depression, and can't go anywhere, so it stagnates there. It's filled with tons of poisonous salts and minerals in which no fish can swim, and no life can exist. The purpose of this illustration is this: we can receive an endless supply of love from the Father, but we must pour it out to others, or else we also will stagnate and die. To be inwardly healthy, the love of the Father must be given away.

More About Love

As we examine more about the Father's love, we see another important attribute: it must be either accepted or rejected. When mankind fell into sin, the Father didn't let us go; His love was so great that He made the decision to draw us back again by sacrificing His own precious Son. In so doing, He placed before mankind the offer to reject the evil one and come back to Him, or to stay in darkness. If we will allow this "giving love" to grip our heart, it will send every demon of mental distress running.

If we examine the negative substances of unforgiveness and hatred, we can glean even more understanding about the Father's nature. He can't allow us to carry these negative substances into Heaven. He knows that they would contaminate it in a very short period of time. Similarly, if we allow hatred and unforgiveness into our hearts in the place of love, they'll also destroy us. It's our choice. Those who allow these tormentors to sit on their soul crowd out the nature of the Father in them. Until they're removed, we'll know the ongoing sting of mental afflictions.

We must never refuse the Father's love and allow ourselves to become like the people in Matthew 25:41-45. They saw the desperate plight of humanity all around, but refused to let the Father's love work through them. They remained filled with their own selfishness. So at the end of time, God sends them to a place prepared for the devil and his angels. The story spelled out in this startling parable makes it clear that we are to receive this love of the Father in great abundance, and then share it all around us. In fact, it's the receiving and giving out of the Father's love that is such a vital component of our mental health. Malachi states that we must also build this heart of the Father into our children, and as they learn to receive the love of the Father through us, they'll be protected from the terrible effects of the worldwide curse that is at work to destroy so many in our day (Malachi 4:6). As we become a part of this love cycle of receiving and giving, we will also protect the lives of future generations.

My wife experienced a rough childhood, barely knowing her mother who passed away when she was four years old. She had an unloving, alcoholic father, and many of her childhood playing days were spent alone inside the back of the family car while her father drank and socialized at the local pub. Even though the social services sent her to live with relatives in her early teenage years, she often felt the pangs of loneliness and rejection. Later in life, a Christian friend gave her some biblical phrases to speak over herself in a mirror. This was a good start, but she wanted to know so much more—so she asked God for a clear revelation of His Fatherhood. He responded, and as He revealed Himself to her, past problems became a distant memory, because the Lord filled her with a true vision of His love and His Fatherhood. She learned from this that old thoughts and feelings don't just disappear—they must be replaced by something so much stronger.

Soul Substance #2—The Holy Spirit

I had a difficult time when my mother came to the end of her life. It seemed like she was wasting away to skin and bones. The doctor put her on an enriched nutritional energy drink diet. For a season this helped to improve her health and strength. At that time, I didn't understand that her greatest lack was the power and anointing of the Holy Spirit. He confirmed this to me in a very unusual way.

When she was on the verge of death, the Holy Spirit said that He'd be pleased to give me a few more days with her. Even though her condition was critical, the Lord told me to use His power to command the spirit of death to lift off of her. It was embarrassing because others were in the room; but I did what He said. When I spoke the command, she sat straight up in bed and asked, "Is that you, David?" It was like she had been filled and energized by a bolt of lightning. She remained filled with life for three or four days, and we set many things in order.

When we were done, we returned home, and left the doctor to tell her that she was very ill and could never return to her home. Within moments, she was dead! It was like the substance of the Spirit that had been keeping her alive lifted, and life left her body. This was hard for me, but I knew that she'd gone to Heaven where she could experience the power of the Holy Spirit first hand.

Our first Biblical introduction to the Spirit of God is found in Genesis 1:2, which states "The earth was without form, and void; and darkness was on the face of the deep. And the Spirit of God was hovering over the face of the waters." In this passage, we learn that the Spirit of God is not just hovering idly over His Creation. He's waiting for the Word of God to be spoken. When it's given by the Father, He springs into action and begins creating and filling. The Holy Spirit now hovers over every life, waiting for us to speak forth the words of God in faith, and with authority. Then He once again springs into action so that He might work though us, so that we can fulfill the high calling of God that has been placed on our lives.

Responding to the Spirit of God

One of the most startling stories about the work of the Holy Spirit is found in the Parable of the Ten Virgins. In this passage, we see that our future with God is determined by our response to the Holy Spirit. If we embrace Him in our lives, we're considered to be wise indeed, and we're filled with His precious anointing oil. But if we're careless and neglect our salvation, we may never build up our inner oil supply. This will leave us with insufficient oil when a dark trial comes upon our lives. If we still don't change our ways, we enter very dangerous waters. We may find ourselves like the five foolish virgins who wasted away their days, and found themselves on the outside looking in. Those who put effort into knowing the Lord will be filled with the rich abundance and strength that only He can offer.

When I'm doing mental health tutoring, I look for things like emptiness, loneliness, or hopelessness. If they're present in the counselee, I know that the Holy Spirit is in short supply, so I can then use the natural to teach about the spiritual. Ephesians 5:18 shows that although natural wine may loosen up one's outward mood, only the Spirit of God can bring lasting peace inwardly. Paul states, "And do not be drunk with wine, in which is dissipation; but be filled with the Spirit." Just as natural things are made of real substances; so it is with spiritual things. God's Holy Spirit can fill the empty places of our soul with anointing oil.

The Praise Revival

In 1946, Pastor Reg Layzell was ready to leave the ministry and return to the business world. As he was fervently praying about this before an evening meeting, the Lord suddenly revealed that the Spirit of God dwelt in man's praises. "But thou art holy, O thou that inhabitest the praises of Israel" (Psalm 22:3). He was shocked. He was a reserved businessman, and this meant that he'd have to praise out loud. He did this very timidly at first, but as his prayer time wore on, he became much bolder. That evening, the Spirit of God began to come upon people mightily, and anoint them. The revival was on. The Holy Spirit was filling and moving in those who were actively praising the Lord. This truth became a life-saver for me about 40 years later.

I had really been enjoying my newfound salvation, but after eight years of freedom, it suddenly ended. Without warning, I entered a particularly deep valley of depression where I became so low in spirit that I knew I couldn't go on much longer. I pleaded with God for help, and suddenly the Lord spoke to me. He said "Son, when you wake up tomorrow morning, I want you to praise Me with all of your heart, and don't stop." I had clearly heard His command, so I obeyed it. After about four hours, the Spirit of God filled my inner man, and I was gloriously delivered.

The depression was on me again the next morning, but this time not as strongly. I repeated this same act of praising for several days in a row until the depression was forced out completely. In looking back, I see that the Spirit of God was at work filling me up and replacing the depression in my soul. This experience kept me free for about eight more years until the oil was used up once again. I still didn't understand that it was my responsibility to continually replenish my spiritual oil—but that's another story.

Soul Substance #3—Wisdom and the Word of God

At the beginning of time, God offered mankind a large variety of fruits to eat. The only restriction was that they couldn't eat from the Tree of the Knowledge of Good and Evil. The fellowship between them and God remained strong for a season, but then one day the test came, and Adam and Eve disobeyed. At that point, humanity's mental health was lost, and they experienced the terrors of physical and spiritual death. But God wasn't about to leave mankind in this state of hopelessness. He had a plan. It involved the death of His Son, and the Tree of Life.

At that early point in history, the Tree of Life disappeared from the pages of Scripture. For a season, mankind headed in a downhill direction…so much so that in Noah's day, almost everyone who was born was heading toward hell. But later on, this amazing Tree of Life reappears in the book of Proverbs. But it was no longer in physical form; it had been given a new name, Wisdom. Proverbs 3:18 tells us that "She [Wisdom] is a tree of life to those who take hold of her, and happy are all who retain her." In this passage, the Lord identifies Wisdom as the most valuable possession we could ever own, and in Proverbs 4:5 we are commanded "Get wisdom! Get understanding!"

Many falter at this point because they don't really know what wisdom and understanding are. However, with a little more detective work, we discover from Proverbs 8:1-11 that these two critical things are wrapped up in the words that the living God offers to all mankind. As we continue investigating, we learn from John 1:14 that "the Word became flesh, and dwelt among us." So now we have a clear connection: the Tree of Life, wisdom, understanding, the Word of God, and Jesus Christ are all very similar in nature.

This is a significant revelation, because the more we eat from the Tree of Life in the form of the words of God, the more we fill ourselves with Jesus Christ. As this process continues, our inner strength will grow mightily. So the thrust of mental health counseling now becomes very clear: if we desire to have success, we must get the words of God inside people. This allows God to fill them with His wisdom so that He might reframe and repair them inwardly. Now, when the words of God pass across their lips, the Holy Spirit will respond to God's words, and create within them the things that they need to bring them into freedom.

The Healing Hospital

Early in my Christian walk, I heard a story that solidified this previous truth. Proverbs 4:20-22 gives us some insights concerning the power of God's Word to heal and repair us. It confirms that whenever the words of God fill us, they will bring life and health to our whole being. Kenneth Hagin further confirmed this in an unusual story about an amazing nineteenth-century healing hospital in New York. This hospital only accepted terminally ill patients who were beyond the reach of medical help. The doctors used unusual medicine…they gave the patients passages from the Word of God to memorize, and to repeat back. One lady who was dying with tuberculosis repeatedly quoted the Galatians passage that "Christ has redeemed us from the curse of the Law" (Galatians 3:13). She spoke out these words thousands of times; but one morning it seemed as if these words went from her head into her heart—when they did, she was gloriously healed.

Joshua was facing a scary future without Moses, yet the same God who had spoken so often to Moses now spoke directly to him. He told him in Joshua 1:8 that the key to success centered around having the words of God fill his mind, and proceed out of his mouth. Joshua was told that he first must engraft the words of God into his soul; this would enable God to be with him wherever he went. If we want to be successful in restoring the mental and emotional health of ourselves and those whom we love, then we must get God's words inside us so that the Holy Spirit can spring into action and do His repair work.

Soul Item #4—The Need for Understanding

Incomplete understanding can have a very humorous side. Many years ago, at a mission station in Africa, a missionary was having trouble with the workers that he had hired to till his garden. They did good work when he was watching, but whenever he would turn his back, they would all lie down and take a nap. This really frustrated the missionary, but there was little that he could do. One day, he had to go into town, and he knew that the natives wouldn't work once he left. He had a brilliant idea. He had a glass eyeball, and much to the surprise and horror of his workers, he popped it out of his socket, and placed it on a rock overlooking the garden. This kept them all working for a time, but when he came back, he found all of the workers sleeping once again. He went to find his eyeball, and discovered that it had been carefully covered with a tin can. Apparently one of the workers had sneaked around behind the eyeball, and placed the tin over it. When they were convinced that the missionary could no longer see them, they went to sleep. Even though this illustration seems amusing, it teaches a lot about the lack of spiritual vision in our day. We see that a tin can has been placed over the eyes of the Church by the professional world. They have said that the principles found in Christ's Word are far too simplistic to be taken seriously. Because of this, many have been lulled to sleep, and have rejected Christ having any part in their mental health discussions. The tragic results of this foolish decision are now playing out in all facets of society. Depression, anxiety, and fear have become rampant, and this won't change until we realize that mental health issues can only be corrected by the One who built the spirit and soul. If we consult Him, He will reveal some incredible principles that will give new understanding about man's inner health.

In Luke 13:11-17, in the story about the woman with the spirit of infirmity, the Lord reveals something startling. In a nutshell, He warned that godly understanding won't be given to the careless or the casual—it will only fill those who have a genuine passion for it. If we're in a hurry all the time, or filled with the cares of this life, we may have little time for His Word. This will block the Holy Spirit from filling us with godly understanding; in fact, if we don't repent, we could be in danger of losing what we already have.

When I was almost dying from my depression attacks, I made the quality decision to pursue God with all of my heart, and fill myself with His Word. To my great joy, my understanding began to increase; hence I could now grasp so much more about my inner health. Soon He was leading me down a very different counseling pathway. I now saw that I had been created with a repairable soul and a rechargeable spirit that could be built up by applying these principles.

Growing Into Maturity

In the infant stage of our walk with Christ, He fills us with the milk of the Word so that we might grow, but it's His desire that we soon grow out of this helpless stage. Next, He feeds us mushy pablum as we become more aware of spiritual things. Later, He moves us on to solid food. As we begin eating more of His solid meat, He reveals to us how spiritual processes are designed to work. He encapsulates this whole process in Proverbs 4:18-19, which states, "But the path of the just is like the shining sun that shines ever brighter unto the perfect day. The way of the wicked is like darkness; they do not know what makes them stumble." As we seek to be filled with understanding, it removes the tin can off of our eyeball, so that we might see. As we wake up, we'll see the desperate plight of those sleeping all around us.

In Proverbs 24:3, the Lord again ties together wisdom and understanding. He states, "Through wisdom the house is built, and by understanding it is established." If we desire our inner man to last for time and eternity, then we need to be built well inside so that we might withstand the surrounding spiritual pressures. As we're being filled with these two valuable things, God adds a third component. He tells us that "knowledge of the Holy One is understanding" (Proverbs 9:10). In other words, the more we gain knowledge of the Holy One in our intimate devotions, the more we grow in understanding. And it is this amazing substance that's designed to fill our soul and solidly establish us in the faith.

Soul Substance #5—Our Need for the Knowledge of God

A close friend married into a family that had previously suffered a great tragedy. The original father had been working on the family car in the garage attached to their home. Because it was winter, and -30 Celsius outside, he had closed the garage door. When he was finishing his repairs, he started the engine to quickly fine-tune it. He must have been certain that he had sufficient time before carbon monoxide poisoning would set in. But he was wrong! A short while later, they found his body nestled against the bottom of the garage door with his nose jammed into the fresh air crack underneath it. What he hadn't known was that once you feel the signs of carbon-monoxide poisoning, it's already too late to save yourself. He had died for his lack of natural knowledge.

It's no different in the spiritual world. God warns us in Hosea 4:6 that His people are too often "destroyed for lack of knowledge." We see this tragedy at work most commonly in the mental health area. God makes a clear claim that He designed the spirit and soul within us, and expects us to turn to Him for first advice. Instead, we have allowed ourselves to become programmed by people who tell us that God is a myth, and that it's only this world's counseling system that can uncover the answers to man's inner needs. As a result of this lack of knowledge, many have perished.

Filling Our Rooms

In Proverbs 24:4, God gives us another incredible piece of advice. Here He states, "By knowledge the rooms are filled with all precious and pleasant riches." He's revealing to us that our soul has rooms, and these rooms cannot be left vacant; they must be filled to overflowing with the knowledge of God. This is very important advice, because Jesus warns us that the enemy will seek to reoccupy those areas from which he has been removed (Matthew 12:44). When the five foolish virgins stood before Heaven's gate, they weren't judged because they had done terrible things; they were judged because they had squandered away their salvation, and were never filled with the knowledge of God (Matthew 25:1-12).

The Lord tells us that we must press in to find this knowledge of God. In Colossians 2:3, He refers to Christ "in whom are hidden all the treasures of wisdom and knowledge." This is going to take some digging, because when the Lord hides a thing, we're going to have to be passionate if we wish to find it. Then in Colossians 1:10, the Lord states, "that you may walk worthy of the Lord, fully pleasing Him, being fruitful in every good work, and increasing in the knowledge of God." The knowledge of God was never designed to be a one-time thing. I believe that we will continue to increase in it throughout the ages of Eternity.

Soul Substance #6—Faith

Over many years, I have watched people malign some of the great teachers of the Bible such as Smith Wigglesworth, Kenneth Copeland, and Kenneth Hagin. Others have copied their teachings to the letter, yet didn't get the results that they expected; they think that their message is far too good to be true. But I'm certain that the great faith message that they preach is not the problem at all. All of these men have prayed the price in their countless hours of watching and waiting before the Lord in order to receive this encouraging message. Sadly, some of those who take in their writings think that they can just grab the gold from their teachings and spend it. But over my 40 years as a Christian, I know that there is no shortcut of God's ways. Over the years, I have heard many different definitions for this mysterious substance called faith, but I noticed that faith formed in me as I ingested God's words, thought about them, and meditated on them. This dovetails with Paul's words in Romans 10:17, "So then faith comes by hearing, and hearing by the word of God." The more I reflected on His words, the more my confidence built in His ability to set me free. I discovered that I couldn't build my faith by any human effort. The Spirit of God built it in me as I fell more and more in love with the Master's words, and meditated on His thoughts.

True Faith

True faith is a definite spiritual substance, and it is formed in us as we spend time before God meditating in His Word. Hebrews 11:1 tells us that "faith is the substance of things hoped for, the evidence of things not seen." People like Copeland and Hagin can encourage us to spend time with the Lord and develop our faith, but they can't do the work for us. Because of my severe trials, I took their words to heart and purposed that if it could work for them in the areas of finances and physical health, then it could also work in the mental health area. As I spent time before the Lord concerning my ongoing bouts of depression, He built the necessary faith in me to press through for my own inner healing. My faith became so strong after a season that

I didn't have to ask if it was 100% God's will to give me peace. I knew it for certain in my heart. As I got to this point, my answer finally began to manifest in full measure. Faith can also be likened to currency. A lot of people try to spend the faith that they don't have and end up in great frustration. Many years ago, an acquaintance had just received salvation, and was full of new convert zeal. He needed a vehicle so he went to a car lot and picked out the exact car that he wanted. He knew that he didn't have the money for it, but as he was writing the check, he told the salesman that he was believing that when he came to draw it out of the bank, God would place the necessary money in his account. The salesman looked at him in shock, and promptly showed him the door. He told him to come back when he had a job and a bit more evidence to back up his faith.

A lot of people expect instant results because they've read material by many different faith teachers. But God wants us to wait in His Word until the substance of faith actually fills up our soul. Then we can go out and spend it. When God warns us in Hebrews 11:6 that "without faith it is impossible to please Him," He's not telling us to drum up our faith by human effort. The verse goes on to say, "for he who comes to God must believe that He is, and that He is a rewarder of those who diligently seek Him." The reward is the deposit of faith He places in our soul.

My heart breaks when I talk to some people about their mental health. They have been so beaten down by inner afflictions that it's a challenge for them just to live from day to day. Thankfully, the Lord is encouraging me not to give up on them, but to understand that it takes a while to get an outboard motor going. It often needs several good sharp pulls on the engine cord. Once the motor is running, the boat is on its way. In the same way, when people finally understand what faith is, some will become unstoppable. When people see that the human soul is the core of their mental health problem, faith enlivens them, and gives them the strength to grab onto their healing. It certainly worked mightily in my life.

Soul Substance #7—Light

Many years ago, when I was teaching in the town of Gibsons, I had a little boy in my school who tried all kinds of crazy stunts. One day, he got off of the school bus, and put a paper bag over his head. He told his sister to shout out verbal directions, and he would find his way home. She kept trying to guide him, but he didn't know left from right very well. It wasn't too long before he stumbled into the ditch, and sank to his ankles in the mud.

This funny story highlights Solomon's warning in Proverbs 4:19 that "the way of the wicked is like darkness; they do not know what makes them stumble." This is a close description of what has happened in the mental health world. The professionals and scientists of our world have cut off the light that Christ offers, and people are stumbling into the ditch everywhere (Luke 6:39).

God uses natural processes to reveal many of His lightly-covered truths. In Romans 1:20 He reminds us that the lessons He has placed in nature are so clear and so revealing that no man will have an excuse on Judgment Day for not believing. In this verse, He's revealing that it's through the working out of these natural processes that we can come to know Him. A number of years ago, when I was struggling to discover the meaning of the seven pillars (Proverbs 9:1) God dropped a question into my spirit that really opened the floodgates. He asked me to describe why light was so critical for the operation of the plant world. This question opened up the mental health world to me. I suddenly realized that it was the receiving of light energy that fuelled the process of photosynthesis.

Let There Be Light

When God spoke His first verbal command, "Let there be light" (Genesis 1:3), He had far more in mind than just natural light. In the spiritual world, a measure of light is given to everyone to guide them toward Christ's salvation. But the real light that makes our Christianity successful is not obtained quite so easily. As we press into God during times of daily devotions, God shines His light on the Word that He finds in us. As we receive His light energy, these are changed into life, wisdom, and strength deep within our soul. That's why the world can't find a permanent cure for mental health—because life isn't produced by natural means. It's a product of spiritual photosynthesis.

As I carefully meditated upon this, I realized that light is a filling substance that must reside within each one of us. Christ tells us in Matthew 6:22-23, "The lamp of the body is the eye. If therefore your eye is good, your whole body will be full of light. But if your eye is bad, your whole body will be full of darkness. If therefore the light that is in you is darkness, how great is that darkness!" When the light is operating correctly in us, our whole body is filled with the products of photosynthesis, and we're filled with the abundant life that Christ desires us to have. But if darkness is operating within us, then we'll often experience feelings of fear, depression, and anxiety.

In the Amazon rain forests, much vegetation has been burned off to permit the growth of crops, and for cattle ranching. However, the soil does not have enough strength, and the heavy rains quickly wash away a large portion of the nutrients that are added. In a short time, the inhabitants move on, and colonizing plants begin springing up everywhere. In time, the plants that spread out their leaves, and create a dense canopy through which little light passes. In time, the other plants shrivel away. This process also happens in our lives. As we come to Christ for salvation and bring Him our ashes, He offers us light. If we allow ourselves to be flooded with this light, we grow mightily in Him. But if we become complacent, we'll wither and stagnate.

Light is one of our most important filling substances, and we must seek it with all of our hearts.

Soul Item #8—Inner Resources

Many valuable lessons about life can be learned from nature. Last spring, I was sitting at my study window watching a mother crow and her baby. She did all of the work to obtain food, and he promptly gobbled up everything she gave to him. This was okay for a time, but soon he became bigger than her, yet he was still demanding she feed him. Finally, she started making him get some of his own slugs and worms. Did he ever squawk at first! But hunger finally drove him to start feeding himself. What a neat type of our spiritual life.

God has planned that our soul should be full of inner resources. At first, He will greatly assist any baby Christian by answering their requests immediately. But as time progresses, He expects them to start digging around and finding some of their own supplies. This is a critical success or failure point for many maturing Christians. Some seek the Lord with all of their hearts, and begin filling up their souls; others become like the baby crow…they loudly squawk and complain. But if they don't yield to the Lord's ways after a long season, they can become like the Children of Israel, and miss out with God completely.

Psalm 1 Insight

In Psalm 1, God lays down a lifetime supply line for all mankind. He contrasts the world's method of gaining inner nutrients with the Christian who quietly feeds himself on the truths of God's Word. The worldly person thinks he has it all together, but when times of trouble come, he has nothing inside him, and he blows away like a piece of chaff before a very strong wind. The godly person, on the other hand, feeds voraciously in God's Word. This enables the Holy Spirit to not only fill him, but also for him to continue to grow and thrive. At the end of time, the two lives are measured. One is filled with life and success, whereas the other has become empty, and failed.

Over my 40 years as a Christian, I have seen many grow mightily in the faith, and press forward to serve the Lord with all of their hearts. Others start out well in their newfound faith, but after a time they become filled with complaints, and begin to find fault with their brethren. The difference between the two is clear. One group recognizes the need to be filled with the things of God, whereas the other group leaves room inside themselves for inner problems to grip the soul. Spiritual pressures like fear, anxiety, and depression are nearby, but if our soul is full of God's Spirit, they have no entrance.

If we look to Biblical examples, there can be no greater contrast than the lives of Jacob and Esau. Esau is described both as a hairy man, and also a man of the field, a cunning hunter. Some might see Esau as a success, but God didn't see him that way at all. Even though he had been taught about the Lord at the feet of Abraham and Isaac, his spiritual senses evaporated in a climate of wine, women, and song. Then, during a time of great hunger, he also became emptied of wisdom. He sold off his precious birthright (the unwritten document that would have placed him in direct lineage to the Lord Jesus Christ). This infuriated the Lord and caused Him to say, "Jacob I have loved, and Esau I have hated" (Romans 9:13). Jacob was a smooth man, dwelling close to his mother, and this portrays the idea of a sissy, but Jacob treasured his godly inheritance, and succeeded greatly because he was hungry for the knowledge of God.

This great need for inner resources is a critical requirement for every Christian life, and the lack of these resources is probably one of the greatest reasons why people are overwhelmed by inner afflictions. When spiritual pressures come, if we have no inner contents, we can be destroyed. Hence, constant soul filling is vital for vibrant inner health.

Soul Item #9—Knowledge of Salvation

Many years ago, during a harsh New England winter, a train crew was desperately trying to break loose a track switch that had locked together during an ice storm. A passenger train was rapidly bearing down on the frantic work crew, and they knew if the switch didn't release, the train and all of its passengers would perish in the Hudson River. There was only one thing to do to save hundreds of lives. Someone would have to climb down into the gear box to break away the ice plug. The problem was that as the gears began to move, they would crush whoever was inside of the gear housing. With no thought for his own life, the son of the foreman hastened into the danger area to free the ice plug. He quickly chipped away the ice, and just in time the gears began to move. The switch closed just as the train reached it, and passed on to its destination. As the boy was dying an agonizing death, he earnestly cried out, "I love you, dad."

Meanwhile, up above, the father was listening to the screams of his son as the brightly lit cars swished by. They were filled with passengers, eating, reading, and laughing—totally unaware of the great sacrifice that had just been made to save their lives. It would be the father's expectation, however, that when they arrived at their destination and were told this story, that they would stop to offer sincere thanks. So it is with our precious salvation. God sent His Son to put us on the rails of life. But He has an expectation that we will embrace Christ's great sacrifice, and seek to fill ourselves with the knowledge of it. Salvation might be described as the new operating system placed within our soul during the time of spiritual birth. The more we learn about it and allow it to work in us, the more successful we'll be in daily life, and in achieving vibrant mental health. It's God's plan to offer the knowledge of His salvation to whoever is hungry so that we might fully embrace it. In Philippians 2:12, Paul states, "work out your own salvation with fear and trembling." In other words, there's a task to be done, and we need to diligently search out the directions that tell us how to live our lives effectively.

A Severe Warning

In Hebrews 2:3 the writer asks, "How shall we escape if we neglect so great a salvation…?" It's the Father's strong desire that salvation should be both the foundation stone and capstone of our soul, as well as the filling material for every space in between. As we aggressively seek to have the knowledge of His precious salvation fill us, it will become the driving force of our lives; and will soon show itself in our actions and reactions. At the end of time, the place that we gave Christ's mighty salvation will determine the success or failure of our lives. In Psalm 91:16, God promises the thing that we all hunger for the most—long life. Then as we search after His salvation, He will reveal to us how life is designed to work. Let me tell another story that better illustrates this point.

Many years ago when floods of immigrants were coming to North America for the promise of free land, a young family told a remarkable story. The father had scraped every possible penny together to book a boat passage for his struggling family. To help them on their voyage, they had then collected many scraps of bread and cheese to eat. About halfway through the voyage, the food ran out, and the family began to starve. In absolute desperation, the father went to the chief steward just before they entered into New York harbor, and asked if he might somehow work to earn some meals for his very hungry family. The surprised steward asked to see his ticket. In shock, he told the passenger that his family had a first class ticket that gave them full rights to daily meals.

We might wonder why this man never checked things out when he first got onto the ship, but he's no different from so many Christians in our day. They come to Christ and receive His salvation, but then they stop searching. Yet the heart of God yearns for us to be filled with the knowledge of His salvation so that we might experience its many benefits. If we don't understand what we have been given, we can live out our lives in near-starvation conditions.

Soul Substance #10—Living Water and Worship (and Praise)

In John 4, the Lord tells us that on His journey to Galilee, Jesus becomes weary and stops to rest beside a well in Samaria. As He's resting, a lady comes by to draw water, and He completely rocks her boat by asking for a drink. For a Jew to ask a favor of a Samaritan is unheard of, so in utter surprise, she asks why He would even notice that she's alive. But Jesus is reaching down through the ages to teach us that we must use natural opportunities if we want to be an effective witness for Him. He uses His own natural need for water to open the way to discuss the inner needs of her soul. In His wisdom, He explains that just as she has a continual need for natural water, she also needs to be filled with spiritual water. She then begins questioning Him on the correct place for people to worship. Now Jesus gets right to the heart of the matter—that the act of worship is very important in providing living water for our souls. Then He reveals the secret longing in God's heart, that we would all be filled with worship.

Her frequent changing of husbands reveals that she has desperate inner needs, and was up to her ears in sin. In fact, Jesus also knows that she is breaking the Jewish Law by living common-law with a man. Yet He uses this conversation with a sinful woman to reveal our deep need to be filled with worship and praise. In our fast-moving culture, many Christians think that worship is something that we do just before we listen to the preacher on Sunday morning. But it's so much more than that. God wants our worship to be how we live each day on this Earth, and our praise to be an expression of our continual thankfulness.

Jesus explains to the Samaritan woman that God hungers to find people whose hearts are filled with worship. In fact, Jesus reveals that this is so important to the Lord that He actually scours the face of the Earth looking to find ones who have put Him first in all that they do. And with good reason! Many eons earlier, before the dawn of time, Satan abandoned his place as the worship leader in Heaven when He saw the love and adoration that was being poured out toward the Lord. In his heart, he became jealous, and craved to have this worship. After a time of careful planning and scheming, Satan became so skilled in the art of deception that he convinced one-third of the angels to follow him. The results were fatal and they were eventually cast down to Earth. This left a huge hole in Heaven, but God was not to be defeated. He set about to raise up a bride for His only Son; a bride that would not only worship, but would also love Him for all of Eternity.

Being Filled With Worship

The importance of being filled with abundant knowledge of God is very important if we're to succeed in our Christianity. This means that our need to be filled with both love and worship must be top priority. The tragic life of Solomon teaches us why. He began his public ministry with a great display of worship. In fact, He worshipped so much that the Lord actually came and spoke some wonderful promises to him in a dream. But even though he had this strong start, he made a serious mistake. He allowed his heart to be divided by wine, women, and song. In his culture, this may not have been considered wrong in moderation, but he was excessive, and it eventually wore down his spiritual strength. In fact, we're told that his wives turned away his worship and his heart after other gods. The book of Ecclesiastes tells a tragic tale. This man who started out as such a prolific worshipper allowed his heart to be corrupted by his undisciplined lifestyle. Now we see him in deep depression wondering if life is even worth living. As the murky water settles, Solomon comes to his senses. In the last two verses of Ecclesiastes 12, he realizes that it's the duty of a man to put God first in every facet of life. It wouldn't surprise me if Solomon returned to his place of worship to again find the God that he had abandoned so many years earlier. In his writings, Solomon paints a vivid picture of what happens inside the souls of those who leave their first love, and demonstrates how mental anguish can overtake their lives. That's why a continual expression of worship is an important component of every vibrant soul. When we're filled with it, we have great peace; when we step away from it, we can become empty like Solomon in his times of disobedience.

In Conclusion

In Luke 11:24, Jesus tells us that the human soul is a continual target for evil spirits. But He doesn't leave us without help. We're also shown that our best defense is to fill our soul with the correct spiritual contents so that there's no room for other things. But this is no small task, and it requires our ongoing involvement. In Proverbs 24:3-4, the Lord teaches that one-third of God's soul rebuilding procedure involves the filling of the rooms of our soul. I have begun to address this need in this chapter, but there's always so much more to be discovered. If we desire to be mentally and emotionally free, it's critical to press into truth and let it be worked out in our lives. As we do, we'll find that vibrant mental health is not an impossible dream. It's just a matter of carefully following God's instructions.

Section IV
A Very Fruitful Soul

    Productivity and fruitfulness are a delight to God. So the purpose of this teaching is that our lives should also blossom and bear much fruit to Him. An amazing transformation from barrenness to fruitfulness has been demonstrated in the land of Israel over the past seventy-five years. I remember my first trip there in 1977 when I stood amazed to see firsthand the effects of diligent cultivation. A land that had once been rocky and barren was now filled with greenery, blossoms, and fruit. On one occasion we stopped at a kibbutz, and were given a fresh grapefruit off a tree. It was extremely juicy and tasty. In another spot, half of a hillside was covered with trees. There had been much tree-planting in that area, and where the trees had been set in the ground for a longer season of time, new soil was beginning to form from the falling pine needles, and there was some water retention. In fact, in one area, the natural creeks were even beginning to trickle once again. The areas that hadn't yet been planted were still hot, barren patches of rock-strewn landscape devoid of all moisture.

    In the Scripture to follow, the Lord is encouraging us that even though our lives were once dry and barren, it's His expectation that they'll come to life, and be filled with fruit as we walk under the canopy of His blessings. As we talk about "coffee-cup counseling" in the next section, we see that we have the opportunity to help those with dry barren lives come to fruitfulness. It's God's expectation that we won't keep His blessings to ourselves.

> *The wilderness and the wasteland shall be glad for them, and the desert shall rejoice and blossom as the rose; it shall blossom abundantly and rejoice, even with joy and singing.*
> *Isaiah 35:1-2*

CHAPTER 11
Coffee Cup Counseling: Sharing Your Freedom

Introducing the Idea

I've often cried out like Paul "that I may know Him" (Philippians 3:10) and stopped there. But the Lord has been alerting me that this verse goes on to say "that I may know Him…and the fellowship of His sufferings…" At one time, I couldn't face this part of the verse because I had already suffered so much from mental health issues. But the Lord revealed that I had been misinterpreting this passage. He advised me that this verse must become an important part of every Christian's mental and emotional makeup because it relates to the suffering that Jesus Christ is presently undergoing as He watches masses of human beings (whom He loves dearly), stumbling headlong toward a Christless eternity. He weeps over every lost soul who has been committed to that place, and yearns for us to be His hands, His feet, and His voice on this Earth, so that He might use us to do something about it. If we'll take hold of the concept of "coffee-cup counseling," we'll be filled with tremendous joy as we embrace His vision to help the lost. Sometimes, I wonder how the Lord must feel as He sees some North American Churches shrinking in size, or closing their doors because His people are fighting with each other. Yet from His vantage point, He can hear the screams of countless lost souls—souls that He wants to be a part of His Bride. Even though we may be fighting our own personal battles, if we'll take on His vision, our troubles will pale as we get some glimpses of the suffering that the Lord is undergoing. When we examine the Parable of the Talents, or the Parable of the Sheep and the Goats, we see that these passages tell us that we're all being held responsible to fulfill the assignment to go forth and help the lost. As I personally took up His burden, it shoved some of the selfishness and self-pity right out of me, and had a huge bearing on the quality of my own mental health.

As we dig deeper in the Parable of the Ten Talents (Matthew 25:14-30), we see that He will judge those who get caught up in selfish living, and ignore what is valuable to Him—human souls. I would like to offer a way that we can all meet this cry of our Savior's heart. I've talked to many people about mental health as I have gone about my daily work, and over the years, I have nicknamed this "coffee-cup counseling." Almost everyone I speak to has been touched by the nightmare of attacks on their mental health in various ways. As I tell them that Christ has an answer for this affliction, it provides a natural opening into sharing the Gospel in a very practical manner.

Our Primary Passion

Because we are in possession of such valuable counseling truths, it's not a time to bury our talents. We must step forward into the busy marketplace and share with a needy world. How to share these truths with a dying world is the subject of this chapter. Firstly, as we survey the Gospels, we see that Jesus Christ didn't hang out a counseling shingle, and neither should we. But open to us all is the possibility of speaking to needy people over the fence, at a Christmas party, at a school board meeting, or over a cup of coffee. These people who would never darken the door of a church or counseling office often feel free to open their hearts in these informal settings. At such times, the Lord doesn't want us to send them down the road for help. He wants to put the tools in our hands to help them.

Our Need to Share

This urge to share is not just something that pertains to counseling. It's part of our human DNA, and we must do it often. Consider the following illustration. In a marriage seminar recently, the story was told of a young man watching an incredibly magnificent sunset over the ocean in California. After it set, he promptly leaped into his car and headed back toward home in the eastern States. When he arrived, he immediately went to his girlfriend's home, and asked her to marry him. She was both delighted and surprised, and asked what had caused him to finally make up his mind. He excitedly told her that as he was watching the most beautiful sunset he had ever seen, he realized that it was not very enjoyable at all because he didn't have anyone to share it with. And so it is with the Gospel. It can be life-changing for both parties.

There's such great joy in sharing it with friends in need, and it's this kind of ongoing vision that will give us a great sense of purpose, and will do such great wonders for our own mental and emotional health.

> *That the sharing of your faith may become effective by the acknowledgment of every good thing which is in you by Christ Jesus.*
> *(Philemon 1:6)*

Approaching This Assignment

At times, we unintentionally force the Gospel onto people in need, but our witness can be so much more effective if we'll slow down and reflect on this verse above. As you've read through this book, you've seen that the life and teachings of Jesus Christ provide the foundation for our "coffee-cup" message, but we now must learn how to deliver that message to those around us. The first obstacle is not to be sidetracked by the complexity of this world's counseling methods. Over 100 years of psychotherapy and medications have shown that their "problem-first" approach to counseling doesn't work well. It may give some relief to troubled individuals for a season, and the medications may sometimes ease their inner soul pain, but it rarely brings about a permanent cure.

Finding a Foundation in Psalm 1

As we embrace this coffee cup method, we can use Psalm 1 to introduce people to God's idea about counseling. In it, God shares with us some of His own very deep thoughts and feelings. It shows us that there are two main types of counseling: godly and ungodly. God stresses that those who respond to His counsel will be happy and prosperous; but He also warns that those who ignore His instructions will become like "chaff which the wind drives away" (Psalm 1:4).

In Psalm 1:1, the Lord is talking to all counselors as He breaks down the world's attitudes toward life's problems. He tells us that there are three reactions from unbelievers. The first group frantically runs everywhere looking for answers, but can't find help in the advice of those around them. The second group has become paralyzed by their ongoing struggles, and is now standing frozen waiting for someone to help them. The third group is the hardest to reach. They've been hurt by life's storms and the thoughtless advice of people, so now oppose Christianity, and have joined the ranks of the ungodly. They're sitting back, openly scorning those who would adopt Christ's ways. All three have real soul challenges, but love can reach even the most resistant sinner when the time is right.

My greatest futility as I went through my bouts of depression was when my own brethren would tell me to simply rise up and "trust God," and demand that I somehow instantly change my thinking. From Psalm 1:2, we see that God doesn't endorse their impossible advice at all. Instead, He tells us to immerse ourselves in His Word and to listen to His Spirit so that He can help us to change the way that we think. All He asks is that we show willingness to change by becoming a lover of His words. As we do, He restructures our thought patterns through the working of His Holy Spirit. This kind of inner transformation doesn't come instantaneously; but in time, change will come. Then in Psalm 1:3, God uses the growth and fruitfulness of a well-watered tree to describe these changes. He tells us how to alter our thinking, and encourages that correct thinking will stabilize our emotions.

Introducing the Concept

In this book, I've set forth a very different approach to mental health—that man is a three-part being with a spirit, soul, and body; and it is the condition of the spirit and soul that determines the strength of one's mental and emotional health. As we study the life and teachings of Jesus Christ, we'll see that He was very much "solution-oriented." He wasn't a problem-chaser; instead, He used a variety of effective teaching parables to instruct the crowds, and then He laid His hands on those who were afflicted with demons and diseases. In His ministering, He set forth a clear pathway for all of those who would desire to step forward and help others. It was His plan that we be ready whenever the opportunity arose to pray for others, and build up their souls through His teachings.

The First Step

Let's begin this discussion with Adam. When he willingly disobeyed the Lord, his inner architecture (spiritual DNA) was badly corrupted, and the link of fellowship with the Lord was broken. So our immediate concern is to restore a person's link with God, and bring them back into relationship with the Lord Jesus Christ. This means that we can discuss their problems for a short season, but we must not spend all of our time there. We want to get them past this and introduce them to Jesus Christ and His salvation. Once we open the discussion about the Lord, we can follow through on the next steps that can guide them toward having a healthy soul. These steps are in a basic order, but can be used as you see fit.

The Second Step

The first and most obvious point is to turn people away from discussing their ongoing problems and feelings, and get them focusing on building quality and consistency into their daily devotions. As I did this, my soul difficulties were replaced by the voice of guidance from the Master, and I received some definite soul touches from the Spirit of God. I soon began to prove the truth of John 8:32 that states, "And you shall know the truth, and the truth shall make you free." Truths found in His Word brought my soul alive, and gave me a burning passion to know more about Jesus Christ. After all, this almost-forgotten Tree of Life was never meant to be a one-time Genesis concept. God expects us to feed from it regularly so that we might fill up our soul with the correct spiritual substances.

The Third Step
This leads directly into the third step of coffee-cup counseling which is to help the individual build an intimate relationship with the Lord Jesus Christ. We're saved and brought into His Kingdom for a definite purpose—so that we might be a pleasure and a delight to His heart. As we grow in intimacy, we're filling up with vital spiritual substances that squeeze troubling things out of the human heart. That's why Psalm 2:12 so clearly states, "Kiss the Son, lest He be angry, and you perish in the way, when His wrath is kindled but a little. Blessed are all those who put their trust in Him." Once you grasp this step-by-step solution-based approach, you'll realize that it's not the counselor who solves the problems of the counselee at all. We're providing them with a pathway of life and hope. It's our message that leads them directly to the Holy Spirit—the repairer of their soul.

A Fourth Step—Mercy and Truth
All of our teachings must be shared with an overflowing of love because this is the oil that opens the door every time. Consider the following example. A well-known pastor from Oregon, Dick Iverson, was sharing a story about mercy and truth. He had put in a hard day's work, and was relaxing in his easy chair after supper. Just as he was drifting off to sleep, he remembered that he had promised to pray with an elderly congregation member in the hospital. She was having a serious operation the next day. So he struggled out of his easy chair and got dressed. He prayed himself awake on the way to the hospital, and made his way up to her ward. When he arrived at the room, she was happy to see him, but said that he hadn't really needed to come…she was fine. He encouraged her anyway, and then prayed his best prayer over her. He talked with her a little longer, and was about to head back home.

Suddenly, this faint voice came from a dark corner of that hospital ward: "Pastor, can you pray with me as well? I'm having a major operation tomorrow, and I'm really scared." He walked over to talk with the lady, and discovered from her conversation that she wasn't a Christian. But this impending operation had opened up her heart, and she was now ready to be introduced to the Lord. He prayed with her, and she accepted Christ as her Savior. Pastor Iverson then emphasized to our Church that as we walk past our personal comforts and show mercy, it'll open up people to the truth. If he hadn't forced himself off that chair, she may very well have gone into a Christless eternity.

The Fifth Step—Seizing the Opportunities Given to You

In everyday life, the greatest opportunities for coffee cup evangelism will not come when you plan for them. That's why you have to be ready at all times to give an account of the truth that lies within you (1 Peter 3:15). When my dad passed away, my mom was an unbeliever and struggling with a lot of emotional pain. Some of the ladies from a nearby Church took her under wing, and helped her to find her feet once again. She didn't accept Christ immediately when she was under their care, but their love and counsel during their frequent coffee times opened the door for her eventual salvation. One of the sections of the Bible where they helped her to find some of her greatest comfort was in the book of Psalms. They weren't seeing the fruit immediately, and she kept saying strange things like, "No one is going to dump a bucket of blood over my head." But love won out, and she eventually changed her mind. All of us need to stretch ourselves to do the work of an evangelist. If we do, we'll reel in many hurting souls.

A Sixth Point—Getting God's Words Inside

As you become a coffee cup evangelist, you most certainly want to show care and concern by listening to the nature of people's many problems, but you don't want to camp there for very long. You must help them to see the importance of getting the words of the living God inside them. When Joshua took over the reins from Moses and was facing the greatest test of his life, God gave very similar advice. He stated, "This book of the Law shall not depart from your mouth, but you shall meditate in it day and night, that you may observe to do according to all that is written in it. For then you will make your way prosperous, and then you will have good success" (Joshua 1:8). God wants us to lead people into His Word so that He might fix it deep within their souls. He knows that as His words live inside them, things will change, and they'll have success.

If we do a bit more detective work, we'll discover in Proverbs 2 that God gives us even more information how to draw life's sustenance out of the Scriptures. There He reveals that we must cry out to God and search for understanding so that we might embrace the essence of His words. The beauty of God's system of counseling is that you don't have to know the contents of hundreds of counseling manuals. We must encourage people to immerse themselves in the Word of God; then as they develop intimacy with Christ, He will reveal what their problem is. If they'll deal with it, He will bring them through to a full and complete healing.

Step #7—Focus on John 3:16

A next key step in our coffee cup counseling is to explain the meaning of John 3:16. Evolutionary teachings have stripped away value from mankind so that young people believe that they're nothing more than a speck of dust in a great cosmic sea. But God wants every individual to know that they are valuable to Him, and that He has given them a definite purpose in this life. Each one was designed to be filled with the love of God, and to walk in close relationship with Him. This changes things dramatically. We now have a reason to live, and it offers very great hope for our future. The Lord never created anyone to be sick or depressed, or to wander aimlessly on the face of this planet. He wants us to teach others about the high calling that has been given, and then help them to embrace His plans for their future. Telling the amazing story of Christ's salvation is the firm foundation on which we can build our counsel.

The desire to be loved and needed is a very important factor in our mental and emotional health, even at a very young age. While I was on duty at the school something occurred that impacted me deeply. As I walked past the main doorway, I saw a tiny child huddled in a corner, sobbing her heart out. So I crouched down beside her and asked what I could do to help. She told me in a very broken voice that no one loved her or cared for her. I prayed with her, and did what I could to get her connecting with the other students, but a few days later, it was the same scenario again. This time, I spoke with her parents, asking them to work with her and teach her how to counteract this spirit of rejection. In our coffee cup counseling, we must teach others about these devious kinds of spiritual pressures, and instruct them how to effectively oppose them.

Step #8—The Seat of Our Mental Health

It isn't the physical part of our makeup that God is excited about. The body is merely a temple or container for our spirit and soul. It's this inner man that has been designed to return God's love, and come into an ever-deepening relationship with Him. And it's also this inner man that is the seat of our mental and emotional health. The world's counseling system has such a hard time helping people because they won't acknowledge that mankind has a soul and spirit, and that they can be fully repaired using the principles of the Word of God. When we teach these principles correctly, people will respond to them, and we'll have the great privilege of seeing them recover their inner health. Their previous abuses will finally lose their grip, and past feelings will have no more strength to afflict them.

Step #9—The Need for Fuel

Once we show people that they're a spirit-being then we can show them that they must have spirit-fuel in order to live and grow. This is where daily Bible meditation has such a huge place. John 6:63 tells us "It is the Spirit who gives life; the flesh profits nothing. The words that I speak to you are spirit, and they are life." Jesus is saying here that the flesh is totally unable to solve inner problems. He then explains that only His words can build spirit and life in the human heart. Most of the mental health problems that we will face in others aren't difficult at all. In so many cases, the person has simply run out of spiritual fuel, and we must show them how to fill up their inner gas tank again. After we come to know something about His Spirit, we must spend time becoming familiar with His words.

Step #10—The Place of Prayer

Once we understand that God loves us, that every human being has a soul, and that we need inner fuel, then we must show people how to relate to Him. After all, how could you love another person if there was no chance to develop intimacy? God has taken care of this need by developing the vehicle of prayer. It's a heart-to-heart love communication between a person and their God. We're encouraged that "the effective, fervent prayer of a righteous man avails much" (James 5:16). Hence prayer is the core of our "knowing" relationship with God, and this "knowing communication" is one of the things that God craves the most from us. In fact, we're told in John 4:23 that He scours the face of the Earth to find those who will worship Him from their hearts. So a major step in our coffee-cup counseling is to emphasize the place of the Word and prayer in the life of each person.

Step #11—The Place of Wisdom and Understanding

The next step comes right on the heels of the first ones, and it's the one that most Christians so often miss. It's our lifetime assignment to gain wisdom and understanding. These two spiritual substances will get us heading in the proper direction in life, and will keep us on our course. Far too many get lost on the trackless seas of time, and they need this compass to make sense out of their very difficult lives. In Proverbs 4:5-7, we're warned that the most important thing in the Christian life is to become a lover of wisdom, and a student who gains understanding. Many long to be helped by God, yet they never give the Lord these building materials to repair their souls. We must carefully explain to each person that wisdom builds up in us as we hear the words of God and obey them. Of equal importance in the regaining of mental health is our passion to gain spiritual understanding. This mysterious substance known as "understanding" could be defined as spiritual sight that enables us to see how things in God's Kingdom are designed to operate. As people gain it, they're truly amazed to see that recovering from depression isn't an impossible dream after all. Understanding becomes a very secure foundation in them, and gives them real hope for their future. But this foundation can only be poured into the footings of their spiritual house as they slow down their lives and take the time to engraft the Word of God. As these words come to live within an individual, the Holy Spirit teaches them their application as they walk through life's experiences.

Step #12—The Knowledge of God

No one can walk around for very long with an empty heart. The human soul has to be filled with something, and God has specifically designed it to be filled with the knowledge of our Savior. In the book of Revelation, God's valuable soul substances are referred to as "hidden manna" (Revelation 2:17). If we don't make the commitment to fill our soul with these mighty provisions, our inner man will soon become a direct target of a very cruel enemy. Proverbs 24:4 states, "By knowledge the rooms are filled with all precious and pleasant riches." The rooms of a man's soul must be filled with the knowledge of God. When that happens, nothing moves us, and we have peace. After God has made such provision, it's tragic that some have ended their lives declaring that they couldn't stand the terrible feelings of emptiness any longer. If only they had known the wonderful riches that the knowledge of God could've added to their inner man. We get a sense of how important the knowledge of God is because He states in Hosea 4:6, "My people are destroyed for lack of knowledge." In other words, because their soul was empty of this filling substance—knowledge—there was nothing in them to stop the enemy from stealing, killing, and destroying. But this knowledge of God doesn't come easily, or all at once. It was during my intimate devotional times that God revealed Himself to me. As He did, I began to gain great hope for my future. In your own sharing, you can help people by giving them your wise counsel, but it's only when they begin to hunger after the knowledge of God for themselves that things will really begin to change in them.

Step #13—Some Inner Construction Secrets

By this time, your coffee-cup friend should be gaining new hope for their future. You have already established that they're made in the image of God, they have a repairable spirit and soul, and that their life needs to be filled with correct spiritual substances. You have also shown them that this world's counselors are struggling greatly because they have no definite reference point to begin their counsel, nor do they have the Word of God as their road map. Because we know that the spirit and soul is the seat of man's mental health, we have a definite place to start. This turning-point revelation came as a real paradigm shift. God opened my eyes to a totally different view of man's mental health. I had studied God's Word for years, but I knew little about His ways until He revealed it. Such precious truths are not available to this world's counselors because they're spiritual in nature, and minister directly to the human soul.

It's vital to know some of these secrets and learn how to apply them to life if we want to see people recover. For many years, I had pondered the meaning of Proverbs 9:1. It states, "Wisdom has built her house, she has hewn out her seven pillars." I knew this passage was important in mental health because it revealed that wisdom was responsible for building up the spiritual house within us; it also revealed that these seven pillars were some sort of internal support. But my understanding stopped there. I had been asking God for further clarification, and one day the Lord explained them to me.

At that time, the Lord also revealed a startling truth. He said, "I want to heal people of their inner afflictions, but very few are willing to slow down their lives sufficiently so that they can accumulate the wisdom material that I need to do inner repairs on their soul." I suddenly saw that man's input into the process of regaining his mental health was very significant. If you discern that your coffee-cup friend is internally weak and has little resistance against surrounding spiritual pressures such as depression, then a good place to begin teaching would be to discuss his or her internal support pillars.

Step #14—Seven Names…Seven Rooms

If the person doesn't really know much about God and His desire to be involved with our lives, it's good to discuss the seven names of God, and the seven rooms of the human soul. These amazing inner construction secrets help show God's passion to be involved in our lives on a daily basis. He's very serious when He states in Proverbs 8:17, "I love those who love me, and those who seek me diligently will find me." God longs to help us and be involved in our lives, but it's a two-way street, and we must grow in this relationship.

Step #15—A Fighting Soul: Its Seven Parts

As a brand new Christian, I grabbed onto Matthew 11:12 like a drowning man. It says, "And from the days of John the Baptist until now the kingdom of heaven suffers violence, and the violent take it by force." I had been through so many struggles already in my life, and I realized that pressing into the Kingdom of Heaven included spiritual warfare. And it seemed that my mental health was dependent on the outcome of those battles. Consequently, I was very determined to build myself up. At that time, the Lord also showed me that there was something about fighting, wrestling, and resisting that builds a man up inside. Jesus clearly tells us in John 10:10, "The thief does not come except to steal, and to kill, and to destroy. I have come that they may have life, and that they may have it more abundantly." If we don't grasp the full meaning of this statement, then we may be in for a rough ride. Many people hold on to the second part of the verse not realizing that you have to fight through the first part in order to take hold of abundant life. The person that you're instructing is feeling the effects of spiritual pressures, but probably doesn't know what they are. It's your task to show them that these forces aren't imaginary, and that they must be fiercely resisted.

Step #16—A Growing Soul: Seven Additions

Just as our body grows in size year by year until we're fully-grown, so the Lord expects our spirit and soul to grow mightily within us. This only occurs as we develop intimacy with the Lord, and continually seek those things that He desires to add to us. It's sad that so many become overly-busy in their lives, and ignore the need for soul growth. In so doing, they leave empty spaces within their inner man, and it is these soul spaces that the enemy seeks to occupy. The pressures exerted by spirits of depression, fear, and anxiety are very real, but if we're keeping ourselves filled with the things of Christ, we have no need to be concerned. These additions add strength to us year by year, and keep the enemy from making inroads.

Many people camp on the high points of our Christian walk such as salvation or an amazing one-time victory, but God wants to add so much more. He wants to see us be consistent in building high moral standards, as well as becoming steadfast in our walk of holiness. This causes Him to reveal His heart so that we might grow in the knowledge of God. He also wants us to become temperate so that we might grow in self-control. Then, as we face the storms that come our way, He can teach us to persevere through these trials, and always overcome them. In preparation for Heaven, He expects to see a continual growth in godliness. A major part of this is genuine kindness toward our brethren. He sums up the soul additions with the greatest addition of all—love. He then encourages us that if we make these additions, we will never fall away from Him (see 2 Peter 1:5-8).

Step #17—An Overcoming Soul

As I look back over my 40 years as a Christian, I see that every person is called to overcome some serious trials in life. As Christians, if we walk side by side with the Master, we'll grow mightily in strength as we work closely with Him to put these obstacles underfoot. This buildup of inner strength isn't common knowledge, and many look in the wrong places for help. As a result, they're overwhelmed by their struggles, and don't overcome. The Parable of the Sower (Mark 4) warns us about several different scenarios. One group embraced Christ excitedly, and because of the many touches and revelations that they received, they brought forth a great abundance of fruit in their lives. But the other group may have embraced Christ at one time, but they became far too busy with life's activities and didn't maintain their closeness with the Master. When life's trials came their way, they hadn't built up their inner rooting system, so they fell away.

This subject of overcoming is also discussed in the Parable of the Talents (Matthew 25:14-30) where each one was given talents according to their ability. Some faced incredible obstacles, but overcame them, and were judged to have used their talents wisely. But one man exhibited no faith, and refused to take any risks. He buried his talent, and had nothing to help him overcome. Because he refused to face life's challenges, he later paid dearly for his lack of diligence. As we examine the seven overcoming challenges of early Revelation, we see that God is very serious about the construction and quality of every human soul. If we meet these challenges correctly, we'll not only overcome in life, but be prepared to "walk with [Him] in white" throughout all of Eternity (Revelation 3:4).

In Conclusion

Every teaching opportunity is somewhat unique, but it's still possible to give some tips on how to best proceed with your own coffee-cup counseling. To do this, you have to assess the situation, whether the problems are caused by depression, death of a loved one, fear, or finances. The trap you must avoid is to begin listening to an ongoing outpouring of problems. If you pause here too long, this will lead down a thousand rabbit trails, and leave you as confused as the person that you're trying to help. You can offer a listening ear for a short while, but your role must become that of a Bible tutor, or you'll soon be stuck on the treadmill of problem-solving and endless counseling.

If you sit down with a person to give coffee-cup counsel, and you tell them that you have a fortune in gold, they might ask to see the goods. If you then reply that you have all of the gravel of the Fraser River at your disposal, people would laugh you to scorn. We all know that even though there's enough gold nestled in that gravel to make thousands of people wealthy beyond belief, there's major work required to recover it, and then convert it into a useful product. In the same way, if you wish to be a good coffee-cup tutor, then you must slow down your life and glean some of the gold ore of wisdom from the Word of God.

The Pharisees memorized reams of the words of God, but only did that so that they could control people. They never allowed their hearts to nestle close to God so that He could transfer His wisdom to them. We also must spend time in the Word and then meditate upon it. As we do, the Holy Spirit will change it into wisdom and life deep within our soul. The world is waiting, so little by little, we must build up a heart of wisdom, and prepare ourselves to be a coffee-cup counselor. As we do the right preparatory things and pray for opportunity, we'll have some great success. In closing, consider the following example.

Dick Iverson once again stretches out the boundary of coffee-cup evangelism for us. His wife had gone to visit a childhood friend. This friend had been an orphan when she connected with her in high school, and she had recently married a young man who had also been an orphan. His wife was greatly concerned about this union, and later in the day, she returned home in tears. She was overwhelmed by the extreme poverty that her friend was now living in. They had a small house on the outskirts of town with almost no furniture, little food, and five children. She asked her husband if the church could do something for this poverty-stricken family. That same night, the church collected food, a small refrigerator, clothing, and some simple furniture. After the service, a bunch of the men arrived at their door with armloads of supplies. The family watched in utter disbelief as bag after bag of groceries filled their kitchen. The men didn't preach to the shocked family…they just showed love.

Several weeks later, this small family appeared at the back of their church. After a few more weeks they all came down to the front to receive salvation. As the years went by, the family prospered, and Dick Iverson said that he had the privilege of being the minister to marry all five of the children. As they were growing up, one of the daughters acquired a keen interest in politics. In time, she was elected to the House in the State of Oregon, and took the position of Speaker in the state legislature. She has now become the second most powerful person in the State of Oregon second only to the Governor. But this success didn't start easily…it all began when the people of a small struggling Church decided to reach out and show a little compassion. Coffee-cup evangelism can also be effective when we close our mouths and demonstrate the same heart of love and compassion.

Chapter 12
Maintaining Our Freedom Forever

The Australian Sailors

A number of years ago, two Australian sailors became completely lost as they wandered about London in a thick, smoky fog trying to find their way back to their ship. By chance, they stumbled across a British colonel decked out in his finest army uniform. One sailor said to him in his thick Australian accent, "Aye, matey! Do you know where we are?" The colonel didn't feel that he had been addressed with the proper military respect by these lowly sailors, so he looked down his long nose and responded back in a distinguished British accent, "Do you know who I am?" One sailor looked at the other and said, "Quick, let's get out of here! We thought we were in bad shape not knowing where we are, but this poor bloke doesn't even know who he is!"

This humorous story can provide us with a valuable counseling truth. Many feel lost in life simply because they don't know who they are, or even where they're going. The secret to gaining then maintaining your freedom forever is to spend intimate time with the Lord so that you might learn these things at His feet. Once you gain that knowledge, you can see that mental health is an inner strength issue, and God has given us the Holy Spirit so that our soul might be repaired, and a book full of dynamic exercises (the Holy Scriptures) so that we might build up our internal strength.

Setting the Stage

I always marvel at the ability of the Queen's guards at Buckingham Palace to remain fixed and unmovable in the face of any adversity. Even though they appear to tourists to just be ceremonial guards, they are fully operational soldiers who could spring into action at a moment's notice. We need to be like that if we desire to maintain the spiritual gold that has been entrusted to us. So as we now consider realistic ways to hold onto our freedom, we should pay close attention to the following Scripture. Solomon tells us in Proverbs 4:23, 26: "Guard your heart with all diligence, for out of it spring the issues of life…ponder the path of your feet, and let all of your ways be established." From previous verses, we know that our heart is guarded as we obey God's words. So these instructions are going to require some serious effort on our part if we desire to fully enjoy the life that God has prepared for us, and then maintain it forever.

Back to the Beginning

Adam and Eve must have been certain that they had been birthed into a perfect world. They were surrounded by a landscape of indescribable beauty, and daily lived amongst a great array of colorful plants and exotic animals. They were able to partake of the delicious fruits hanging from many trees, and also had the wonderful privilege of fellowshipping with God in the cool of the evening. There were no mental health issues, and their future looked very bright. In fact, they felt so comfortable and secure in their environment that they had no concept about contrary spiritual pressures, nor did they know that a test would soon be coming against them that would rock their world. They were told not to eat of the fruit of the Tree of the Knowledge of Good and Evil, and for a time, this wasn't a problem. But Eve was filled with curiosity. As Satan told his deceptive lies, Eve was caught off-guard, and a strong challenge to her obedience suddenly unfolded. She became convinced that she was missing out on life, and soon became confused. As Satan continued to unleash his deception against her, and combined it with an array of strong soul pressures, she eventually succumbed. Yet it is God's certain will that we shouldn't buckle under these pressures. We must learn how to maintain the many good things that God has given to us, remembering that God has said that He will never allow us to be tempted above what we're able to bear (1 Corinthians 10:13).

In Our Present Day

Today we're in the same predicament as Adam and Eve. In fact, we're told in 1 Corinthians 10:11 that the things that happened to our ancestors were written for our learning. I see this first test as being eternal in its significance, and it can teach us a very real truth about maintaining ourselves. I assume that Adam and Eve had been eating lots of the delicious fruit from the other trees in the Garden, but were not partaking sufficiently from the Tree of Life. Consequently, when spiritual opposition came against them, they didn't have the strength to withstand an array of contrary spiritual pressures. They believed Satan and soon began to feed from the Tree of the Knowledge of Good and Evil. This direct disobedience opened up a very poisonous revelation—so much so that it seriously damaged their spiritual DNA. At that very instant, mental health problems entered the human race.

A New Feeding Ground

This created a problem for mankind because we suddenly had two streams of information available to us. One stream built strength into mankind as it pointed us toward eternal life with God; the other alternative stripped away our strength as it pointed us toward the evil one, and the lustful pleasures that he was offering. This brings us to a major truth concerning soul maintenance: If we desire to maintain our souls forever, then we must eat voraciously from the Tree of Life, and shun the fruit from the tree that caused such destruction of man's mental health.

It grieves me deeply as I work to help people in the mental health area as I see starving souls scrabbling around under the wrong tree trying to find some morsels of food to fill their famished souls. So without any hesitation I can say that eating from the Tree of Life is one of the first and most important steps in our ongoing soul maintenance. If I went even further and proposed solutions for the modern day mental health crisis, I would look very hard at people's personal feeding habits, and recommend strong doses of Scripture. We must give priority to feeding often from sources that will build up the soul. Hence, let me suggest that eating from the Tree of Life is an absolute necessity, not a preference.

Learning Obedience the Hard Way

I love to watch nature shows on the National Geographic channel. The other day, I saw a clip about a shark attack that really startled me. In South Africa, they have shark watchers that guard many of the local swimming beaches. One day a 12-foot Great White shark was spotted in the bay and the alarm was sounded. Everyone left the water, but one fellow was determined to have a quick dip. Unknown to him, he swam right into the jaws of the shark, and lost both of his legs below the knee. It was a horrible spectacle, but it should remind us that there is zero room for error when it comes to spiritual obedience. The second step toward soul freedom is to obey those in authority over us. They are placed there for our protection (Hebrews 13:17).

Becoming Intimate with God

In the same way, if we hunger to maintain spiritual freedom, then we must submit ourselves to the authority of God's Word. And for good reason! John Bevere, in his studies concerning the Holy Spirit, discusses the three levels of intimacy. The physical level between a man and woman would be the first level. It is a wonderful physical union, but not enough to make a marriage work for very long. The personality connection between people is the second level of intimacy where the sexual attraction is not involved at all. This is where people seem to relate really well to each other from the heart, and are what Anne of Green Gables calls "kindred spirits" (e.g. David and Jonathan).

The third level is the deep spiritual connection between a human being and God. Five virgins knew the Lord, and had an abundant entrance into Heaven, whereas the other five neglected their salvation, and had no connection with His heart. When we move into these higher levels of intimacy with God, the likelihood that we will ever fall away becomes much less. It's also at this level where human mental health continually improves as we're ever more filled with Christ.

I have entitled my seventh daily devotional, 'Maintaining Your Soul'. I used the analogy of an automobile repair shop to explain how ongoing maintenance of our complex hidden parts can have a huge bearing on preventing future soul troubles. For example, we must not neglect our salvation, but rather search it out to discover its many benefits. Through prayer, we will also be in constant communication with the One that we love, and as we continually feast on the Tree of Life, we will be filled to overflowing with the knowledge of God.

Overcoming Obstacles

History is filled with exciting adventures where men have had an obstacle to conquer such as an impenetrable castle, yet they somehow found a way to get in and take the city. For example, the Jebusites taunted David's armies that even the weak and the lame could keep the city from him. Through the wisdom of God, David figured out a way to climb through a watercourse, and soldiers were able to open the city gates from the inside. In this case, wisdom took the city. In another place, the city of Troy had withstood a siege from the Greek armies for over ten years. At the end of that time, the Greek armies pretended to sail away, and left a large wooden horse as an offering. History tells us that hidden inside of that horse were select soldiers who crept out at night, and opened the gates for the returning Greek armies. Trickery caused Troy to fall, and it should be no surprise that Satan often uses trickery in his assaults against us.

The Value of Strength and Wisdom

One story that truly astounds me occurred in the city of Babylon many thousands of years ago. The Medes and the Persians had tried often to devise a way to take this impregnable fortress without any success. But they now had a plan. One night, they created a very obvious diversion where a group of soldiers distracted the guards up on the walls of Babylon. Meanwhile, the Persians were diverting the course of the mighty Euphrates River into a nearby drainage canal. When the water levels of the Euphrates dropped sufficiently, they simply walked into the city through the river passage underneath the wall. Their unexpected entrance led to a great victory for the Persians. In this case, the use of wisdom caused the corrupt Babylonian Empire to fall, and allowed the city to be taken. Hence we must never become proud of our lofty position in Christ, because at the most unexpected time, we can become prey to a sudden attack from the enemy (see Romans 11:19-21; 1 Corinthians 10:12).

Inner Storms and Pressures

Many Christians spend their days trying to maintain their Christianity, and not be overwhelmed by inner pressures. But these troubled people are barking up the wrong tree. If we really want to stay strong and hold on to what we have, then the secret is to draw near to Christ so that He might help us. I can say this from much experience because my life was spiraling down into absolute futility, but when I finally abandoned all other attempts and drew near to the Lord, He began to heal me. From this I learned that His heart longs for intimacy, and it causes Him to draw near to us, and build us up so that we become stronger than the spiritual bullies who are targeting our soul. Once again, consider the following warning.

Jesus tells this powerful story in Matthew 12:43-45 that should serve as the centerpiece of our soul maintenance strategy. He warns, "When an unclean spirit goes out of a man, he goes through dry places, seeking rest, and he finds none. Then he says, 'I will return to my house from which I came.' And when he comes, he finds it empty, swept and put in order. Then he goes and takes with him seven other spirits more wicked than himself, and they enter and dwell there; and the last state of that man is worse than the first. So shall it be with this wicked generation." When the Lord delivers us from relentless enemy pressures, He expects us to get busy and build ourselves up spiritually so that we might maintain ourselves as well as being fully prepared for the return of the bully.

The Dangerous Consequences of Being Spiritually Weak

In this illustration, the man had used up the spiritual materials that had been given to Him by the Lord, and was doing nothing to resupply himself. When the demonic bully finally did return to check out his previous home, the man didn't have the strength or the inner resources to stop a full reinvasion of his soul. This same scenario can happen to all of us in various degrees, but thankfully, it doesn't have to be the end of the journey, because I endured this several times. Finally, I became serious enough to really take the Lord's message to heart, and when I did, He was able to build me up and then fill me up. In fact, Matthew tells us in Matthew 11:12 that "violence" will surround the establishing and the maintaining of the Kingdom of God in our lives, and we must be in a condition to maintain ourselves. Those who are stuck on the concept of a "gentle Jesus" aren't going to be able to maintain themselves as spiritual violence confronts their soul.

At school, we've been very proactive to stop bullying. This has been a good thing, but we've seen that it's only half the solution. The children being bullied also need to be taught how to stand up for themselves—and know to call out for help when it happens. In real life, the bully will always come back again and again unless he is beaten at his own game. It's no different in the spiritual world because the enemy knows that if he can invade our soul, then he has found a home. Thankfully, the greatest antidote is taking hold of the life that Christ offers by becoming intimate with the Master. Then when he comes to attack us, the Master goes to the door, and he will flee in terror.

Spiritual Boredom

Satan has many tricks up his sleeve, and often uses boredom to pry many away from the Master. Some people never uncover the excitement and wonder that has been hidden in our salvation, and it's easy for the enemy to then steer them toward worldly things. In time, they know that they're unsatisfied, but they get caught up in the pull of meaningless activities. Some will even live out the old English nursery rhyme concerning Solomon Grundy. It goes like this: "Solomon Grundy, born on a Monday, christened on Tuesday, married on Wednesday, took ill on Thursday, grew worse on Friday, died on Saturday, buried on Sunday; that was the end of Solomon Grundy." What a description of some Christian's lives. Yet the Lord says exactly the opposite in Psalm 91:16. He tells us, "With long life will I satisfy him, and show him my salvation." If we search for His treasures, we'll be so busy finding our fulfillment in Him that there's no danger that we'll ever fall away.

The Parable of the Sower

After we have passed from this life, the Parable of the Sower, found in Mark 4 could either be read over us in praise, or it could be read in condemnation. It is our call. Verses 14-15 states, "The sower sows the word. And these are the ones by the wayside where the word is sown. When they hear, Satan comes immediately and takes away the word that was sown in their hearts." These people never made the Word of God their passion; hence they didn't guard it. A perfect example would be the Children of Israel. They were delivered from Egypt and heard the Word of the Lord, but they didn't respond in faith, and treated the Lord with contempt.

Verses 16-17 continues, "These likewise are the ones sown on stony ground who, when they hear the word, immediately receive it with gladness, and they have no root in themselves, and so endure only for a time. Afterward when tribulation or persecution arises for the word's sake, immediately they stumble." It's our responsibility to take hold of the Word of God and set it deep in our hearts where we can use it often, and experience its miracle-working power. By frequent use, roots of confidence are set down within us, and we become secure in our faith.

Verses 18-19 continue, "Now these are the ones sown among thorns; they are the ones who hear the word, and the cares of this world, the deceitfulness of riches, and the desires for other things entering in choke the word, and it becomes unfruitful." Another thing that keeps us from maintaining our freedom is allowing ourselves to be distracted by other things. If this happens, then we never let the Word of God enter deeply into us so that it can be used to bring home many souls for the Master.

Verse 20 is what the Master desires the most of all, and is the most certain way that we can maintain our freedom. It states, "But these are the ones sown on good ground, those who hear the word, accept it, and bear fruit; some thirtyfold, some sixty, and some a hundred." These people set themselves to hear the Word of God, believe it, and make the best use of it in their lives. I know that when I took hold of the Word and really called out to the Lord with it, some incredible things happened in my life, and I received healing. I found that bearing spiritual fruit has a profound effect on our mental and emotional health. In so doing, we're able to maintain our freedom and walk with the Master in genuine closeness.

The Parable of the Two Builders

The ongoing saga of man's mental health is brought into clear focus in this parable, and it takes us right back to our first charge from the Lord—that we must feed continually from the Tree of Life. Matthew 7:24-25 states, "Therefore, whoever hears these sayings of Mine and does them, I will liken him to a wise man who built his house on the rock: and the rain descended, the floods came, and the winds blew and beat on that house; and it did not fall, for it was founded upon a rock." The Lord is giving soul-building instructions here, and those who honor Him by hearing and obeying them will succeed in all areas of life. The correct building of the human soul results in strong inner health.

The second builder described in Matthew 7:26-27 discovered the nightmare of ignoring the Word of God, and disobeying its commands. "But everyone who hears these sayings of Mine, and does not do them, will be like a foolish man who built his house on the sand: and the rain descended, the floods came, and the winds blew and beat on that house; and it fell. And great was its fall." We live in a world filled with people who have little or no respect for the Word of God. Yet obedience to His words will eventually determine the strength and resiliency of our mental health. In this case, this man's house (spirit/soul combination) collapsed; in modern language we might call it a complete nervous breakdown, or a series of severe panic rushes that incapacitates the individual. It's our response to God's Word that determines whether we're able to maintain our freedom or not.

When Problems Do Return

We need to be aware of Satan's devices. If we've been delivered from inner pressure, we can be almost certain that these same pressures will eventually assail our hearts once again (Matthew 12:43-45). But if we've been maintaining our freedom, the enemy will find our house put in order and filled with the correct spiritual substances. This allows us to face the problem squarely, and not back down. When he does come, we must increase our devotional times and intimacy with Jesus Christ until the inner pressure is gone once again. In my life, the old pressures have tried to return from time to time, but because I now keep myself strong in spirit, after a short battle, the enemy disappears.

In Conclusion

There are many clues given to us in the Word of God that instruct us how to maintain the precious freedoms that have been given to us. It all begins with a commitment to feed from the Tree of Life in Genesis 2, and ends with our hunger to guard the words of life entrusted to us (Revelation 22:7). Then all throughout the Word of God, we see that our salvation contract is no light matter. It is to be studied thoroughly, and its precepts understood. As we do this, we become strong internally, and are to make this precious contract known to our brethren. This filling of our hearts with the Word of God, the vision it creates, and the sense of purpose it gives to us, is a huge part of our ongoing soul maintenance.

My greatest revelation in mental health was to stop chasing after the enemy, and start pursuing intimacy with the Lord. In this place of intimacy, He reveals to us how to stay free. Many ignore any advice that entails effort. They go from person to person trying to get bits of advice. But all to no avail. We must not be like a weakling in a weight room asking everyone about the exercise machines, their manufacturers, and how they function. Instead of ever getting their hands dirty and doing the exercises, they just talk endlessly about them. To maintain freedom, we must draw close to the Master, and heartily obey Him.

CHAPTER 13
Conclusion: the "What If" Questions Answered

The "What if" Game

When we were kids, we used to love to play the "what if" game. My favorite question was, "What if I won the lottery and had a million dollars to spend? What would I do with all of the prize money?" (I no longer ask this question.) My wife's mother died when she was only four years old, so she often used to wonder, "What if my mother had lived? How would it have affected my life?" Right now as Christians, the "what if" question is two-fold, and it is no longer a game. I often speculate, "What if I had not found Christ? Would I have gone to a Christless eternity?" But the second question is even more pressing. It is this: "What if my loved ones don't change their ways? Will they lose out with Christ forever?" These many "what if" questions can never be answered in this lifetime, but this book poses a "what if" question about Christian counseling that can be answered, and it most certainly deserves some serious consideration.

The Full Question

When we look at the subject of mental health counseling, the "what if" question is no longer a game. Hence, the full title of this book is "What if Freud was wrong to remove Jesus Christ from the counseling arena?" As we study the works of men like Darwin, Nietzsche, Freud, and Jung, we see that they didn't believe that man was crafted in the image of our God, nor did they believe that man had a soul and spirit. They also completely rejected God's most powerful mental health truth—that this God-given spirit/soul combination was the seat of man's mental and emotional health, and that it was fully repairable. So because this world's system wholeheartedly embraced incorrect human ideas, mankind was left without a reference point for mental health counseling, and people were now placed in a dangerous position of having no solid ground underfoot.

As time went on, a whole host of other followers proposed a potpourri of counseling ideas using some of the philosophical teachings and "roller-coaster" ideas of these men. As a consequence, we see the counseling concept in the world today that man doesn't really need God either in scientific studies, or in complex psychiatric teachings. And the results on human mental health have been nothing short of tragic. But let's not just focus on Sigmund Freud and his incorrect teachings. "What if Charles Darwin had recognized that species boundaries had not been crossed when he wrote *On the Origin of Species*? Would it have slowed down the steamroller of evolution, and prevented the lack of purpose that we see in our young people today? There is much strong evidence that a Great Creator and an Intelligent Designer exist—so much so that God emphatically declares in Romans 1:20 that His handiwork is so clearly displayed in nature that no one can offer an excuse for rejecting His Son when they stand before Him.

"What if Friedrich Nietzsche had tempered his words, and not declared that 'God is dead'?" Would he have still gone completely insane? And would it have avoided the carnage caused by Adolf Hitler who used these words as a driving force of the Third Reich? "What if Carl Jung had not been Freud's disciple?" Would he have had a better perspective on mental health, and would it have prevented him from losing his own sanity, and seeking the occult for some of his revelations?

These are philosophical questions that are difficult to answer, but let's look at what is real. Jesus Christ is still knocking on the door of human hearts even today declaring that He has a much better way to counsel. If we will open to Him, a completely different style of counseling will open before us.

The Lord's introduction would be to reveal His amazing salvation contract signed and sealed in His own blood. Then He would introduce us to the mighty Holy Spirit who has been given to mankind to be the Great Counselor. After He had made it clear to us that we are indeed crafted in the image of God, and that He desires to make our soul and spirit strong, He will uncover the truth that the demonic realm is real, and that there is a war raging all around us.

It is then that we go where the world refuses, and face the fact that we are in an all-out war against this demonic realm, and that spiritual pressures are very real, and that can be very uncomfortable. God opens up this hidden realm so that He can reveal to us that true mental health only comes as the Holy Spirit makes us whole inside. Then we learn that our spirit man is made strong as we obey Him in the areas of spiritual exercise and nutrition. That is when He can teach us that we won't find our answers by chasing down complex human problems.

Psalm 1 Re-visited

With these many "what if" questions in mind, let's now return to Psalm 1 and see if it has been written for the express purpose of helping us to answer these questions. In it, God strongly advises that we would be blessed if we would reject the counsel of the ungodly, and adhere to the sure counsel of His Word instead. The Lord saw down through the eons of time, and knew that ungodly men would forcefully proclaim their own humanistic ideas, and try to destroy the precious counsel that His words offer to mankind.

"What if we ignore the counsel of the ungodly, and accept His words at face value?" Then Psalm 1:3 clearly teaches that we would find the inner health for which we have longed, and that we'd be able to walk through the remainder of our lives in glorious peace. He tells us in Psalm 1:4 that those who reject His counsel are blown about like chaff in a wind storm because there is nothing in them to hold their feet on the ground. The question remains, "What if they don't repent?" Then it doesn't matter that they seem to be in charge of world affairs; there will come a day when their lives fall apart, and they'll be in great fear.

God Has His Own Strategies

Let's get down to the heart of the matter. This manuscript answers the "what if" question, and states that Freud was wrong in his philosophical writings. It also reveals that our God has His own effective strategy for curing the inner ills of mankind. The Lord's main thrust is to put our myriad of complex problems on His back-burner, and concentrate on restructuring and building up our human soul. To do so, He uses the many soul-building strategies and exercises that are clearly set forth in the Word of God. He knows that as our soul becomes ever stronger within us, it will then have the capacity to resist the strong spiritual pressures that are being targeted against it. As we gain this ability, our problems will fade away like mist pouring forth from a steam kettle on a very chilly day.

Where Do We Go From Here?

So this now leaves us with the question, "Where do we go from here?" I have attempted to give this direction, and have set forth the idea that God built the human spirit and soul; therefore, it makes perfect sense to return to this amazing Creator, and give the honor due to Him. We do this by acknowledging that only He knows why the thoughts and feelings collapse within the heart of a man. This means that we must go to a place where worldly men dare not go: the early book of Genesis. As we walk this almost forbidden pathway, we will discover that mankind has indeed been crafted in the image of our God: spirit, soul, and body. This is our immovable reference point for all mental health counseling, and a sure place to tie our lifeline. But this is just the first step. We soon realize that the body can be seen, but the soul and spirit are the mysterious parts of our complex inner makeup, and only by means of the words of our God can they ever be understood.

What About Genesis 2 & 3?

In Genesis 2 we learn even more about this hidden inner construction. We see that a man lay on the ground in a physical body that contained a soul. At a set time, the Lord breathed spirit into the man, and he rose up "a living being" (Genesis 2:7). Then in Genesis 3 of this long-ignored book, we learn even more details about the spiritual world that surrounds us. We're introduced to a spirit being that philosophers have mocked for centuries: Satan. Our first introduction to him gives away his character. He is a liar and a deceiver, and is in the process of applying spiritual pressure to Eve. Then Adam and Eve buckle under his onslaught of spiritual pressures; and when they do, it opens the door for mental health problems to enter into the human race. So the die is now cast. We see God and Satan contending for the souls of men, and it becomes our challenge to accept Jesus Christ, and help others to also make the right choice.

Our Primary Counseling Manual

So let me close this by re-visiting the questions that are so important to our future. "What if the invisible spirit/soul combination is the seat of our inner health?" Then it means that they can be re-structured and fully recharged. It also means that the Word of God must become our primary counseling manual, and that the ideas and the works of men must fade in their significance. To those who are proud in heart, this is absolute nonsense; but to those who are humble of soul, this is the gold that they've long been seeking after.

It fulfills Solomon's words in Proverbs 8:34-35 that state, "Blessed is the man who listens to me, watching daily at my gates, waiting at the posts of my doors. For whoever finds me finds life, and obtains favor from the LORD." Life is God's antidote for our mental health woes, so as we find the Master, we also find the answers to the complex inner problems that we have been seeking for so long.

Where Do We Go From Here?

So after assessing these "what if" questions, the question arises, "Where do we go from here?" How should we structure our counsel so that we can touch the desperate human needs that we see around us? I stress the great value of our salvation contract, the importance of daily devotions, and the need for intimacy with Jesus Christ. Then we must feed from the Tree of Life, and anchor His words in our soul. This gives us the means to fight against the pressures of an unseen enemy. The list could go on, but if we will give importance to these first things, then it will start us on the right track, and as we continue to seek the knowledge of God and learn more of His truths, it will bring us safely home to our destination.

Once we arrive home, we'll know for certain that Freud was wrong, and that worldly philosophies can never answer the deepest questions of life. We have undergone a paradigm shift in our thinking, and a brand new counseling landscape stretches out before us. This gives real hope in our hearts that we can help those who are hurting so much.

Chapter 14
Wrapping It All Up

The question might be asked, "Who am I to challenge the mighty bastions of Darwinian evolution and Freudian counsel?' But I have walked the walk, and I was given my "outside-the-box" answers by the Holy Spirit. I can see so clearly that unless we, as Christians, strongly declare that the Lord Jesus Christ provides mankind with a far better structure for scientific study and mental health counseling, then men will always lack purpose for living, and these counseling truths will be hidden from those who so desperately need them.

These pillars of society need to be strongly challenged by men and women who love Jesus Christ. The problem-chasing method of counseling leads troubled souls into a hopeless maze of rabbit trails, whereas this solution-based method of counseling works well provided we keep the Holy Spirit at the center of our discussions. I find it tragic indeed that those who would suppress the truth still have the loudest voice, and Jesus Christ and His effective soul-building methods continue to remain on the backburner of our society. Souls are screaming out in pain, yet this world's system continues to proclaim that there are no counseling solutions in sight that can provide men with a permanent cure.

I know from many agonizing trials and much practical experience what works and what doesn't. There is no question in my mind that there's an Intelligent Designer, and a mighty solution-based Counselor to be reckoned with. It is His passion to set damaged people on their feet once again, give them purpose in their daily living, and provide them with an eternal destiny. So the "what if" question is vital if we desire to connect with those who have been taught all of their lives that the God of Heaven has no relevance in the fields of science and counseling.

I am bridging that gap by setting forth the testimony of my own life where I was fully healed and restored by the Master after many long years of life-threatening depression. This book also has several other purposes in mind: firstly, to reveal some long-hidden biblical counseling truths, and also to prepare us for our God-assigned task of coffee cup evangelism. We must realize that God doesn't heal and restore any person just so they can live the rest of their lives seeking their own pleasures. He expects that our personal testimony will become the springboard that will enable us all to minister effectively to many others. So let's listen to the cries of a dying humanity, and now let's go forward, knowing that Freud was completely wrong. And let's proclaim these powerful truths to all who will listen so that we might help those who are in such desperate need.

www.ingramcontent.com/pod-product-compliance
Lightning Source LLC
Chambersburg PA
CBHW071707090426
42738CB00009B/1700